Mooting

Mootin   le,
interacti   ed
academi   lle
complex   nt
and vital   his
book, E   he
various   cal
and prac   ng
competi

Onlin   ng
alive and   ue
as well a   its
of interes   presentations,
identifyi   they use
cases and   nen be
re-enacted, incorporating the suggestions for improvements to help you to see
how the overall performance could have been improved.

This definitive guide will equip you with a complete grasp of mooting from the
initial preparatory stages through to advocacy in the moot itself.

Eric Baskind is Senior Lecturer in Law at Liverpool John Moores University.
He served as National Adjudicator to the English-Speaking Union Essex Court
Chambers National Mooting Competition in 2008, 2009 and again for 2013–
2015, and is now Chair of the Advisory Board to the Competition.

Mooting
The Definitive Guide

Eric Baskind

Routledge
Taylor & Francis Group
LONDON AND NEW YORK

First published 2018
by Routledge
2 Park Square, Milton Park, Abingdon, Oxon OX14 4RN

and by Routledge
711 Third Avenue, New York, NY 10017

Routledge is an imprint of the Taylor & Francis Group, an informa business

British Library Cataloguing-in-Publication Data
A catalogue record for this book is available from the British Library

Library of Congress Cataloging-in-Publication Data
Names: Baskind, Eric, author.
Title: Mooting : the definitive guide / Eric Baskind.
Description: Abingdon, Oxon ; New York, NY : Routledge, 2017. |
Includes bibliographical references and index.
Identifiers: LCCN 2017006098 (print) | LCCN 2017006204 (ebook) |
ISBN 9781138851160 (hardback : alk. paper) | ISBN 9781138851177
(pbk. : alk. paper) | ISBN 9781315724317 (Master) |
ISBN 9781317530589 (Adobe Reader) | ISBN 9781317530572 (ePub) |
ISBN 9781317530565 (Mobipocket)
Subjects: LCSH: Moot courts—England.
Classification: LCC KD440.A2 B37 2017 (print) |
LCC KD440.A2 (ebook) | DDC 340.071/142—dc23
LC record available at https://lccn.loc.gov/2017006098

ISBN: 978-1-138-85116-0 (hbk)
ISBN: 978-1-138-85117-7 (pbk)
ISBN: 978-1-315-72431-7 (ebk)

Typeset in Galliard
by Keystroke, Neville Lodge, Tettenhall, Wolverhampton

Visit the companion website: www.routledge.com/cw/baskind

Printed and bound in the United States of America by
Edwards Brothers Malloy on sustainably sourced paper

Contents

Foreword

For centuries, advocates have played a fundamental role in the administration of justice in courts and tribunals as well as through arbitration and other forms of dispute resolution. Mooting is one of the best means by which aspiring advocates can learn to develop the preparatory and presentational skills that will enable them to advance their case in its best way, and deal effectively with judicial questioning. Mooting provides students with the opportunity to gain both experience and confidence as advocates in a courtroom setting, thus helping to develop real court presence. In taking part in a moot, students show not only their knowledge and skill in researching and handling legal materials, but also their ability to practise the art of forensic and persuasive argument in a concise and effective manner. Mooting is the ideal environment in which to learn and hone the skills that as advocates one needs in practice. It enables students to appreciate the importance of thorough preparation and effective time management, as well as being able to present their material clearly, in both oral and written forms.

Our professional education is designed to give us the skills to know or be able to find, and understand, the legal principles that should govern the issues pertaining to any legal problem. Equally important is learning the skills of being able to present the facts and the law in a way that is persuasive. Mooting is an important element in that educative process.

Mooting is fun and those who engage in it enjoy the experience and find it enormously rewarding. Mooting also provides students with a positive step on the road to securing pupillage or a training contract. Essex Court Chambers has for many years been proud to be associated with the National Mooting Competition and to contribute to assisting the advocates of the future to develop their skills.

Mooting: The Definitive Guide sets out in a clear and logical manner all the information needed to make a success of mooting as well as providing comprehensive guidance on organising and running a mooting event. We commend this book to anyone involved in mooting.

Richard Jacobs QC
Graham Dunning QC
Co-Heads of Essex Court Chambers
March 2017

About the English-Speaking Union

ENGLISH-SPEAKING UNION

The English-Speaking Union is an international educational charity and membership organisation that believes in the power of spoken communication. Through its educational programmes, competitions, cultural exchanges and advocacy, it provides people with the skills to realise their full potential, helping them become confident communicators, critical thinkers and empowered citizens. The ESU believes that good communication is essential to individual, community and cross-cultural development and understanding, and endeavours to ensure it is recognised as such.

About Essex Court Chambers

ESSEX COURT CHAMBERS
BARRISTERS

Essex Court Chambers is a leading set of barristers' chambers, specialising in commercial and financial litigation, arbitration, public law and public international law.

Members of Chambers are recognised specialists in all areas of commercial law and handle disputes across the full spectrum of the business and financial world, including banking and finance, civil fraud, corporate/chancery and offshore, insurance and reinsurance, energy, trade, shipping, revenue and employment. The members have a reputation for exceptional talent, top-class advocacy and a client-oriented approach.

Members act in the full spectrum of UK-based litigation, from County Court hearings to substantial High Court trials and appeals before the Court of Appeal, Supreme Court and Privy Council, as well as before specialist tribunals and public inquiries. They also regularly appear before the European Courts, and advise on and act in arbitrations and disputes around the world, including in Africa, the Caribbean, Europe, the Middle East and Asia.

1 Introduction to mooting

Introduction

This book is aimed at everyone who is involved in mooting whether as a mooter, organiser, coach or judge. It provides a complete guide to every aspect of mooting from considering the mooting problem through to researching the issues, practising your advocacy and participating in the moot itself. Additionally, there is a chapter dealing with organising a moot or mooting competition which includes advice on setting moot problems and judging a moot.

Chapters 1 and 2 deal with a range of preliminary issues and cover an introduction to mooting and key aspects of the English legal system, with specific emphasis on how it relates to mooting. **Chapters 3, 4 and 5** examine the preparation stage of a moot and cover legal research, case preparation, preparing your skeleton argument, putting together your list of authorities and preparing your bundle for the moot. **Chapter 6** is the part of the book that deals with practising your moot and covers lawyers' skills, advocacy, presentation and personal skills. **Chapter 7** deals with oral submissions. This is arguably the most important part of the moot, and it is often said that a good performance on the day will go a long way to winning the moot. **Chapter 8** puts into practice all we have covered in the previous chapters to enable you to participate successfully in a moot and covers all aspects of the moot itself. **Chapter 9** will be of interest to those organising a moot or mooting competition and includes guides for organising and judging a moot as well as drafting moot problems. **Chapter 10** sets out a number of moot problems covering a range of different law subjects. **Chapter 11** accompanies the online resource which analyses a complete moot with interactive advice discussing and helping you to understand good and poor mooting practice. Finally, **Chapter 12** provides a host of useful resources that will prove invaluable to any serious mooter or mooting organiser.

What is mooting?

A moot is an argument on points of law that aims to simulate an appeal court hearing before a judge or panel of judges. The participants, known as 'mooters', argue the legal merits of appealing a fictitious case that has been decided in a lower court.

A moot is not concerned with an argument over the facts of the case as these are deemed to have been settled at the original hearing. For this reason, witnesses or juries do not feature in moots and this distinguishes a moot from a mock trial. As a result, the style of advocacy is different in a moot to that seen in a trial and is much less impassioned. Both can be contrasted with the trials of yesteryear where the conduct and language used was rather different to even the most flamboyant language used in jury trials of today. For example, during Sir Walter Raleigh's treason trial in 1603, Sir Edward Coke, the Attorney General, addressed the defendant, who was about to speak in his own defence:

> Thou art a scurvy fellow; thy name is hateful to all the realm of England for thy pride. I will now make it appear to the world that there never existed on the face of the earth a viler viper than thou art . . . Thou art a monster; thou hast an English face and a Spanish heart. Thou viper! For I thou thee, thou traytor.[1]

The style of advocacy a mooter should be aiming for is that seen in an appellate court such as the Court of Appeal or Supreme Court, where the vast majority of moots are notionally set. Anyone unfamiliar with this style of advocacy would do well to observe a case being argued. Fortunately, this is made easy as the Supreme Court streams cases live from its website. In addition to the live streaming service, footage from most hearings is also uploaded to the Supreme Court's website the day after the hearing takes place and this footage remains available to view for approximately one year after the hearing.

Mooting is also different to debating, not least because a debate can be on any subject matter whereas a moot is limited to legal issues. Both, of course, involve public speaking, where the participants make and respond to points made by their opponent. This, however, is where the similarity ends.

The history of mooting

Mooting is one of the original forms of legal education. It can be traced back at least to the fourteenth century where it was used by the Inns of Court as a means of training lawyers in the rigours of pleading and advocacy, and formed a fundamental component in the system of legal education. Books were, in those early days, almost non-existent, and the opinions expressed by the eminent lawyers of the day were often treated with as much respect as those of the judges. One of the key roles of the Benchers of the Inns was to act as the judge during a moot, and such was their seniority that their opinions were sometimes cited in the courts. This method of passing down legal knowledge and experience has been described as 'a constant rehearsal and preparation for the life of the advocate and judge'.[2]

1 Trial of Sir Walter Raleigh, 1 State Trials (1730) 205–212
2 Sir William Searle Holdsworth, 'A History of English Law' 1903–1972 (1965) London, Methuen/Sweet & Maxwell, vol. 2, p. 508

An extract from one of the earliest-known moots from the fourteenth-century *Kyppocke's Case* is shown below:

Kyppocke's Case
A man has issue a son and a daughter by one marriage and a son by another; the elder son marries and purchases certain land to him and his wife and their heirs in fee; and then he aliens the same land to his sister in tail, with warranty; and afterwards the father, the elder son and his sister purchase certain land unto the father in fee, the son in tail and the sister for life; the father and son die; the sister holds over, against whom the son's wife brings cui in vita; she vouches herself by a strange name, and enters into the warranty, pleads and loses, so that the demandant has judgment to recover, and she over; the demandant sues execution, but she does not; then the daughter gives a moiety of other land to the son of the half blood and has issue, and dies seised of the other moiety; the son of the half blood enters in this moiety; the donor ousts him from the whole; the sister's issue brings scire facias against the donor and recovers by default, and then re-enfeoffs him in tail; the son of the half blood has issue a son and dies; the issue brings a writ of entry in the quibus and recovers by default; the sister's issue has issue and dies.

Anyone struggling with a modern-day moot might be well advised to read over *Kyppocke's Case* and then consider themselves rather fortunate that they were not studying law in the fourteenth century.

The importance of mooting

Mooting will help improve your academic performance as well as enhance your employability profile. The value of mooting is perhaps best captured by the following:

Advocacy lies at the core of the common law adjudicative system. It is for that reason that moots have been an important part of legal education not only by the profession and professional providers but by university law schools. As a judge of the Court of Appeal of England and Wales and a former law professor and member of Essex Court Chambers, I can attest to the continuing importance of gaining experience in the art of persuasion which participating in mooting provides. Mooting helps to develop the ability to work as a member of a team, to present factual and legal material clearly and concisely, and to be responsive to questions from the judge(s).
(The Rt. Hon. Lord Justice Beatson, Welcome address to the
43rd annual final of the English-Speaking Union–Essex Court
Chambers national mooting competition, 23 June 2015)

Moots . . . are a small but firm step on the road to a place in chambers or a training contract.
(*The Times Student Law Supplement*, 19 October 2004)

Mooting . . . provides law students from universities and colleges throughout the United Kingdom with the opportunity to gain experience in their future role as advocates. In taking part in a moot, students do not just show their knowledge and skill in handling legal materials, but also their ability to practise the art of forensic and persuasive argument in a concise and effective manner. Furthermore, mooting enables students to gain confidence as advocates in a courtroom setting.

(Essex Court Chambers, London, 2013)

[E]ncouraging young lawyers to hone their advocacy skills at an early stage . . . [is] effectively investing in the future . . .

(Lord Collins of Mapesbury, 2010)

The benefits of mooting are numerous and include:

Mooting enhances your research and analytical skills as well as your ability to learn the law

In order to present your moot in a satisfactory and persuasive manner, you will need a thorough understanding of the legal issues involved in the moot problem. To do this properly, you will need to read and understand a significant number of cases and be able to identify and apply the legal principles appropriately in the moot. This can be contrasted with preparing for an exam where, although not recommended, reading a few pages from a student textbook and some headnotes from key cases might just be enough to get you through the earlier stages of your studies. This will not be nearly enough to succeed at mooting. The additional time spent in preparing for a moot can pay dividends in another way. Moot problems, just like exam questions, are often set to reflect topical legal issues, and mooting students frequently report having to spend much less time revising for their exams on topics they have researched for their moots.

There is one important additional point to make. Mooting requires you to engage properly with primary sources of law such as decided cases and statutes rather than relying on the secondary sources of textbooks. Engaging with primary sources helps you to construct your arguments in the same way practising lawyers would construct their arguments, thus enabling you to be creative with your submissions rather than merely repeating what a textbook author has said about a case. Additionally, some moots are written to test a novel point of law where a textbook will be of very limited assistance to you in any event.

Mooting enhances your CV

As you will have noted from the above quotations from *The Times Student Law Supplement* and from Lord Collins, mooting adds significant weight to your CV. Legal recruiters frequently remind us that evidence of mooting is crucial for any candidate wishing to pursue a career as an advocate because it confirms their commitment to advocacy and legal practice. This is even more important for students wishing to pursue a career at the Bar. Participating in mooting competitions is also a valuable addition to your CV as this demonstrates your commitment to those extra-curricular activities that complement your chosen career. In summary, there can be no better way of demonstrating your interest and commitment to advocacy than to add mooting to your CV.

Mooting boosts your confidence

Mooting is often a student's first experience of applying their legal skills in a practical context. Quite understandably, some students will query whether they have what it takes to become a lawyer and whether they will succeed in the profession. Mooting is one of the best activities for boosting your confidence and putting your practical skills into practice.

Mooting provides excellent public speaking experience

Moots are often performed in front of an audience. This can be anything from a small number of your fellow students, your family and friends, your lecturers or tutors, to a larger audience in the case of a competition. Standing up in front of any audience can, at first, be quite a daunting experience, but once you have done this a few times it can be extremely enjoyable and rewarding. Having the confidence to get up and speak in front of any audience is a valuable experience for anyone, no matter what career you ultimately decide to pursue.

Even outside of the law, being able to stand up and deliver presentations, chair meetings, deliver training and the like are real assets for anyone.

Mooting will help your teamwork

Mooting is an excellent team activity where both members of the team work together to present their case in a way that complements the other. No matter how good your submissions are, they will not serve your team at all well if they damage or contradict those of your partner. Working with your teammate during the preparatory stage of putting your submissions together is therefore essential. Using your teammate as a critical sounding board can also pay dividends. A submission that struck you as a good one may not be that attractive once you have discussed it critically with your teammate.

Remember that in order to win a moot, your team needs to be better than your opponent's team. Any help that you can give each other is likely therefore to bear fruit.

Mooting will improve your skills as an advocate

There can be no better activity than mooting to improve your advocacy skills. By participating in a moot, you will learn skilfully how to persuade a court that your client's case is correct and should succeed.

Mooting will improve your ability to think on your feet

Being able to deal well with judicial interventions requires you to think on your feet. This is a skill that improves with practice and is one that all good lawyers possess.

Mooting makes you think and act as a lawyer in practice would think and act

From the moment you receive your 'brief' you will take on an identical role to the practising lawyer in getting your case ready for hearing. You will use all the various skills you have learned and apply them in a practical legal exercise.

Taking all of the above points together, you can see that mooting really does make you think and act the same way a lawyer in practice would think and act.

We considered above the importance of engaging thoroughly with primary sources of law rather than relying on secondary sources. Just as a practising lawyer would not base his submissions on what a textbook writer had to say about a particular case, neither should you when preparing your submissions. The judge (whether in a real court or a moot court) will expect you to have read and thoroughly understood a case and be able to refer to particular passages in the judgments that support your arguments.

Good lawyers are not afraid of getting to grips with primary sources of law and appreciate the advantages of being able to interpret the decided cases themselves and adapt them in their submissions. This is a skill that you will pick up as a mooter.

In addition to the skills and experience that mooting will bring, it will also expose you to the kind of life you might expect as a practising advocate, whether at the Bar or as a solicitor advocate. You can then make an informed decision about whether advocacy, in any form, is really for you.

The participants and their roles

A moot typically has the following participants.

Mooters

There are four mooters in a moot: two for the appellant and two for the respondent. They are referred to as leading counsel and junior counsel. These titles are not (insofar as the participants are concerned) intended to indicate seniority – they are just titles given for the purpose of the moot. Each of the mooters has a different role:

Appellant

Leading counsel	• opens the moot and introduces all parties to the judge(s) • opens the appellant's case and addresses the first ground of appeal • (in some moots) exercises the appellant's right to reply[a]
Junior counsel	• follows leading counsel and addresses the second ground of appeal • concludes the appellant's case by inviting the court to allow the appeal

a Although it is customary for the right to reply to be given by leading counsel, it is generally permissible (unless the rules or judge say otherwise) for this to be given by junior counsel.

Respondent

Leading counsel	• opens the respondent's case and addresses the first ground of appeal. This includes responding to submissions made by the appellant's leading counsel
Junior counsel	• follows leading counsel and addresses the second ground of appeal. This includes responding to submissions made by the appellant's junior counsel • concludes the respondent's case by inviting the court to dismiss the appeal

In the case of an appeal and cross-appeal, the order of the mooters is different. To see what is meant by an appeal and cross-appeal, see the moots on pages 253–256. With this type of moot, the appeal is dealt with first, followed by the cross-appeal. The format is best explained by the following table:

Leading counsel for the appellant	• opens the moot and introduces all parties to the judge(s) • opens the appellant's case and addresses the first ground of appeal
Leading counsel for the respondent	• opens the respondent's case and addresses the first ground of appeal. This includes responding to submissions made by the appellant's leading counsel
Junior counsel for the cross-appellant	• addresses submissions on the cross-appeal on behalf of the cross-appellant
Junior counsel for the cross-respondent	• addresses submissions on the cross-appeal on behalf of the cross-respondent. This includes responding to submissions made by the cross-appellant
Reply by the appellant	• exercises the appellant's right to reply
Reply by the cross-appellant	• exercises the cross-appellant's right to reply

Mooting tip

When you first receive the moot problem, it might not be that clear which side or party you are representing. For example, you might be told that you are representing 'the appellant' without being told who the appellant is. Conversely, you might be given the name of the party you are representing without being told whether they are appellant or respondent. In the case of an appeal and cross-appeal, you will also need to work out where the cross-appellant and cross-respondent fit into the moot. It might be easier when you first get the moot problem to ignore the various terms 'appellant', 'respondent', 'cross-appellant' and 'cross-respondent', and instead look to see which side is appealing the judgment from the court below and leave for a moment the question of which side is cross-appealing. Looking at the moot on pages 254–256, you will see at paragraph 5 that 'permission has been granted by the Supreme Court for an appeal by Sloth Inc and cross-appeal by Pear Inc on the following points . . .'. Paragraph 5 makes clear, therefore, that Sloth Inc are the appellants.

In Scotland, the order in which the mooters speak is different to that in England and Wales:

Speaker No.	
1	Junior counsel for the appellant/reclaimer
2	Junior counsel for the respondent
3	Senior counsel for the appellant/reclaimer
4	Senior counsel for the respondent

Judge(s)

The judge is in overall charge of the moot. At the end of the moot, the judge will usually deliver a short judgment on the law before announcing the winner of the moot. Winning the legal arguments should have no bearing on the team that wins the moot. Some moots have a panel of judges, especially for the final rounds.

Clerk

The clerk sits with the judge and assists him with the bundles and papers. The clerk also calls on the case and instructs the court to stand when the judge enters and is ready to retire/leave the court.

Timekeeper

The timekeeper keeps the time. The rules of the moot will state how long each mooter has to present their arguments and whether or not the clock stops for judicial interventions.

The moot room

Moot rooms vary in size and facilities, ranging from a classroom to a purpose-built moot room. Sometimes a moot will take place in a real courtroom. In all cases, the layout of the room will be similar. The judge's bench is often on a platform so that it is elevated from the remainder of the court.

The figure below shows a typical layout of a moot room in England and Wales.

The Moot Room in the Redmonds Building at
Liverpool John Moores University

Scottish moot rooms are laid out differently to those in England and Wales to reflect the different layout of Scottish courts. The figure below illustrates a typical layout of a Scottish moot room.

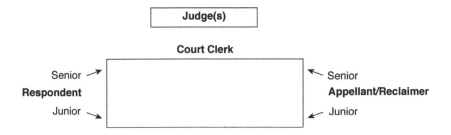

The grounds of appeal

The grounds of appeal are the most important parts of the moot as these determine the basis of your arguments. All moot problems will set out the grounds of the appeal and it is important that these are adhered to – you must not deviate from them. A typical moot will have two grounds of appeal which are divided between the two mooters in each team. You will be told which side you will be representing, usually at the same time as the moot problem is circulated.

What makes a good mooter?

A good mooter is an effective advocate – someone who has thoroughly prepared and knows their material inside out. Mooting often involves complex legal issues with no single or straightforward answer. A good mooter is someone who is able to make their submissions in a logical and easy-to-follow manner while remaining a pleasure to listen to. Good mooters exude confidence and are well organised. Overall, good mooters are able to make their submissions in a persuasive manner and make effective use of the limited time available to them.

Before reading this book in detail, and by way of a general introduction to the skills you will need in order to succeed at mooting, you might find it helpful to review the following advice that is provided to mooters in the English-Speaking Union–Essex Court Chambers National Mooting Competition Handbook.

Introduction

A successful mooter is one who manages to persuade the judge of the superiority of his or her legal arguments.

A good legal argument:

- is clearly and, if possible, concisely stated;
- is well reasoned and logical;
- is supported, so far as possible, by legal principles established in previous cases; and
- is directly applicable to the facts of the case.

A successful mooter is likely:

- to be familiar with the facts but will not speculate upon them;
- to offer well-structured and clear arguments without reading them from a prepared script;
- to be able to engage with the judge in unscripted discussion about the strengths and weaknesses of the argument; and
- to refer to case law to support his or her arguments but will avoid lengthy quotations, or quotations taken out of context, and will acknowledge the relative weight of different authorities.

Preparing for the moot

Preparing for a moot is a different exercise to preparing for a tutorial or other abstract legal discussion. While the skills of legal research and legal problem-solving which you have developed as a law student are useful, mooting requires something extra. It is an argument in which you have to persuade the judge by force of legal reasoning. One of the rewards of mooting however is a deepened understanding of the nature of legal reasoning and its application within our legal system.

You should benefit not just in terms of your professional future but also in terms of your intellectual and academic skills.

When preparing for a moot:

- familiarise yourself thoroughly with the facts and the grounds of appeal;
- become equally familiar with the legal reasoning adopted in the authorities relevant to your grounds of appeal (including the authorities upon which your opponent will rely);
- construct a legal argument which is consistent with the authorities upon which you will rely and which is applicable to the facts of the case;
- ensure that in adopting your argument, the court is not being asked to act beyond its powers, e.g. do not expect the Court of Appeal to overrule a House of Lords decision (although it could distinguish it);
- draft a skeleton argument which summarises accurately your arguments and which refers appropriately to your authorities;
- anticipate your opponent's likely arguments and think how you will counter them during the moot.

There is nothing wrong in seeking advice from tutors or others, nor in asking them to act as a coach.

Conduct of the moot

Speakers should dress soberly as if in a court. Gowns may be worn but only if all four speakers are able to do so. Try not to deflect attention away from what you are saying by fiddling with coins in pockets, shuffling about, walking up and down, leaning on the desk and so on.

The first speaker in the moot must introduce himself or herself and the three other speakers, and should say, 'May it please your Lordship/Ladyship, I am [Caroline Whitmore] and I appear in this matter on behalf of the [Appellant], together with my learned friend [Miss Sally Webb], and the [Respondent] is represented by my learned friends [Mr William Postgate] and [Miss Mary White].' Always end your submission by asking the judge if there are any questions to be asked by saying, 'Unless I can help your Lordship/Ladyship any further . . .', wait to see if you can, then thank the judge and sit down.

Address the judge directly as 'My Lord'/'My Lady' and indirectly as 'Your Lordship'/'Your Ladyship'. Refer to other speakers as 'My learned friend' or 'My learned junior/leader'. In court an advocate will never say

'I think . . .' or 'In my opinion . . .' in the presentation of their arguments; the correct form is that which connotes the advancement of opposing ideas, such as 'I submit . . .' or 'It is my submission that . . .' or even 'I suggest . . .'. Do not interrupt the judge when you are being asked questions. If the judge interrupts you, let him. When responding to the judge's questions or interruptions, be deferential but firm; whether agreeing or disagreeing, always do so 'with respect . . .'. If the judge directs you to address a particular point, say, 'If your Lordship/Ladyship pleases'.

General

You are strongly advised to read the guidance for judges so that you are familiar with the kinds of things that the judge is looking for in a mooter. The judge will be particularly interested in your ability to present your submissions on the law while at the same time dealing with questions arising all within the relevant time-frame. The judge is likely to be aware of the facts of the problem, though the first speaker should enquire about this and be prepared to provide to the judge an accurate or balanced summary. Do not spend time on this unless it is necessary. The facts of a moot problem are never in dispute and should not be argued over.

'Hot air' and oratory do not win moots, but the style in which an argument is presented is nevertheless important. As the object of the moot is to persuade the judge to find for your side, you must first make sure that the judge can hear and see you; so speak deliberately and audibly and try to establish eye contact. Do not speak in a rushed or mumbled manner. You should never read your speech or write it out word for word. Detailed notes are fine, but be prepared at any stage to be told by the judge that he wants you to move on. A rigid script will limit your flexibility to do so. Speeches that are read tend to be given in a dull monotone and eye contact is not achieved. The structure and development of your argument should also be presented slowly and concisely – your judge will certainly be taking notes and may know little of the area of law to which you refer. In particular, cite any authority slowly, giving the judge time to find and read the passage. Indicate when you are finished with one point by saying, 'If I may move on'.

Watch out for 'leads' from the bench and be ready to make immediate use of them, even if it means re-arranging or amending your argument. In particular, if the judge has indicated he is with you on a point, or does not wish to hear further argument upon it, move on to the next one.

If the judge asks you a question which you cannot answer on the spur of the moment, you may ask for leave to return to the point later or even to confer with your teammate. If you cannot answer, it is best to be honest about it rather than provide a hopeless response or promise to come to the point later in your argument and then fail to do so. Try to ensure that, so far as is possible, your argument can stand by itself and has no excessive dependency upon authority. Authorities are a tool, not an end in themselves. Use them to support your argument rather than making your argument a connection between a list of quotations. However, always be prepared to support any point in your argument with authority if called upon to do so, which authority should be contained in your list. If you refer to a dictum in passing you should cite the portion of it on which you rely. Do not cite a case without offering to tell the judge, however briefly, of the facts and the decision.

Always ensure the clerk to the court has all the cases you have listed present in court for the use of the judge. As there are often omissions, it is wise to prepare an unmarked copy that can be handed to the judge. When citing cases, the full reference should always be given e.g. [1966] 1 W.L.R. 1234 is: 'reported in the first volume of the Weekly Law Reports for 1966 at page 1234'. Cases should be cited as e.g. 'Hills and Duhig' or 'The Crown against Dixon'. Do not say 'versus' or 'v'.

Do not refer to judges in a case by their abbreviated titles, but rather as 'Mr Justice Kirk' or 'Lord Justice Sheridan'. Do be concise; the timing of a moot is very limited, so ensure you do not waste your or the court's time by reading out unnecessarily long passages from authorities. The effective use of your time is rewarded by judges. Do not exceed the time allotted to you or you may risk being told to sit down by the judge.

A speaker must never mislead the court. The most likely occasion for this is to cite a case without referring to other relevant but opposing authorities. Tactically, it is better for you to bring them to the attention of the judge than for your opponent to do so.

In short, your role as an advocate is to structure your client's case to form cogent legal arguments and to make persuasive representations to the court to obtain the best possible outcome.

These, and many more skills of the good mooter, are what this book is about.

2 Key aspects of the English legal system

Introduction

It should go without saying that you will need a good understanding of the English legal system or, if the moot is held in a different jurisdiction, the legal system pertaining to that jurisdiction. Although it is unlikely that judges will question you specifically on this, it will be apparent from your submissions if you present your case without such an understanding.

This chapter is not intended to be a substitute for other texts on the English legal system. Although the chapter will prove invaluable to any student of law, its primary purpose is to provide clear practical guidance on the English legal system as it relates specifically to mooting.

Upon initial receipt of the moot problem, many mooters will understandably rush to the textbooks to try to find the answer. Many moots don't have an answer as such but a range of possible arguments that can sensibly be made. However, your research will make little sense unless you have a good knowledge of the relevant legal system that underpins the area of substantive law pertaining to the moot. Even basic legal principles which students learn at the beginning of their studies are sometimes overlooked in the rush to find the solution to the moot. For example, mooters sometimes quote from dissenting judgments without realising that they have done so, or read from the case headnote believing it to be part of the judgment. A good background knowledge of the relevant legal system will ensure these basic mistakes are not made, especially when the mooter is under the pressure of judicial questions which may take them away from the security and comfort of a prepared speech. The question of prepared speeches is discussed at length in Chapter 6.

Sources of English law

Submissions made to the moot judge should be based on appropriate legal authority. Without this, they will be little more than your own opinions or the opinions of others, which will do little to persuade the court to accede to them. You will need to understand not only the sources of English law but also what weight the court should attach to them.

Primary sources of law

(a) Primary legislation

The most important source of English law is statute law (also known as Acts of Parliament). You should remind yourself of the doctrine of parliamentary supremacy which holds that Parliament is the supreme legal authority in the UK and can create or abolish any law it wishes. In general terms, the courts cannot overrule legislation passed by Parliament and no parliament can pass laws that future parliaments cannot change. Conversely, legislation can be passed by Parliament that can amend or abolish any rule or principle of the common law. As Salmon LJ explained in *Blackburn v The Attorney-General:*[1]

> Parliament . . . can enact, amend and repeal any legislation it pleases. The sole power of the Courts is to decide and enforce what is the law and not what it should be – now, or in the future.

In *AXA General Insurance Ltd v The Lord Advocate,*[2] the Supreme Court indicated that there may be exceptional circumstances where, should Parliament enact a law that was contrary to the rule of law or fundamental rights, the courts might refuse to apply it.[3]

(b) Secondary legislation

Secondary (or delegated) legislation is law that has been made by bodies or persons to whom Parliament has granted law-making powers through an enabling statute which lays down the basic framework of the law while leaving the detail to others. These include by-laws and statutory instruments and they are considerable in number. Bodies or persons who have been given the power to pass delegated legislation may only do so within the confines of the limited powers extended to them under the enabling statute. Any laws passed outside of these powers are *ultra vires* and can, therefore, be declared invalid by the courts.

An example of the relationship between primary and secondary legislation is the Health and Safety at Work Act 1974 (an Act of Parliament) and the Lifting Operations and Lifting Equipment Regulations 1998 (secondary/delegated legislation). The introduction to these Regulations provides that:

> The Secretary of State, in exercise of the powers conferred on him by sections 15(1), (2), (3)(a) and (5)(b), 49 and 82(3)(a) of, and paragraphs 1(1), (2) and (3), 14, 15(1) and 16 of Schedule 3 to, the Health and Safety at Work

1 [1971] 1 WLR 1037, 1041
2 [2012] 1 AC 868, [2011] UKSC 46
3 See, for example, Lord Hope at [97] and Lord Reed at [135] and [149]–[153]

etc. Act 1974 and of all other powers enabling him in that behalf and for the purpose of giving effect without modifications to proposals submitted to him by the Health and Safety Commission under section 11(2)(d) of the 1974 Act after the carrying out by the said Commission of consultations in accordance with section 50(3) of that Act, hereby makes the . . . . Regulations.

Mooting tip
The key point to remember is that although the courts have no power to declare statutes invalid, they are able to quash secondary legislation if they have been passed outside of the powers granted under the statute.

(c) Case law

Case law (or common law) is something that features extensively in moots. It is typically concerned with the development, application and interpretation of existing legal principles to cases coming before the courts rather than creating entirely new laws which, as we have just seen, is a matter for Parliament itself.

Case law is extremely important due to our system of binding precedent and is discussed separately below.

Secondary sources of law

You should not confuse secondary legislation (discussed above) with secondary sources of law, such as textbooks and journal articles. Although secondary sources can prove invaluable in helping you to understand legal principles, they have no binding effect on a court and should not be cited as authority: legal authority is confined to primary sources of law, such as statute and case law. That said, textbooks and journal articles are sometimes cited in court and referred to with approval in some judgments. If you do decide to refer to textbooks or articles, you should consider making it clear to the court that you are aware that they have no binding effect. You should also select your texts with care. You should refer to material that is as authoritative as you can find. These texts are typically the leading practitioner texts on the subject and are often referred to with approval in judgments. You should always make sure that you cite from the most up-to-date editions. The following table sets out a number of the key practitioner texts:

Subject	Title
Agency	Bowstead and Reynolds on Agency
Company law	Gore-Browne on Companies
Conflict of laws	Dicey, Morris and Collins on the Conflict of Laws
Contract law	Chitty on Contracts
Criminal law	Archbold Criminal Pleading, Evidence and Practice

Subject	Title
Damages	McGregor on Damages
Encyclopaedia of law	Halsbury's Laws of England
Equity	Snell's Equity
Land law/real property	Megarry and Wade: The Law of Real Property; Emmet and Farrand on Title
Negligence and nuisance	Charlesworth and Percy on Negligence
Private international law	Dicey, Morris and Collins on the Conflict of Laws
Restitution	Goff and Jones on the Law of Restitution
Tort law	Clerk and Lindsell on Torts
Trusts and trustees	Underhill and Hayton, Law of Trusts and Trustees

Additionally, for a Scottish law moot, the relevant practitioner texts include the following:

Subject	Title
Company law	Gore-Browne on Companies
Contract law	McBryde, The Law of Contract in Scotland
Criminal law	Gordon, The Criminal Law of Scotland
Delict	Walker, The Law of Delict in Scotland
Encyclopaedia of law	The Laws of Scotland: Stair Memorial Encyclopaedia
Land law	Gordon and Wortley, Scottish Land Law
Private International Law	Anton and Beaumont, Private International Law
Trusts and succession	Meston, Scottish Trusts and Succession Service

Although student textbooks should generally be avoided, there are exceptions, such as *Smith & Hogan's Criminal Law* which is occasionally cited in criminal cases. Similarly, with journal articles, you should select from the main journals (such as the *Law Quarterly Review, Modern Law Review, Criminal Law Review* or specialist subject journals such as the *Construction Law Journal*) rather than those that publish in newspaper or magazine format.

It should not add any more weight to an article if the author also happens to be a judge. Megarry J explained the reasons for this in *Cordell v Second Clanfield Properties Ltd*:[4]

> It seems to me that words in a book written or subscribed to by an author who is or becomes a judge have the same value as words written by any other reputable author, neither more nor less. The process of authorship is entirely different from that of judicial decision. The author, no doubt, has

4 [1969] 2 Ch 9

the benefit of a broad and comprehensive survey of his chosen subject as a whole, together with a lengthy period of gestation, and intermittent opportunities for reconsideration. But he is exposed to the peril of yielding to preconceptions, and he lacks the advantage of that impact and sharpening of focus which the detailed facts of a particular case bring to the judge. Above all, he has to form his ideas without the aid of the purifying ordeal of skilled argument on the specific facts of a contested case. Argued law is tough law. This is as true today as it was in 1409 when Hankford J. said: '*Home ne scaveroit de quel metal un campane fuit, si ceo ne fuit bien batu, quasi diceret, le ley per bon disputacion serru bien conus*' [Just as it is said 'A man will not know of what metal a bell is made if it has not been well beaten' so the law shall be well known by good disputation]; and these words are none the less apt for a judge who sits, as I do, within earshot of the bells of St. Clements. I would, therefore, give credit to the words of any reputable author in book or article as expressing tenable and arguable ideas, as fertilisers of thought, and as conveniently expressing the fruits of research in print, often in apt and persuasive language. But I would do no more than that; and in particular I would expose those views to the testing and refining process of argument. Today, as of old, by good disputing shall the law be well known.[5]

Law Commission reports should also be cited with caution. They can be very illuminating in setting out the (then) current state of the law and its defects, together with their proposals for reform. The difficulty with citing such material is that if the proposals for reform are substantial, the court is likely to say that any such changes are a matter for Parliament rather than the courts. In all cases, you will need to provide cogent reasons why the court should accede to your submissions.

Because the Supreme Court is not bound by its own previous decisions (or those of its predecessor, the House of Lords) there may be greater scope for referring to the writings of leading authors in your attempt to persuade the court to depart from one of its own previous decisions. However, just because the Supreme Court *may* depart from one of its own previous decisions it does not mean that it will easily do so. We will consider the principles of precedent below, but for present purposes it should be noted that decisions of the Supreme Court are normally *binding* on itself but may be departed from *when it appears right to do so*. For this reason, you must justify fully your reasons if you are to stand any chance of persuading the Supreme Court to depart from one of its previous decisions or one from the House of Lords. The task will be made much easier if you can show significant criticism to the previous decisions from judges, practitioners or leading academics. Such criticism was one of the reasons why the House of Lords in *R v G & Another*[6] was persuaded to overrule its previous

5 Ibid., 16
6 [2004] 1 AC 1034

decision in *R v Caldwell*[7] on the meaning of recklessness in criminal law. Lord Bingham expressed the point this way:

> I do not think the criticism of *R v Caldwell* expressed by academics, judges and practitioners should be ignored. A decision is not, of course, to be overruled or departed from simply because it meets with disfavour in the learned journals. But a decision which attracts reasoned and outspoken criticism by the leading scholars of the day, respected as authorities in the field, must command attention. One need only cite (among many other examples) the observations of Professor John Smith . . . and Professor Glanville Williams. . . . This criticism carries greater weight when voiced also by judges as authoritative as Lord Edmund-Davies and Lord Wilberforce in *R v Caldwell* itself, Robert Goff LJ in *Elliott v C* [1983] 1 WLR 939 and Ackner LJ in *R v Stephen Malcolm R* (1984) 79 Cr App R 334. The reservations expressed by the trial judge in the present case are widely shared. The shopfloor response to *R v Caldwell* may be gauged from the editors' commentary, to be found in the 41st edition of *Archbold* (1982). . . . The editors suggested that remedial legislation was urgently required.[8]

Mooting tip

For the reasons explained above, although secondary sources can prove invaluable in helping you to understand legal principles, you should cite them with caution and never as authority. That said, it is often helpful to begin your research using secondary sources as a 'funnel approach'. This enables wider reading of and around the subject and will provide a helpful overview of the issues as well as help identify the primary source(s) of the relevant law.

Statutory interpretation and the construction of statutes

Many moot problems will concern to a greater or lesser degree the correct interpretation of a statute. In such a case, you will need to understand how the courts approach the matter.

Aids to interpretation

There are several aids that can assist the court in interpreting a statute, both intrinsic and extrinsic.

---

7 [1982] AC 341
8 Ibid., [34]

(a) Intrinsic aids

An internal aid is one found within the piece of legislation itself. Examples of internal aids are the literal and golden rules of interpretation which will be discussed below. They also include the following:

THE STATUTE

The court may draw comparisons with provisions elsewhere in the same statute. The long title, the short title and the subheadings in the statute may also provide assistance as to the meaning of a particular provision, although it cannot overrule a clear statement to the contrary within the wording of the statute itself.

THE PREAMBLE AND EXPLANATORY NOTES

Older statutes contain a preamble which sets out its purpose, often in some detail. Where a statute contains a preamble, it may be used as an aid to interpretation. Since 1999, explanatory notes have been published at the same time as the statute and these may also be used to explain the main purposes and meaning of the legislation.

THE MARGINAL NOTES

When they appear, marginal notes do not form part of the legislation but are added by the draftsman solely for facility of reference. Marginal notes have been known to be rather misleading; for example, the marginal note to s 143 of the Criminal Justice and Public Order Act 1994 refers to 'male rape and buggery' whereas the section refers only to the latter. The traditional rule held that marginal notes were not permitted as aids to construction even in the case of ambiguity.[9] The reason for this has been said to be because marginal notes are not inserted by Parliament but by 'irresponsible persons'.[10] However, in *Stephens v Cuckfield Rural District Council*,[11] Upjohn LJ stated that

> the marginal note to a section cannot control the language used in the section, it is at least permissible to approach a consideration of its general purpose and the mischief at which it is aimed with the note in mind.[12]

9 See, for example, *Chandler v Director of Public Prosecutions* [1964] AC 763.
10 *Re Woking Urban District Council (Basingstoke Canal) Act 1911* [1914] 1 Ch 300, 322, Phillimore LJ. However, in *R v Montila* [2004] 1 WLR 3141 Lord Hope disagreed with this and said: 'It is not true that headings and side notes are inserted by "irresponsible persons", in the sense indicated by Phillimore LJ. They are drafted by Parliamentary Counsel, who are answerable through the Cabinet Office to the Prime Minister' [33].
11 [1960] 2 QB 373
12 Ibid., 383

More recently, it has been held that marginal notes can be considered. In *R v Montila*,[13] Lord Hope explained that:

> The question then is whether headings and side notes, although unamendable, can be considered in construing a provision in an Act of Parliament. Account must, of course, be taken of the fact that these components were included in the Bill not for debate but for ease of reference. This indicates that less weight can be attached to them than to the parts of the Act that are open for consideration and debate in Parliament. But it is another matter to be required by a rule of law to disregard them altogether. One cannot ignore the fact that the headings and side notes are included on the face of the Bill throughout its passage through the Legislature. They are there for guidance. They provide the context for an examination of those parts of the Bill that are open for debate. Subject, of course, to the fact that they are unamendable, they ought to be open to consideration as part of the enactment when it reaches the statute book.[14]

THE SCHEDULES

Usually appearing at the end of a statute and dealing with matters such as transitional provisions and things that have been repealed by the statute, the Schedules can be referred to in the event of ambiguity or uncertainty about any of the statute's provisions.

INTERPRETATION SECTIONS

The majority of statutes contain interpretation sections which provide guidance as to how certain words or phrases used in the statute should be interpreted.

THE RULES OF LANGUAGE

Courts have also been assisted by the rules of language that have been developed over the years, including *ejusdem generis* (general words which follow specific words are taken to include only things of the same kind), *noscitur a sociis* (a word can draw its meaning from other words around it) and *expressio unius exclusio alterius* (express reference to one thing implies the exclusion of another). We will return to these rules at page 28.

(b) Extrinsic aids

An extrinsic aid is one that is external to the statute. Some external aids, such as dictionaries, are straightforward and the court is able to refer to them where

13 [2004] 1 WLR 3141
14 Ibid., [34]

necessary in order to ascertain the meaning of a non-legal word. Courts may also refer to textbooks in appropriate circumstances and also to earlier statutes when ascertaining the mischief that the statute under consideration is attempting to remedy. The Interpretation Act 1978 may also be referred to when considering particular words that are used in various statues.[15]

HANSARD

Following the decision of the House of Lords in *Pepper (Inspector of Taxes) v Hart*,[16] the court is entitled, in certain circumstances, to refer to parliamentary materials. These circumstances were explained by Lord Browne-Wilkinson:

> [T]he exclusionary rule should be relaxed so as to permit reference to Parliamentary materials where (a) legislation is ambiguous or obscure, or leads to an absurdity; (b) the material relied upon consists of one or more statements by a Minister or other promoter of the Bill together if necessary with such other Parliamentary material as is necessary to understand such statements and their effect; (c) the statements relied upon are clear.[17]

Although the principle in *Pepper v Hart* was extended in *Three Rivers District Council v Governor and Company of the Bank of England (No 2)*[18] to include cases where the legislation under consideration was not in itself ambiguous but where guidance was needed on the general purpose of legislation, caution was emphasised in *Wilson v First County Trust Ltd (No. 2)*[19] where Lord Nicholls explained:

> I expect that occasions when resort to Hansard is necessary as part of the statutory 'compatibility' exercise will seldom arise . . . Should such an occasion arise the courts must be careful not to treat the ministerial or other statement as indicative of the objective intention of Parliament. Nor should the courts give a ministerial statement, whether made inside or outside Parliament, determinative weight. It should not be supposed that members necessarily agreed with the minister's reasoning or his conclusions.[20]

The point in *Wilson* that concerns us here is the way in which *Pepper v Hart* was used in relation to a question about the Human Rights Act 1998. To this, the court said that it would be rare that resort to *Hansard* would be appropriate in deciding the compatibility of an Act of Parliament with the Convention, and the possible interpretations that could be given to that Act. The role of the court is

---

15 Despite its somewhat misleading title, the Interpretation Act 1978 does not provide guidance for interpreting legislation.
16 [1993] AC 593
17 Ibid., 640
18 [1996] 2 All ER 363
19 [2004] 1 AC 816
20 Ibid., 843

to interpret the legislation as it stands and it will only be in limited circumstances that the court should have recourse to *Hansard* in its effort to find the meaning of a statute.

JUDICIAL APPROACHES TO STATUTORY INTERPRETATION

When determining the meaning of a statute, the court is required to ascertain the intention of Parliament. There are different approaches to this task. The Interpretation Act 1978 can prove helpful here as it provides certain definitions that are found in various statutes.

For example, section 5 provides that:

> In any Act, unless the contrary intention appears, words and expressions listed in Schedule 1 to this Act are to be construed according to that Schedule.

Schedule 1 defines various words and expressions.

Section 6 deals with gender and number and provides:

> In any Act, unless the contrary intention appears –
>
> (a) words importing the masculine gender include the feminine;
> (b) words importing the feminine gender include the masculine;
> (c) words in the singular include the plural and words in the plural include the singular.

Section 8 deals with distance and provides:

> In the measurement of any distance for the purposes of an Act, that distance shall, unless the contrary intention appears, be measured in a straight line on a horizontal plane.

Apart from the specific guidance provided by the Interpretation Act 1978, it is a matter for the court to determine how to interpret statutes. Three main rules or approaches have been devised to assist the courts, although the decision as to which, if any, of these approaches to use rests with the individual court.

Mooting tip

Because there is no rule of law that determines which of these approaches the court should follow, you can, within reason, be somewhat creative in selecting which of them best suits your submissions. Having said this, you will need to do this with caution and be alert to the possibility that the judge will ask you why you have chosen the approach you have rather than one of the others and whether the outcome would be different if the court decides to adopt one of the alternative approaches.

The literal rule As its name suggests, the literal rule gives all words in the statute their literal, ordinary and natural meaning. The basis for this rule is that the best way of identifying the will of Parliament is by adhering strictly to the literal words used.[21]

If the court follows the literal rule and 'the words of an Act are clear, you must follow them, even though they lead to a manifest absurdity. The court has nothing to do with the question of whether the legislature has committed an absurdity.' However, 'if the words of an Act admit two interpretations, and if one interpretation leads to an absurdity, and the other does not, the Court will conclude the legislature did not intend the absurdity and adopt the other interpretation'.[22] If an absurdity does arise as a result of the use of the literal rule, its devotees hold that any remedy is a matter for Parliament and not the courts (although this approach does nothing to support justice in the instant case). Lord Bramwell was one such devotee of the literal rule. In *Hill v East and West India Dock Co*,[23] he stated that 'it is infinitely better to adhere to the words of an Act of Parliament and leave the legislature to set it right than to alter these words according to one's notion of an absurdity'.

The practical problems with adopting the literal rule can be seen in cases such as *Fisher v Bell*.[24] Following several serious violent incidents in which flick knives were used to inflict injury, Parliament passed legislation to ban their sale. The Restriction of Offensive Weapons Act 1959 created an offence to 'sell or offer for sale' any flick knives. The defendant shopkeeper displayed a flick knife in his window for sale together with the price. He was charged with offering it for sale, contrary to the 1959 Act. The words 'offer for sale' were not defined in the Act and the magistrates gave the words their normal meaning under the general law of contract which meant that the shopkeeper had merely issued an invitation to treat. Dismissing the appeal, Lord Parker CJ explained:

> It is perfectly clear that according to the ordinary law of contract the display of an article with a price on it in a shop window is merely an invitation to treat. It is in no sense an offer for sale the acceptance of which constitutes a contract.[25]

---

21 Sometimes, though, the way in which an instrument has been drafted can make it extremely difficult to follow. See, for example, Schedule 2 of the Teachers (Compensation) (Advanced Further Education) Regulations 1983 which provides: 'In these Regulations a reference to a Regulation is a reference to a Regulation contained therein, a reference in a Regulation or the Schedule to a paragraph is a reference to a paragraph of that Regulation or the Schedule and a reference in a paragraph to a sub-paragraph is a reference to a sub-paragraph of that paragraph.'

22 *R v City of London Court Judge* [1892] 1 QB 273, 290, per Lord Esher MR

23 (1884) 9 App Cas 448

24 [1961] 1 QB 394

25 Ibid., 399

The shopkeeper was therefore not guilty of offering the flick knife for sale despite the fact that this was the exact kind of behaviour that the 1959 Act sought to prohibit.

The golden rule   The golden rule may be applied in cases where the application of the literal rule would lead to an absurdity. In such a case, the court may decide to depart from a literal interpretation and instead give the words a meaning that avoids an absurd result. *R v Allen*[26] concerned the meaning of s 57 of the Offences Against the Person Act 1861 which created the offence of bigamy. The section reads:

> Whosoever, being married, shall marry any other person during the life of the former husband or wife, whether the second marriage shall have taken place in England or Ireland or elsewhere, shall be guilty . . .

A literal interpretation of s 57 would make the offence of bigamy impossible to commit because it is impossible in law for a person who is already married to marry another person. To avoid this absurdity, the court in *Allen* applied the golden rule and held that the word 'marry' in the section should be interpreted as meaning 'to go through a marriage ceremony'. As a result, the defendant's conviction was upheld.

Similarly, in *Adler v George*[27] the defendant was charged under s 3 of the Official Secrets Act 1920 which created an offence of obstructing a member of the armed forces 'in the vicinity of' any prohibited place. The defendant had committed the obstruction in an air force station which was the prohibited place itself. Because a literal interpretation might have excluded any obstruction *in* the prohibited place, and it would be absurd for a person to be liable if they were near to a prohibited place but not if they were actually in it, the court held that 'in the vicinity of' should be interpreted to mean in or near the prohibited place.

The mischief (purposive) rule   The mischief rule is the oldest of the rules dating back to the sixteenth-century *Heydon's Case*.[28] It was described in 1969 by the Law Commission on Statutory Interpretation as a 'rather more satisfactory approach' to interpretation than either of the other two rules. In *Heydon's Case*, Lord Coke described the process through which the court must interpret the legislation. He explained that the court must consider the following questions:

1. What was the common law before making the Act under consideration?
2. What was the mischief and defect for which the common law did not provide?
3. What was the remedy Parliament passed to cure the mischief?
4. What was the true reason for the remedy?

---

26 (1872) LR 1 CCR 367
27 [1964] 2 QB 7
28 (1584) 76 ER 637

After considering these questions, the court should try to ascertain the intention of Parliament and apply the interpretation which corrects the mischief that the statute intended to put right.

The mischief rule was restated by the House of Lords in *Jones v Wrotham Park Settled Estates*[29] where Lord Diplock identified three necessary conditions for the rule to apply:

1. It must be possible to determine, from a consideration of the provisions of the Act read as a whole, precisely what the mischief was that it was the purpose of the Act to remedy.
2. It must be apparent that the draftsman and Parliament had by inadvertence overlooked, and so omitted to deal with, an eventuality that required to be dealt with if the purpose of the Act was to be achieved.
3. It must be possible to state with certainty what were the additional words that would have been inserted by the draftsman, and approved by Parliament, had their attention been drawn to the omission before the Bill was passed into law.

Lord Diplock explained that unless the third condition is fulfilled, any attempt by a court to repair the omission in the Act cannot be justified as an exercise of its jurisdiction to determine 'the meaning of a written law which Parliament has passed. Such an attempt crosses the boundary between construction and legislation. It becomes an usurpation of a function which under the constitution of this country is vested in the legislature to the exclusion of the courts.'[30]

The mischief rule helps avoid injustice and absurdity while promoting judicial flexibility. This flexibility, and the controversial nature of the rule, can be seen in *Royal College of Nursing of the United Kingdom v Department of Health and Social Security*.[31] The RCN challenged the legality of the involvement of nurses in carrying out abortions. It was an offence under s 58 of the Offences Against the Person Act 1861 for any person to carry out an abortion, while s 1 of the Abortion Act 1967 provided an absolute defence for a registered medical practitioner to carry out abortions provided certain conditions were satisfied. As a result of advances in medical science, surgical abortions were largely replaced with drug-induced ones and it was common for these to be administered by nurses. The question that arose is: since nurses were not medical practitioners, were these nurses acting unlawfully? By a majority, the House of Lords held that the Act was intended to provide for safe abortions, the mischief being to rid society of back-street abortions where no medical care was available, and that nurses could therefore lawfully carry out such procedures. Lord Wilberforce said that the House was not construing or interpreting the legislation but was

29 [1980] AC 74
30 Ibid., 105
31 [1981] AC 800

rewriting it, while Lord Edmund-Davies described it as 'redrafting with a vengeance'.[32]

The purposive approach is based on the mischief rule and involves seeking an interpretation of the law which best gives effect to its general purpose. This approach was explained by Lord Denning MR in *HP Bulmer Ltd v Bollinger SA*:[33]

> [W]hat are the English Courts to do when they are faced with a problem of interpretation? . . . No longer must they examine the words in meticulous detail. No longer must they argue about the precise grammatical sense. They must look to the purpose or intent. . . . They must not confine themselves to the English text. . . . If they find a gap, they must fill it as best they can. They must do what the framers of the instrument would have done if they had thought about it. So we must do the same.[34]

More recently, the House of Lords recognised the importance of the purposive approach in *R v Secretary of State for Health ex parte Quintavalle*.[35] This case concerned the interpretation of s 1(1) of the Human Fertilisation and Embryology Act 1990. Lord Steyn explained:

> [T]he adoption of a purposive approach to construction of statutes generally, and the 1990 Act in particular, is amply justified on wider grounds. In *Cabell v Markham* (1945) 148 F 2d 737, 739 Learned Hand J explained the merits of purposive interpretation:
>
> > 'Of course it is true that the words used, even in their literal sense, are the primary, and ordinarily the most reliable, source of interpreting the meaning of any writing: be it a statute, a contract, or anything else. But it is one of the surest indexes of a mature developed jurisprudence not to make a fortress out of the dictionary; but to remember that statutes always have some purpose or object to accomplish, whose sympathetic and imaginative discovery is the surest guide to their meaning.'
>
> The pendulum has swung towards purposive methods of construction. This change was not initiated by the teleological approach of European Community jurisprudence, and the influence of European legal culture generally, but it has been accelerated by European ideas . . . In any event, nowadays the shift towards purposive interpretation is not in doubt. The qualification is that the degree of liberality permitted is influenced by the context, eg social welfare legislation and tax statutes may have to be approached

32 Ibid., 831
33 [1974] Ch 401 (CA)
34 Ibid., 426
35 [2003] 2 AC 687

somewhat differently. For these slightly different reasons I agree with the conclusion of the Court of Appeal that section 1(1) of the 1990 Act must be construed in a purposive way.[36]

Mooting tip

You should note that once a court has determined the meaning of a statute (or part of a statute), that decision becomes part of case law in the same way as any other decision. Subject to the rules of precedent, a lower court is therefore bound to follow that interpretation.

Principles and presumptions of statutory interpretation

A number of principles and (rebuttable) presumptions have been developed to assist the courts in determining the meaning of a statute. These include:

- Statutes should be read as a whole.
- A presumption in favour of words taking their meaning from the context in which they are used.

    These two points are related and should be considered alongside the 'rules of language' noted at page 21. In short, other sections within the same statute might shed some light on the meaning of the words under consideration. This is why you should not try to interpret words within one section in isolation of the words used elsewhere in the statute.

    o   *Ejusdem generis* – general words which follow specific words are taken to include only things of the same kind. For example, in *Powell v Kempton Park Racecourse*[37] the House of Lords had to consider whether Tattersall's ring at a racecourse was an 'other place' within the meaning of s 1 of the Betting Act 1853 which made it an offence to keep a 'house, office, room or other place' for the purposes of betting. Tattersall's ring was an outside area and the House of Lords held that the general words 'other place' should be restricted to indoor places because the other words in the list were all references to places inside.

    o   *Noscitur a sociis* – a word is known by the company it keeps and can draw its meaning from other words around it. This rule was applied by the House of Lords in *Inland Revenue Commissioners v Frere*[38] where the word 'interest' had to be interpreted. The Income Tax Act 1952 allowed 'the amount of interest, annuities or other annual interest' to

---

36 Ibid., 700
37 [1899] AC 143
38 [1965] AC 402

be deducted from income. It was held that this related only to annual interest as the other items related to annual payments. As the respondent's interest payment was not an annual interest payment, he could not deduct it from his income for the purposes of calculating the income tax to be paid. Similarly, in *Pengelly v Bell Punch Co Ltd*[39] the statute required 'floors, steps, stairs, passages and gangways' to be kept clear. It was held 'floors' in this context referred to parts used as a passageway and not to the part of a factory floor used statically for storage.

o   *Expressio unius exclusio alterius* – express reference to one thing implies the exclusion of another. In *R v Inhabitants of Sedgely*,[40] a statute sought to raise taxes on 'lands, houses, tithes and coal mines'. It was held that it did not apply to limestone mines as these were impliedly excluded by the specific mention of coal mines.

- A presumption that a statute does not change the common law. Parliament can, of course, alter the common law but must expressly say so in the legislation.
- A presumption in favour of a *mens rea* requirement for statutory criminal offences. In *Sweet v Parsley*[41] a teacher rented out her house to some students. Unbeknown to her, the students were smoking cannabis in the house. She was charged with an offence of being concerned with the management of premises which were being used for the purposes of smoking cannabis contrary to s 5(6) of the Dangerous Drugs Act 1965. The wording in the section did not state any *mens rea* requirements. The House of Lords reviewed the pre-statute common law position which required knowledge of the activities in order to impose criminal liability. The presumptions that statutes do not change the common law and that *mens rea* is required were applied in cases, such as this one, where the offence is a 'real' crime as opposed to a regulatory offence.
- A presumption against the retrospective effect of new laws.
- A presumption against ousting the jurisdiction of the courts.
- A presumption against the deprivation of liberty. If Parliament intended to impose a sanction which deprives the individual of his liberty, then it must expressly say so in the legislation. In *R v Secretary of State for the Home Department, ex parte Khawaja*,[42] Lord Scarman explained the position in the following way:

> My Lords, in most cases I would defer to a recent decision of your Lordships' House on a question of construction, even if I thought it

39 [1964] 1 WLR 1055 (CA)
40 (1831) 2 B & Ad 65
41 [1970] AC 132
42 [1984] AC 74

wrong. I do not do so in this context because for reasons which I shall develop I am convinced that the *Zamir* reasoning gave insufficient weight to the important (I would say fundamental) consideration that we are here concerned with, the scope of judicial review of a power which inevitably infringes the liberty of those subjected to it.[43]

- A presumption against application to the Crown. Unless the statute states clearly to the contrary, it will be presumed not to apply to the Crown.
- A presumption that Parliament does not intend to violate international laws. Wherever possible, the court should interpret legislation in such a way as to give effect to existing international legal obligations.

Hierarchy of the court system

You will need to understand the court structure and the various routes to an appeal, including the specific route to the appeal in which you are appearing. It is important not to focus on your grounds of appeal in isolation of the procedural history of the case which you may well be questioned about.

Mooting tip

You should understand where the case originated and how it got to the moot court. For example, if it is a criminal case, is the appeal from a decision of the Crown Court or Court of Appeal or is it an appeal by way of a case stated on a point of law? Has the case followed the ordinary hierarchy of the court structure or is it a 'leapfrog' appeal? Even if the moot judge does not ask you specific questions about this, it may be apparent from the way you argue the case that you are unfamiliar with the origins and procedural history of the case. By ensuring that you understand these points, you will not be wasting time (or losing marks) during the moot by attempting to deal with such basic matters which might affect your ability to deal with the substantive points you need to deal with.

You should also appreciate that the test which the Supreme Court applies when considering granting permission to appeal is a strict one. Permission is only granted for applications that, in the opinion of the Justices, raise an arguable point of law of general public importance which ought to be considered by the Supreme Court at that time, bearing in mind that the matter will already have been subjected to judicial scrutiny and may have already been reviewed on appeal.

43 Ibid., 109

England and Wales

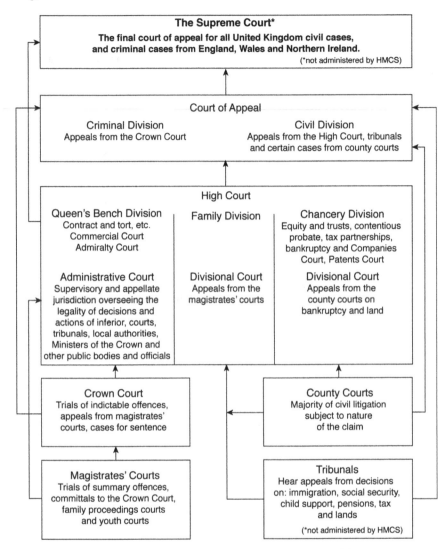

Hierarchy of the court system. Diagram reproduced from
Her Majesty's Courts Service.

Scotland

The court structure in Scotland is different although it still follows a hierarchical system. The Court of Session and the High Court of Justiciary are Scotland's Supreme Courts. The Court of Session is Scotland's highest civil court. It is divided into the Outer House and the Inner House. The Outer House hears cases at first instance whereas the Inner House is primarily an appeal court, hearing civil appeals from both the Outer House and Sheriff Courts. Appeals from the Inner House may go to the UK's Supreme Court sitting in London.

The High Court of Justiciary is Scotland's supreme criminal court. When sitting as a first instance trial court, it hears the most serious criminal cases, such as murder and rape. At first instance, it sits in cities and larger towns around Scotland; as an appeal court, it sits mostly in Edinburgh. The High Court hears criminal appeals from first instance cases from the High Court itself, Sheriff Courts and Justice of the Peace Courts.

The majority of cases are dealt with in the country's Sheriff Courts unless they are of sufficient seriousness to go to the Scottish Supreme Courts at first instance. The Sheriff Appeal Court was established in September 2015 to hear appeals arising out of summary criminal proceedings from both the Sheriff and Justice of the Peace Courts. Less serious criminal matters are heard at first instance in the Justice of the Peace Courts (in Glasgow, also the Stipendiary Magistrate Court). From 2008 to early 2010, Justice of the Peace Courts gradually replaced the former District Courts which were operated by local authorities.

The principles of binding precedent

The doctrine of precedent (*stare decisis*) lies at the heart of the English legal system. In short, decisions made by a higher court will be binding on a lower court.

> **Mooting tip**
>
> As Buxton LJ pointed out in *R (Kadhim) v Brent LBC Housing Benefit Review Board*,[44] it is the reasons and not the outcome that determine the status of a decision.

Although the rules of precedent serve to a large extent in achieving certainty, they should not be considered so rigid that they are unable to evolve so as to serve the needs of justice. This was explained by Lord Woolf CJ in *R v Simpson*:[45]

> The rules as to precedent reflect the practice of the courts and have to be applied bearing in mind that their objective is to assist in the administration of justice. They are of considerable importance because of their role in achieving the appropriate degree of certainty as to the law. This is an important requirement of any system of justice. The principles should not, however, be regarded as so rigid that they cannot develop in order to meet contemporary needs.

44 [2001] QB 955 at 965
45 [2004] QB 118 at 128

In *Willers v Joyce*,[46] a nine-justice Supreme Court explained the general principles of precedent in the following terms:

> In a common law system, where the law is in some areas made, and the law is in virtually all areas developed, by judges, the doctrine of precedent, or as it is sometimes known *stare decisis*, is fundamental. Decisions on points of law by more senior courts have to be accepted by more junior courts. Otherwise, the law becomes anarchic, and it loses coherence clarity and predictability . . . The doctrine is, of course, seen in its simplest and most familiar form when applied to the hierarchy of courts. On issues of law, (i) Circuit Judges are bound by decisions of High Court Judges, the Court of Appeal and the Supreme Court, (ii) High Court Judges are bound by decisions of the Court of Appeal and the Supreme Court, and (iii) the Court of Appeal is bound by decisions of the Supreme Court. (The rule that a Circuit Judge is bound by a decision of a High Court Judge is most clear from a 'Note' included at the end of the judgment in *Howard De Walden Estates Ltd v Aggio* [2008] Ch 26).
>
> The position is rather more nuanced when it comes to courts of co-ordinate jurisdiction.
>
> Until 50 years ago, the House of Lords used to be bound by its previous decisions (see e.g. *London Tramways Co Ltd v London County Council* [1898] AC 375). However, that changed in 1966 following the *Practice Statement (Judicial Precedent)* [1966] 1 WLR 1234, which emphasised that, while the Law Lords would regard their earlier decisions as 'normally binding', they would depart from them 'when it appears right to do so'. The importance of consistency in the law was emphasised by Lord Wilberforce in *Fitzleet Estates Ltd v Cherry* [1977] 1 WLR 1345, 1349, when he explained that the *Practice Statement* should not be invoked to depart from an earlier decision, merely because a subsequent committee of Law Lords take a different view of the law: there has to be something more. Having said that, the *Practice Statement* has been invoked on a number of occasions in the past half-century, most recently in *Knauer v Ministry of Justice* [2016] 2 WLR 672, where, at paras 21–23 it was emphasised that, because of the importance of the role of precedent and the need for certainty and consistency in the law, the Supreme Court 'should be very circumspect before accepting an invitation to invoke the 1966 Practice Statement'. The Court of Appeal is bound by its own previous decisions, subject to limited exceptions. The principles were set out by the Court of Appeal in a well-known passage (which was approved by the House of Lords in *Davis v Johnson* [1979] AC 264) in *Young v Bristol Aeroplane Co Ltd* [1944] KB 718, 729–730:
>
> > '[The Court of Appeal] is bound to follow previous decisions of its own as well as those of courts of co-ordinate jurisdiction. The only exceptions to this rule . . . are . . . (1) The court is entitled and bound to decide

which of two conflicting decisions of its own it will follow. (2) The court is bound to refuse to follow a decision of its own which, though not expressly overruled, cannot, in its opinion, stand with a decision of the House of Lords. (3) The court is not bound to follow a decision of its own if it is satisfied that the decision was given per incuriam.'

So far as the High Court is concerned, puisne judges are not technically bound by decisions of their peers, but they should generally follow a decision of a court of co-ordinate jurisdiction unless there is a powerful reason for not doing so. And, where a first instance judge is faced with a point on which there are two previous inconsistent decisions from judges of co-ordinate jurisdiction, then the second of those decisions should be followed in the absence of cogent reasons to the contrary: see *Patel v Secretary of State for the Home Department* [2013] 1 WLR 63, para 59. I would have thought that Circuit Judges should adopt much the same approach to decisions of other Circuit Judges.[47]

Before examining in detail the principles of *stare decisis*, it is important to recognise that no matter how powerful a judgment, it should never be read as if it were a statute. This caution was explained by Lord Nicholls in *Royal Brunei Airlines Sdn Bhd v Philip Tan Kok Ming*[48] where he criticised the tendency to elevate to the status of statute the much-quoted dictum of Lord Selborne LC in *Barnes v Addy*[49] in relation to the liability of trustees. Lord Nicholls explained what appears to have gone wrong is that:

[T]here has been a tendency to cite and interpret and apply Lord Selborne's formulation as though it were a statute . . . This approach has been inimical to analysis of the underlying concept.[50]

Mooting tip
When your opponent cites strong judicial authority against you, you should consider whether they are attempting to elevate it to the status afforded only to statute. If they are, the above passage from Lord Nicholls might prove useful.

We will start by considering the consequences of rulings made by the European Court of Justice and those made by the European Court of Human Rights. Only

---

47 The judgment goes on to consider the principles of precedent in relation to the Privy Council – indeed, this was the principal question for the court. This will be discussed below.
48 [1995] 2 AC 378 (PC)
49 (1874) LR 9 Ch App 244
50 Ibid., 386

rulings made by the former are binding. Lord Bingham explained this in *Kay and others v Lambeth London Borough Council:*[51]

> The mandatory duty imposed on domestic courts by section 2 [of the Human Rights Act] . . . is to take into account any judgment of the Strasbourg court and any opinion of the commission. Thus they are not strictly required to follow Strasbourg rulings, as they are bound by section 3(1) of the European Communities Act 1972 and as they are bound by the rulings of superior courts in the domestic curial hierarchy.[52]

European Court of Justice

Decisions of the European Court of Justice (ECJ) are binding on UK courts insofar as Community law matters are concerned. The ECJ is, in relation to such matters, the court of last resort. The ECJ generally follows its own previous decisions but is not bound to do so.

European Court of Human Rights

The European Court of Human Rights (ECtHR) is an international court, based in Strasberg, and rules on individual or State applications alleging violations of the European Convention on Human Rights.

Section 2(1) of the Human Rights Act 1998 provides that 'a court or tribunal determining a question which has arisen in connection with a Convention right must take into account any judgment, decision, declaration or advisory opinion of the European Court of Human Rights'. The words in the section 'must take into account' make clear that decisions of the ECtHR are not strictly binding on UK courts, although having taken the ECtHR jurisprudence into account they would usually be followed.

This position was confirmed by the Supreme Court in *Manchester City Council v Pinnock*[53] where Lord Neuberger MR observed:

> This court is not bound to follow every decision of the European court. Not only would it be impractical to do so: it would sometimes be inappropriate, as it would destroy the ability of the court to engage in the constructive dialogue with the European court which is of value to the development of Convention law . . . Of course, we should usually follow a clear and constant line of decisions by the European court . . . But we are not actually bound to do so or (in theory, at least) to follow a decision of the Grand Chamber. As [has been pointed out] section 2 of the 1998 Act requires our courts to 'take into account' European court decisions, not necessarily to follow them.

51 [2006] 2 AC 465 (HL)
52 Ibid., 490
53 [2011] 2 AC 104 (SC)

Where, however, there is a clear and constant line of decisions whose effect is not inconsistent with some fundamental substantive or procedural aspect of our law, and whose reasoning does not appear to overlook or misunderstand some argument or point of principle, we consider that it would be wrong for this court not to follow that line.

In the present case there is no question of the jurisprudence of the European court failing to take into account some principle or cutting across our domestic substantive or procedural law in some fundamental way. That is clear from the minority opinions in *Harrow London Borough Council v Qazi* [2004] 1 AC 983 and *Kay v Lambeth London Borough Council* [2006] 2 AC 465, and also from the fact that our domestic law was already moving in the direction of the European jurisprudence in *Doherty v Birmingham City Council* [2009] AC 367. Even before the decision in *Kay v United Kingdom* [2011] HLR 13, we would, in any event, have been of the opinion that this court should now accept and apply the minority view of the House of Lords in those cases. In the light of *Kay v United Kingdom* that is clearly the right conclusion.[54]

In *Kay and others v Lambeth London Borough Council*,[55] the House of Lords had to decide which decision should be followed in a case where a judgment made by a court which binds a lower court is inconsistent with a subsequent decision of the ECtHR. By a majority, it was held that although domestic courts were not strictly required to follow the rulings of the ECtHR, they were obliged to give practical recognition to the principles it expounded. The House of Lords also acknowledged that although it was a matter for the ECtHR to interpret Convention rights as they were uniformly to be understood by all member states, it was for domestic courts to determine initially how the principles it laid down were to be applied in the domestic context. Their Lordships also said that adherence to precedent was a cornerstone of the domestic legal system by which a degree of certainty in legal matters was best achieved and that judges could grant leave to appeal where they considered a binding precedent was inconsistent with Strasbourg authority and that, save in an extreme case where the decision of a superior court could not survive the introduction of the Human Rights Act 1998, they should follow the ordinary rules of precedent. Accordingly, the Court of Appeal had acted correctly when it followed a decision of the House of Lords (in favour of a conflicting decision of the ECtHR) and granted permission to appeal.

In exceptional circumstances, a court may be correct to follow a decision of the ECtHR rather than one from a court which would normally bind it. For example, in *D v East Berkshire Community NHS Trust and Others*,[56] the Court of Appeal declined to follow a decision of the House of Lords which was incompatible

54 Ibid., 125
55 [2006] 2 AC 465 (HL)
56 [2004] QB 558 (CA)

with the Convention on grounds *inter alia* that the ECtHR had disagreed with the House of Lords when it made an earlier decision in the same case and that the House of Lords' decision predated the Human Rights Act 1998.

Supreme Court/House of Lords

The Supreme Court replaced the Judicial Committee of the House of Lords in October 2009 and, like its predecessor, sits at the pinnacle of the court structure in England and Wales, with its judgments having the same binding effect as those made by its predecessor.

Decisions made by the Supreme Court are binding on all inferior courts. The rules on whether its decisions are binding on itself are the same as those that applied in the House of Lords – that is, they are 'normally binding' but may be departed from 'when it appears right to do so'. This was set out in the Practice Statement (Judicial Precedent) made in the House of Lords by Lord Gardiner LC:[57]

> Practice Statement (Judicial Precedent)
> House of Lords
> 26 July 1966
>
> Lord Gardiner LC, Viscount Dilhorne, Lord Reid, Lord Denning, Lord Parker of Waddington, Lord Morris of Borth-y-Gest, Lord Hodson, Lord Pearce, Lord Upjohn and Lord Wilberforce
>
> Judicial Precedent—House of Lords—Modification of practice—Former decisions of House normally binding—Departure from previous decision when appearing right to do so.
>
> Before judgments were given in the House of Lords Lord Gardiner LC made the following statement on behalf of himself and the Lords of Appeal in Ordinary:
>
> LORD GARDINER LC: Their Lordships regard the use of precedent as an indispensable foundation upon which to decide what is the law and its application to individual cases. It provides at least some degree of certainty upon which individuals can rely in the conduct of their affairs, as well as a basis for orderly development of legal rules.
>
> Their Lordships nevertheless recognise that too rigid adherence to precedent may lead to injustice in a particular case and also unduly restrict the proper development of the law. They propose, therefore, to modify their present practice and, while treating former decisions of this House as normally binding, to depart from a previous decision when it appears right to do so.
>
> In this connection they will bear in mind the danger of disturbing retrospectively the basis on which contracts, settlements of property and fiscal

57 [1966] 1 WLR 1234

arrangements have been entered into and also the especial need for certainty as to the criminal law.

This announcement is not intended to affect the use of precedent elsewhere than in this House.

The Supreme Court has not reissued this Practice Statement as a fresh statement of practice in the court's own name because

> it has as much effect in [the Supreme Court] as it did before the Appellate Committee in the House of Lords. It was part of the established jurisprudence relating to the conduct of appeals in the House of Lords which was transferred to [the Supreme Court] by section 40 of the Constitutional Reform Act 2005.[58]

It is important for the Supreme Court to have the ability to reconsider its previous decisions and those of the House of Lords as this enables it to reflect on changing social conditions as well as consider the decisions from the courts in the Commonwealth. The practice also reflects that of the ECJ and the ECtHR, neither of which is bound by a rigid doctrine of precedent, although in practice, as we have seen, neither of them easily disregards its previous decisions.

Even though the Supreme Court *may* depart from a previous decision 'when it appears right to do so', it is important to appreciate that its (and the House of Lords') previous decisions are 'normally binding'. The House of Lords exercised its power deriving from the 1966 Practice Statement sparingly and no doubt the Supreme Court will continue to act in a similar way.

Just because an earlier decision of the House of Lords or Supreme Court was wrong, it should not be thought that this, without more, is a sufficient reason for the Supreme Court not to follow it.[59] This was explained by Lord Reid in *Knuller (Publishing, Printing and Promotions) Ltd v Director of Public Prosecutions.*[60]

> I have said more than once in recent cases that our change of practice in no longer regarding previous decisions of this House as absolutely binding does not mean that whenever we think that a previous decision was wrong

---

58 *Austin v Southwark London Borough Council* [2011] 1 AC 355 (SC), per Lord Hope DPSC at 369. See also Supreme Court Practice Direction 3, para 3.1.3.

59 Although *R v Shivpuri* [1987] AC 1 is a rare example of where the House of Lords did overturn its previous decision (in *Anderton v Ryan* [1985] AC 560) simply because it accepted that its earlier decision was wrong. As Lord Bridge explained (at 23): 'If a serious error embodied in a decision of this House has distorted the law, the sooner it is corrected the better. Secondly, I cannot see how, in the very nature of the case, anyone could have acted in reliance on the law as propounded in *Anderton v. Ryan* in the belief that he was acting innocently and now finds that, after all, he is to be held to have committed a criminal offence.'

60 [1973] AC 435, 455, HL

we should reverse it. In the general interest of certainty in the law we must be sure that there is some very good reason before we so act . . . I think that however wrong or anomalous the decision may be it must stand and apply to cases reasonably analogous unless or until it is altered by Parliament.

So, if a wrong decision is unlikely to be enough to persuade the Supreme Court not to follow it, what might be considered enough? In *Jones v Secretary of State for Social Services*,[61] the House of Lords thought that it might be appropriate to do so if to adhere to the previous decision would produce serious anomalies or other results which were plainly unsatisfactory. Lord Reid explained the position in these terms:

> My understanding of the position when [the Practice Statement] was adopted was and is that there were a comparatively small number of reported decisions of this House which were generally thought to be impeding the proper development of the law or to have led to results which were unjust or contrary to public policy and that such decisions should be reconsidered as opportunities arose. But this practice was not to be used to weaken existing certainty in the law. The old view was that any departure from rigid adherence to precedent would weaken that certainty. I did not and do not accept that view. It is notorious that where an existing decision is disapproved but cannot be overruled courts tend to distinguish it on inadequate grounds. I do not think that they act wrongly in so doing: they are adopting the less bad of the only alternatives open to them. But this is bound to lead to uncertainty for no one can say in advance whether in a particular case the court will or will not feel bound to follow the old unsatisfactory decision. On balance it seems to me that overruling such a decision will promote and not impair the certainty of the law.[62]

In *Rees v Darlington Memorial Hospital NHS Trust*,[63] Lord Steyn felt that, without trying to be exhaustive, 'a fundamental change in circumstances' or experience showing that a decision of the House results in 'unforeseen serious injustice' may permit such a departure.[64]

A case that demonstrates a 'fundamental change in circumstances' is *Miliangos v George Frank (Textiles) Ltd*,[65] where the House of Lords overruled its previous decision in *Re United Railways of Havana and Regla Warehouses Ltd*[66] which had held that an award of damages in an English civil case had to be made in sterling.

---

61 [1972] AC 944
62 Ibid., 966
63 [2004] 1 AC 309 (HL)
64 Ibid., 324
65 [1976] AC 443 (HL)
66 [1961] AC 1007 (HL)

In *Miliangos*, the House of Lords held that the instability which had overtaken sterling and other major currencies since its earlier decision in *United Railways*, as well as the procedures evolved in consequence by the English courts and by arbitrators to secure payment of foreign currency debts in foreign currency, justified departure from that decision since a new and more satisfactory rule could be stated to enable the courts to keep step with commercial needs and would not involve undue practical and procedural difficulties.

In *R v Secretary of State for the Home Department, ex parte Khawaja*,[67] Lord Scarman acknowledged that the Practice Statement is an affirmation of the importance of precedent 'as an indispensable foundation upon which to decide what is the law and its application to individual cases'.[68] However, he recognised that 'too rigid adherence to precedent may lead to injustice in a particular case and also unduly restrict the proper development of the law'.[69] To illustrate when the House might depart from one of its previous decisions he propounded a two-stage test:

> The House must be satisfied not only that adherence to the precedent would involve the risk of injustice and obstruct the proper development of the law, but also that a judicial departure by the House from the precedent is the safe and appropriate way of remedying the injustice and developing the law.[70]

Lord Scarman also pointed out that

> the possibility that legislation may be the better course is one which, though not mentioned in the Statement, the House will not overlook . . . Provided, however, due attention is paid to the dangers of uncertainty in certain branches of the law (especially the criminal law) the House, as it has already in a number of cases made clear, will, if it thinks it right, depart from a previous decision whether the decision be ancient or modern and whether the point of law arises upon the construction of a statute or in the judge-made common law or equity.[71]

In relation to the *Khawaja* case, Lord Scarman said that the loss of a person's liberty might amount to a ground for departing from or overruling one of the House's own decisions and explained that

> in most cases I would defer to a recent decision of your Lordships' House on a question of construction, even if I thought it wrong. I do not do so

---

67 [1984] AC 74
68 Ibid., 106
69 Ibid.
70 Ibid.
71 Ibid.

in this context because for reasons which I shall develop I am convinced that the . . . reasoning gave insufficient weight to the important (I would say fundamental) consideration that we are here concerned with, the scope of judicial review of a power which inevitably infringes the liberty of those subjected to it . . .'[72]

In *Horton v Sadler*,[73] Lord Bingham stated the position more generally. He said that 'over the past 40 years the House has exercised its power to depart from its own precedent rarely and sparingly. It has never been thought enough to justify doing so that a later generation of Law Lords would have resolved an issue or formulated a principle differently from their predecessors'[74] and confirmed that although former decisions of the House of Lords are normally binding, 'too rigid adherence to precedent may lead to injustice in a particular case and unduly restrict the development of the law. The House will depart from a previous decision where it appears right to do.'[75]

It is also important to consider the potential consequences of the Supreme Court overruling an earlier decision. Where such consequences are 'incalculable', the court may refuse to do so. For example, the Supreme Court refused to overrule an earlier decision of the House of Lords where that earlier decision had been assumed to be right and been acted upon in many tens of thousands of subsequent cases.[76]

On a practical level, if an application for permission to appeal is to ask the Supreme Court to depart from one of its own decisions or from one made by the House of Lords, this should be stated clearly in the application and full details must be given.[77]

Privy Council

The function of the Judicial Committee of the Privy Council is somewhat different to the other appellate courts. It is not a court of the United Kingdom but acts as a final appellate court for a number of Commonwealth countries, among others. It is the court of final appeal for the UK overseas territories and Crown dependencies, and for those Commonwealth countries that have retained the appeal to Her Majesty in Council or, in the case of republics, to the Judicial Committee. It sits in the Supreme Court building in London and although consisting of judges of the Supreme Court it remains a separate legal entity.

---

72 Ibid.
73 [2007] 1 AC 307 (HL)
74 Ibid., 323
75 Ibid.
76 See, for example, *Austin v Southwark London Borough Council* [2011] 1 AC 355 (SC), per Lord Hope DPSC at 371.
77 Supreme Court Practice Direction 3, para 3.1.3

Subject to the recent judgment of the Supreme Court in *Willers v Joyce*,[78] decisions of the Privy Council are not binding on the English courts although do have strong persuasive authority. Some doubt was, however, cast on this principle by the Court of Appeal in *R v James*[79] which sat five-strong because of the novel and important question of the law relating to precedent that was raised in the appeal. The case concerned whether the Court of Appeal (Criminal Division) was bound by a decision of the House of Lords[80] or the conflicting decision of the Privy Council.[81]

Lord Phillips CJ stated:

> The rule that this court must always follow a decision of the House of Lords and, indeed, one of its own decisions rather than a decision of the Privy Council is one that was established at a time when no tribunal other than the House of Lords itself could rule that a previous decision of the House of Lords was no longer good law. Once one postulates that there are circumstances in which a decision of the Judicial Committee of the Privy Council can take precedence over a decision of the House of Lords, it seems to us that this court must be bound in those circumstances to prefer the decision of the Privy Council to the prior decision of the House of Lords. That, so it seems to us, is the position that has been reached in the case of these appeals.
>
> What are the exceptional features in this case which justify our preferring the decision in *Holley*'s case to that in the *Morgan Smith* case? We identify the following. (i) All nine of the Lords of Appeal in Ordinary sitting in *Holley*'s case agreed in the course of their judgments that the result reached by the majority clarified definitively English law on the issue in question. (ii) The majority in *Holley*'s case constituted half the Appellate Committee of the House of Lords. We do not know whether there would have been agreement that the result was definitive had the members of the Board divided five/four. (iii) In the circumstances, the result of any appeal on the issue to the House of Lords is a foregone conclusion.[82]

The Lord Chief Justice went on to express a doubt as to whether the Court of Appeal will often, if ever again, be presented with the circumstances that presented themselves in the appeal and emphasised that it was only those unique circumstances which justified the court in taking the decision it did. His Lordship also pointed out that the decision 'should not be taken as a licence to decline to follow a decision of the House of Lords in any other circumstances'.[83]

78 [2016] UKSC 44. This case is discussed below.
79 [2006] QB 588
80 *R v Smith (Morgan)* [2001] 1 AC 146
81 *Attorney General for Jersey v Holley* [2005] 2 AC 580
82 Ibid., 601
83 Ibid., 602

The traditional approach to precedent was re-emphasised by the Court of Appeal in *Sinclair Investments (UK) Ltd v Versailles Trade Finance Ltd (in administrative receivership)*[84] where Lord Neuberger MR stated:

> We should not follow the Privy Council . . . in preference to decisions of this court, unless there are domestic authorities which show that the decisions of this court were *per incuriam* or at least of doubtful reliability. Save where there are powerful reasons to the contrary, the Court of Appeal should follow its own previous decisions, and in this instance there are five such previous decisions. It is true that there is a powerful subsequent decision of the Privy Council which goes the other way, but that of itself is not enough to justify departing from the earlier decisions of this court.
>
> I do not suggest that it would always be wrong for this court to refuse to follow a decision of the Privy Council in preference to one of its own previous decisions, but the general rule is that we follow our previous decisions, leaving it to the Supreme Court to overrule those decisions if it is appropriate to do so.[85]

The Master of the Rolls explained the court's justification when deciding to follow a Privy Council decision 'on the proposition that it was a foregone conclusion that, if the case had gone to the House of Lords,[86] they would have followed the Privy Council decision'.[87]

In 2016, a nine-justice Supreme Court in *Willers v Joyce*[88] clarified the position of precedent in relation to the status of decisions of the Privy Council in the courts of England and Wales. The principal question for the court was whether a claim in malicious prosecution could be brought in relation to *civil* proceedings by one private person against another private person. The trial judge was faced with a House of Lords decision which conflicted with a later decision of the Privy Council. In *Gregory v Portsmouth City Council*,[89] the House of Lords rejected the contention that a claim in malicious prosecution could be brought in relation to civil proceedings, although in the later case of *Crawford Adjusters v Sagicor General Insurance*[90] the Privy Council reached the opposite conclusion. The trial judge concluded that if there was a decision of the House of Lords (or the Supreme Court) which was binding on her as a first instance judge, she could only follow a decision of the Privy Council to the opposite effect if, for all practical purposes, it was a foregone conclusion that the Supreme Court would itself follow

---

84 [2012] Ch 453
85 Ibid., 478
86 Or, now, the Supreme Court.
87 Ibid.
88 [2016] UKSC 44
89 [2000] 1 AC 419
90 [2014] AC 366

the decision of the Privy Council. The judge did not consider it a foregone conclusion and therefore followed the decision of the House of Lords and struck out the claim.

Lord Neuberger delivered the unanimous judgment of the Supreme Court. In short, Lord Neuberger confirmed the position that, unless there is a decision of a superior court to the contrary effect, a court in England and Wales can normally be expected to follow a decision of the Privy Council, but there is no question of it being bound to do so as a matter of precedent. Further, he explained that a court should not, at least normally, follow a decision of the Privy Council if it is inconsistent with the decision of another court which would otherwise be binding on it. Lord Neuberger explained that there is an important exception to this principle. In an appeal to the Privy Council that involves an issue of English law on which a previous decision of the House of Lords, Supreme Court or Court of Appeal is challenged, the judges in the Privy Council can, if they think it appropriate, not only decide that the previous decision was wrong, but also expressly direct that domestic courts should treat their decision as representing the law of England and Wales. This reflects the fact that the Privy Council judges normally consist of the same judges as the Supreme Court.

Lord Neuberger:

> The appeal in *Willers v Joyce* raises an important issue, namely the status of decisions of the Judicial Committee of the Privy Council ('the JCPC') in the courts of England and Wales . . . Although the function of the JCPC has varied somewhat since its creation . . . this case is concerned with its function as the final appellate court for a number of Commonwealth countries, the 14 British Overseas Territories, the Channel Islands and the Isle of Man . . . Accordingly, the JCPC is not a court of any part of the United Kingdom.
>
> Having said that, the JCPC almost always applies the common law, and either all or four of the five Privy Counsellors who normally sit on any appeal will almost always be Justices of the Supreme Court. This reflects the position as it has been for more than 100 years, following the Appellate Jurisdiction Act 1876, which created the Lords of Appeal in Ordinary (i.e. the Law Lords), who thereafter constituted the majority of the Privy Counsellors who sat in the JCPC, until the creation of the Supreme Court in October 2009.
>
> Three consequences have been held to follow from this analysis, at least as a matter of logic. First, given that the JCPC is not a UK court at all, decisions of the JCPC cannot be binding on any judge of England and Wales, and, in particular, cannot override any decision of a court of England and Wales (let alone a decision of the Supreme Court or the Law Lords) which would otherwise represent a precedent which was binding on that judge. Secondly, given the identity of the Privy Counsellors who sit on the JCPC and the fact that they apply the common law, any decision of the JCPC, at least on a common law issue, should, subject always to the first point, normally be regarded by any Judge of England and Wales, and indeed any Justice of the Supreme Court, as being of great weight and persuasive value. Thirdly,

the JCPC should regard itself as bound by any decision of the House of Lords or the Supreme Court – at least when applying the law of England and Wales. That last qualification is important: in some JCPC jurisdictions, the applicable common law is that of England and Wales, whereas in other JCPC jurisdictions, the common law is local common law, which will often be, but is by no means always necessarily, identical to that of England and Wales.

In *Tai Hing Cotton Mill Ltd v Liu Chong Hing Bank Ltd* [1986] AC 80, 108, Lord Scarman, giving the advice of the JCPC said '[o]nce it is accepted . . . that the applicable law is English', the JCPC 'will follow a House of Lords decision which covers the point in issue'. As he explained, the JCPC 'is not the final judicial authority for the determination of English law. That is the responsibility of the House of Lords in its judicial capacity.' On the other hand, when the issue to be determined by the JCPC is not a point of English law, the JCPC is not automatically bound by a decision of the Law Lords (or the Supreme Court) even if the point at issue is one of common law, not least because the common law can develop in different ways in different jurisdictions (although it is highly desirable that all common law judges generally try and march together). This is well illustrated by the decision of the JCPC in the Hong Kong case of *Mercedes-Benz AG v Leiduck* [1996] AC 284, where the majority refused to follow the House of Lords decision in *The Siskina* [1979] AC 210.

In *In re Spectrum Plus Ltd (In liquidation)* [2005] 2 AC 680, the House of Lords had to consider a point on which the Court of Appeal had expressed one view in two cases (*Siebe Gorman & Co Ltd v Barclays Bank Ltd* [1979] 2 Lloyds Rep 142 and *In re New Bullas Trading Ltd* [1994] 1 BCLC 485), and the JCPC had expressed the opposite view in a subsequent New Zealand appeal (*Agnew v Comr of Inland Revenue* [2001] 2 AC 710). In *Spectrum Plus* at first instance, the trial judge followed the JCPC decision, but the Court of Appeal held that he has been wrong to do so, as he was bound by the earlier Court of Appeal decisions, and they reversed him on the ground that they were equally bound.

Although the House of Lords reinstated the trial judge's decision in *Spectrum Plus* and overruled the Court of Appeal decisions in Siebe *Gorman v Barclays* and in *New Bullas*, the majority of the Law Lords made it clear that the trial judge was wrong in not regarding himself as bound by those decisions and in treating himself as entitled to follow the more recent decision of the JCPC. Thus, at para 93, Lord Scott said that the Court of Appeal had 'correctly' said that the trial judge's 'test was in conflict with the Court of Appeal's decision in *In re New Bullas* . . . and concluded that the rules of binding precedent enabled neither [the judge] nor a subsequent Court of Appeal to rule that that case had been wrongly decided'. Lord Walker expressed himself more elliptically at para 153, where he said that the trial judge 'was correct on every point in his judgment except one, which does not present any obstacle to your Lordships (that is as to the relative authority as precedents of the *New Bullas* and *Agnew* cases)'. Lord Nicholls, Lord Steyn and Lord Brown agreed with the opinions of both Lord Scott and Lord Walker.

There is no doubt that, unless there is a decision of a superior court to the contrary effect, a court in England and Wales can normally be expected to follow a decision of the JCPC, but there is no question of it being bound to do so as a matter of precedent. There is also no doubt that a court should not, at least normally, follow a decision of the JCPC, if it is inconsistent with the decision of a court which is binding in accordance with the principles set out . . . above.

The difficult question is whether this latter rule is absolute, or whether it is subject to the qualification that it can be disapplied where a first instance judge or the Court of Appeal considers that it is a foregone conclusion that the view taken by the JCPC will be accepted by the Court of Appeal or Supreme Court (as the case may be). . . . Nonetheless, I have concluded that it is more satisfactory if, subject to one important qualification which I deal with [below], the rule is absolute – i.e. that a judge should never follow a decision of the JCPC, if it is inconsistent with the decision of a court which is otherwise binding on him or her in accordance with the principles set out [above].

First, particularly given the importance of the doctrine of precedence and 'highly centralised nature of the hierarchy' of the courts of England and Wales, the doctrine should be clear in its terms and simple in its application. Secondly, as the very careful judgment of [the trial judge] in the present case shows, there can be much argument and difference of opinion as to whether it is 'a foregone conclusion' that the Court of Appeal or Supreme Court will follow a particular JCPC decision which is inconsistent with an earlier decision of the domestic court. If there is a strict rule, there need be no such argument. Thirdly, even apart from this second point, there should be no more delay or cost in having a strict and clear rule rather than a more flexible rule. Thus, if the first instance judge follows the decision of a superior court in this jurisdiction, she can grant a 'leapfrog certificate', and, if it is appropriate, the Supreme Court can then decide to consider the issue directly. It is hard to see why, if such a course is appropriate, it would be beneficial in terms of time or costs for the issue to be considered by the Court of Appeal. Having said that, there may well be a case where the Supreme Court will consider that it would benefit from the views of the Court of Appeal, and in such a case it can refuse to entertain the appeal pursuant to the certificate.

Having said that, I would adopt a suggestion made by Lord Toulson which may, in terms of strict logic, be inconsistent with the above analysis, but which is plainly sensible in practice and justified by experience . . . There will be appeals to the JCPC where a party wishes to challenge the correctness of an earlier decision of the House of Lords or the Supreme Court, or of the Court of Appeal on a point of English law, and where the JCPC decides that the House of Lords or Supreme Court, or, as the case may be, the Court of Appeal, was wrong. It would plainly be unfortunate in practical terms if, in such circumstances, the JCPC could never effectively decide that courts of England and Wales should follow the JCPC decision rather than the earlier decision of the House of Lords or Supreme Court, or of the Court of Appeal. In my view, the way to reconcile this practical concern with the principled approach identified [above] is to take advantage of the fact that the President of the JCPC is the same person as the President of the Supreme Court, and the fact that panels of the JCPC normally consist of Justices of the Supreme Court.[91]

Lord Neuberger then went on to consider the position in the courts of Scotland and of Northern Ireland:

The traditional view in Scotland has been that, subject to some possible exceptions, judgments of the House of Lords in English appeals are at most highly persuasive rather than strictly binding, and I find it impossible to see how decisions of the JCPC on English law can have greater authority than that. As for Northern Ireland, given that the common law applies in the same way as it does in England and Wales, I would have thought that precisely the same principles should apply as they do in England and Wales.[92]

The decision in *Willers v Joyce* should be considered the final word on the matter.

Court of Appeal

The Court of Appeal is split into Civil and Criminal Divisions, neither of which bind the other. They are both bound by decisions of the Supreme Court and House of Lords and in turn bind the relevant courts below.

Civil Division

Subject to a number of exceptions, the Court of Appeal (Civil Division) is generally bound by its own previous decisions. These exceptions were set out by Lord Greene MR in *Young v Bristol Aeroplane Co Ltd*:[93]

- Where there is a conflict between two previous decisions of the Court of Appeal. In such a situation, the Court of Appeal must decide which of these cases to follow.

---

91 Ibid., [1], [10]–[19]
92 Ibid., [22]
93 [1944] KB 718 (CA)

- Where a previous decision of the Court of Appeal cannot stand with a decision made by the House of Lords or Supreme Court whether or not its own previous decision has been expressly overruled.
- Where a previous decision of the Court of Appeal was made *per incuriam*. In *Morelle v Wakeling*,[94] Sir Raymond Evershed MR explained that:

> As a general rule the only cases in which decisions should be held to have been given *per incuriam* are those of decisions given in ignorance or forgetfulness of some inconsistent statutory provision or of some authority binding on the court concerned: so that in such cases some part of the decision or some step in the reasoning on which it is based is found, on that account, to be demonstrably wrong. This definition is not necessarily exhaustive, but cases not strictly within it which can properly be held to have been decided *per incuriam* must, in our judgment, consistently with the *stare decisis* rule which is an essential feature of our law, be . . . of the rarest occurrence.[95]

A further exception to the *Young v Bristol Aeroplane per incuriam* rule was made by the Court of Appeal in *R (Kadhim) v Brent London Borough Council Housing Benefit Review Board*:[96]

- a proposition of law which, although part of the *ratio decidendi* of an earlier decision, had been assumed to be correct by the earlier court and had not been the subject of argument before, or consideration by, that court.

Criminal Division

The Court of Appeal (Criminal Division), established initially by the Criminal Appeal Act 1966 and thereafter by the Criminal Appeal Act 1968, replaced the Court of Criminal Appeal[97] and, as did its predecessor court, provides a mechanism (among other things) for the review of a conviction recorded in the Crown Court on the grounds that it is unsafe. It focuses on misdirection of law or irregularity in the conduct of the trial and, as a result, the approach of the judge to all aspects of the trial falls under particular scrutiny.[98]

The Criminal Division of the Court of Appeal is bound in the same way as the Civil Division and the same general principles apply before either Division can depart from a previous decision. However, since the Criminal Division deals with the liberty of the individual, it may not follow a previous decision where

---

94 [1955] 2 QB 379 (CA)
95 Ibid., 406. See also *Williams v Fawcett* [1986] QB 604
96 [2001] QB 955 (CA)
97 Which was set up by the Criminal Appeal Act 1907
98 *Webster v Lord Chancellor* [2015] EWCA Civ 742

the interests of justice to that individual require an earlier authority not to be followed,[99] and this is especially the case where the court is of the opinion that the law has been misapplied or misunderstood in an earlier decision of the court.[100]

In *R v Taylor*,[101] Lord Goddard MR explained the position in the following terms:

> This court . . . has to deal with questions involving the liberty of the subject, and if it finds, on reconsideration, that, in the opinion of a full court assembled for that purpose, the law has been either misapplied or misunderstood in a decision which it has previously given, and that, on the strength of that decision, an accused person has been sentenced and imprisoned it is the bounden duty of the court to reconsider the earlier decision with a view to seeing whether that person had been properly convicted. The exceptions which apply in civil cases ought not to be the only ones applied in such a case . . .[102]

The constitution of the court was considered in *R v Simpson*.[103] It was held that the Criminal Division of the Court of Appeal had a degree of discretion when deciding whether a previous decision should be treated as a binding precedent when there were reasons for saying that the decision was wrong and that when exercising that discretion regard should be made to the constitution of the court which had made the decision. *Simpson* was distinguished in *R v Magro*[104] which held that even if a previous decision was wrong, the Court of Appeal is still bound by it. While appreciating the practical value of the approach adopted in *Simpson* which underlines the discretion available to a five-judge constitution of the court, circumspectly exercised, to decide that a previous decision of the Court of Appeal should not be treated as a binding decision when it is wrong, Lord Judge CJ nevertheless explained that *Simpson* does not establish that a five-judge constitution is entitled to disregard or deprive the only previous decision of the three-judge constitution of the court of its authority on a distinct and clearly identified point of law, reached after full argument and close analysis of the relevant legislative provisions.[105]

99 *R v Spencer* [1985] QB 771
100 *R v Gould* [1968] 2 QB 65
101 [1950] 2 KB 368 (CCA)
102 Ibid., 371
103 [2004] QB 118 (CA)
104 [2011] QB 398 (CA)
105 Ibid., 411

Mooting tip

You should bear in mind that a decision made by a court will have the same binding effect irrespective of the number of judges sitting. Therefore, decisions given by a full court of five or seven judges will carry no greater weight, and decisions by a two-judge court will have no less weight, than a normal three-judge court.[106]

Divisional Courts

The Divisional Courts consist of the Queen's Bench Division, which hears criminal appeals and cases involving judicial review, and the Chancery Division and Family Division, both of which hear civil appeals.

The Divisional Court is bound by the decisions of all superior courts and binds all courts below, including the 'ordinary' High Court. In civil cases, the Divisional Court is usually bound by its own previous decisions although it may avail itself of the exceptions available to the Court of Appeal in *Young v Bristol Aeroplane Co Ltd*.[107] In criminal cases, and in cases relating to judicial review, the Queen's Bench Divisional Court may decide not to follow its own previous decision where it is satisfied that such decision was wrongly made.[108]

High Court

The High Court is bound by the decisions of all superior courts. Decisions of individual High Court judges bind all inferior courts. Although such decisions do not bind other High Court judges, they are of strong persuasive authority and for reasons of consistency tend to be followed.

Where different High Court judges have reached different decisions, and where the later of these decisions has considered the earlier one and explained the reason for not following it, then, for reasons of certainty, it is usually that later decision that is followed.[109]

Where the High Court judge is faced with conflicting judgments of a superior court, then he is required to follow the later of these decisions.

Circuit judges

In the 'Note' included at the end of the judgment in *Howard De Walden Estates Ltd v Aggio*,[110] it was made clear that a Circuit Judge is bound by a decision of a High Court judge.

---

106 *Langley v North West Water Authority* [1991] 3 All ER 610
107 [1946] AC 163
108 *DPP v Butterworth* [1995] 1 AC 381 (HL)
109 *Colchester Estates (Cardiff) v Carlton Industries Plc* [1986] Ch 80
110 [2008] Ch 26

Crown Court

Decisions of judges made in the crown courts do not form binding precedents although they are themselves bound by decisions of the superior courts. When High Court judges sit in the crown courts, their rulings are seen as persuasive but not binding in later cases. Because crown courts do not form binding precedents they are not bound by their own previous decisions.

County Court

Decisions made in the county courts are usually unreported and do not produce binding precedents. They are not bound by their own previous decisions but are bound by all superior courts.

Magistrates' Court

Decisions made in the magistrates' courts do not produce binding precedents. They are not bound by their own previous decisions but are bound by all superior courts.

Persuasive authority

Having considered the rules of *stare decisis*, it is worth considering the principles of persuasive authority. A persuasive authority is one that is not binding on a court but which the court may nevertheless decide to follow. The following are examples of decisions that might be considered persuasive:

*   Decisions of English courts lower in the court hierarchy. The Supreme Court may, for example, choose to follow a decision of the Court of Appeal or High Court, and the Court of Appeal may choose to follow a decision of the High Court, although neither is bound to do so.
*   Decisions of the Judicial Committee of the Privy Council (discussed above).
*   *Obiter dicta* of English judges (discussed below).
*   Decisions made by the courts in Scotland, Ireland, the Commonwealth (especially Australia, Canada and New Zealand) and the USA. These may be particularly helpful where there is a shortage or lack of English authority on a specific point.

Finally, where there is no direct authority in the form of decided cases, persuasive authority may be found in legal textbooks and journals.

Ratio decidendi and obiter dicta

Ratio decidendi – the reason for deciding. Thus, the *ratio decidendi* of a case is not the court's decision itself but the principle of law upon which the decision is based.

Obiter dictum – a statement made by the way (plural, *obiter dicta*). Those parts of the judgment which do not form the *ratio decidendi* are known as *obiter dicta*. These might be discussions about hypothetical situations such as occurred in *Rondel v Worsley*.[111] This case concerned whether a barrister was liable in tort for the negligent presentation of a criminal case in a court and the preliminary work associated with it. The House of Lords unanimously held that a barrister is not so liable. Lords Reid, Morris, Pearce and Upjohn went on to state that a solicitor when acting as an advocate in court was entitled to identical immunity from suit. These statements were, therefore, necessarily *obiter*. *Obiter dicta* do not form part of the binding precedent of a case although judges in subsequent cases might find them persuasive. Further, in *Rondel*, Lords Reid, Morris and Upjohn stated that barristers would not be entitled to this immunity in relation to matters that were not connected with cases in court and the preliminary work associated with them. These *dicta* were followed by the majority of the House of Lords in *Saif Ali v Sydney Mitchell & Co*[112] which had to consider whether a barrister's immunity covers pre-trial acts or omissions in connection with civil proceedings brought by his lay client. This involved a reconsideration of *Rondel* in order to see what rule of law was to be extracted from it. The result was that *dicta* from *Rondel* was elevated to a status nearing that of *ratio decidendi*. Lord Wilberforce explained:

> *Rondel v Worsley* gave rise to a restatement of the traditional principle of barristers' immunity. . . . Previously an important if not the main reason for the immunity was supposed to lie in the fact that a barrister could not sue for his fees: this reason, if valid, would of course have thrown a blanket of immunity over all barristers' actions, in or out of court, whatever their nature. This House, however, in 1967 took the inevitable view that this reason no longer applied: liability for negligence might exist in the absence of a contract for reward. Nevertheless the immunity was held to exist on grounds, essentially, of public policy; mainly upon the ground that a barrister owes a duty to the court as well as to his client and should not be inhibited, through fear of an action by his client, from performing it; partly upon the undesirability of re-litigation as between barrister and client of what was litigated between the client and his opponent. This necessarily involved a removal of the total blanket immunity and a restriction of it to such cases as might fall within the area of public policy.
>
> *Rondel v Worsley* was concerned and only concerned with matters taking place in court which resulted in an outcome unfavourable to the client. But the speeches contain considered observations as to the extent of barristers' immunity for matters taking place outside court and in barristers' chambers.

111 [1969] 1 AC 191
112 [1980] AC 198

Since the case was not concerned with such matters, these observations have the status of *obiter dicta*. However, not all *obiter dicta* have the same weight, or lack of weight, in later cases. Of those then made in the House two things may be said. First, they were considered and deliberate observations after discussion of the same matters had taken place in the Court of Appeal and in the light of judgments in the Court of Appeal. It may be true that the counsel in the case did not present detailed arguments as to the position outside the court room – they had no interest in doing so – but I cannot agree that this invalidates or weakens judicial pronouncements. Judges are more than mere selectors between rival views – they are entitled to and do think for themselves. Secondly, it would have been impossible for their Lordships to have dealt with the extent of barristers' immunity for acts in court without relating this to their immunity for other acts, ... These factors, in my opinion, tell in favour of giving considerably more weight to their Lordships' expressions of opinion than *obiter dicta* normally receive. We may clarify them, but we should hesitate before disregarding them.[113]

The weight a subsequent court should attach to persuasive authority depends on a number of factors. These include the position of the court in the court hierarchy, whether the judgment was given *ex tempore* or was reserved,[114] whether the judgment was unanimous or whether there were any dissenting opinions, the age of the case,[115] whether the point in issue was fully argued by counsel and, to some extent, the reputation of the individual judge concerned. This latter point is not without controversy because, in theory, the status of all judges in the same court is equal and it has been described by Lord Diplock as 'invidious' to make any distinction between judges based on their reputation as jurists.[116] That said, judgments made by judges who are regarded as particular authorities or 'heavyweights' are often given more respect than those made by other judges. A particularly good example of this is Lord Atkin's 'neighbour principle' in *Donoghue v Stevenson*.[117] Although this is clearly *obiter*,[118] it has been followed in a long line of subsequent cases. In *Home Office v Dorset Yacht Co Ltd*,[119] Lord Reid acknowledged that *Donoghue v Stevenson* was a 'milestone' and that Lord Atkin's neighbour test should be regarded as 'a statement of principle'. Although Lord Reid emphasised that the test should not be treated as if it were a statutory definition he explained that 'the time has come when we can and should

---

113 Ibid., 212
114 A judgment that is delivered after being reserved will often carry greater weight than one that is made *ex tempore*. A reserved judgment is indicated in the law reports by the words *curia advisari vult* (the court will consider), often abbreviated to *cur. adv. vult* or *c.a.v.*
115 Discussed below.
116 *Saif Ali v Sydney Mitchell & Co* [1980] AC 198, 217, HL
117 [1932] AC 562 (HL)
118 For the reason explained below.
119 [1970] AC 1004 (HL)

say that it ought to apply unless there is some justification or valid explanation for its exclusion'.[120]

The reason Lord Atkin's neighbour principle is *obiter* is that it was a far wider explanation of the law than was necessary to decide the case and was not directly related to its facts. That said, for the reasons just explained, subsequent courts have tended to elevate the principle to one of *ratio decidendi* with the result that a claimant whose relationship with the defendant satisfies the neighbour test is presumed to have established that the defendant owed him a duty of care which can then be applied to the particular circumstances of the case.

The age of a case

The age of a case is something that can be used either to support or weaken its value as a precedent. Old cases remain good law unless and until they have been overruled either by a subsequent case or by an Act of Parliament. This reflects the declaratory theory of the common law which provides that judges do not create law but merely declare what the law is, and has always been. A consequence of this theory is that no case is too old to be considered good law. Indeed, many old and practically forgotten cases still appear in the law reports.

An example of this can be seen in *Cambridge Water Company v Eastern Counties Leather plc*[121] where Mann LJ felt unable to distinguish the barely cited case of *Ballard v Tomlinson*[122] and followed it despite the result meaning that a polluter of a water source could be held liable for nuisance even in a case where the harm caused was not a foreseeable result of his actions. Although this decision was subsequently reversed by the House of Lords,[123] it demonstrates how old cases can prove invaluable in modern-day litigation.

Whether or not a court will follow a case of such antiquity is a matter open for argument and is something a good mooter should be aware of.

Although some judges take the view that older cases that have been neither overruled nor disturbed over a very long time should be afforded particular respect, other judges take a different approach and are open to being persuaded that given a case's age it may have become outdated and as a consequence ought not be afforded the same status it once enjoyed. This position is confirmed in the explanatory note to the House of Lords' Practice Statement[124] which explains that:

> An example of a case in which the House of Lords might think it right to depart from a precedent is where they consider that the earlier decision was influenced by the existence of conditions which no longer prevail, and that in modern conditions the law ought to be different.

120 Ibid., 1027
121 [1993] Env LR 287
122 (1885) 29 Ch D 115
123 [1994] 2 AC 264
124 [1966] 1 WLR 1234. Discussed at page 37.

The main argument in support of following a more recent decision is that it represents the most up-to-date pronouncement on the law and, therefore, the current thinking of the court.

Precedent and methods used to avoid it

To follow

The rules of *stare decisis* require a judge to follow a decision of a higher court in a case where the facts and circumstances are sufficiently similar. Some courts are also required to follow their own previous decisions.

To distinguish

A court is not bound to follow a previous decision where the facts or the point of law of a case are sufficiently different to the case under consideration.

> **Mooting tip**
> Since the facts of two cases are unlikely to be identical, a good mooter might attempt to avoid an awkward precedent by persuading the judge to distinguish it so that the rule laid down in the earlier case does not apply. To do this, however, you must be able to identify how the cases differ and why any such difference is important. As you will have seen above, you can also ask the court to distinguish a case even where the facts are reasonably similar, provided that the point of law that was considered in the earlier case was sufficiently different. Similarly, you might be able to persuade the court to give a narrow meaning to the *ratio decidendi* of an earlier case. Judges don't identify which part of their judgment forms the *ratio decidendi* so this can be a fertile area for argument. Finally, where a number of judges have each delivered their own substantive judgment, each giving a different reason for coming to their decision, it might be possible to argue that the case has no clear *ratio decidendi* or no clear single *ratio decidendi*.

To reverse

On appeal to a higher court, the higher court can reverse a decision made by the lower court in the same case if it concludes that the lower court has misapplied the law.

To overrule

Where a higher court disagrees with a statement of law made by a lower court in a previous case, the higher court can overrule it. Although this does not affect the position of the parties to the earlier decision, it does mean that the proposition laid down in the earlier case will no longer be followed.

Per incuriam

It might be possible to argue that the earlier decision was made *per incuriam* (through lack of care) and should not therefore be followed. It was noted at pages 47–48 that in *Young v Bristol Aeroplane Co Ltd*[125] the Court of Appeal established the principle that it was not bound to follow its own earlier decision if it had been made *per incuriam*. This generally means that the decision was reached in circumstances where some relevant statutory provision or precedent, which would have affected the court's decision, had not been brought to the court's attention, thus rendering the decision flawed. This principle has since been applied in other courts.[126]

The most obvious way of finding out whether a case or statutory provision has been cited is to consult the law report. The key cases that were cited in argument will usually be referred to in the text of the judgment although some other cases may not be, especially where counsel has cited a number of cases in support of a proposition where a single leading case would have sufficed. To address this point, some law reports list all of the cases that were cited in argument (whether orally or in the parties' written skeleton arguments) but not referred to in the judgment itself. This practice is particularly helpful as it enables subsequent courts to ascertain whether or not an important authority had been cited to the earlier court and, if not, to consider whether any decisions reached were made *per incuriam*.

125 [1944] KB 718
126 See, for example, *R v Northumberland Compensation Appeal Tribunal, ex parte Shaw* [1951] 1 KB 711

3 Legal research and case preparation

Introduction

Your first task is to read the moot problem very carefully so as to get a good appreciation of the factual matrix and the legal issues involved. Do not think for one moment that you will be able to blag yourself through the moot. Mooting is a serious business; if you want to succeed, you must be committed to it and be prepared to work hard.

The research process

By the time most students get into mooting, they will have already found their own way around the process of legal research. Researching for a moot is a little different to exam preparation – often narrower but more detailed. Whichever way you feel comfortable about researching, you should make sure that you cover the following five stages, each one building on the previous stage. Specific details about what is involved in each of these stages is examined throughout the book.

Stage 1 – Understand the issues

Although this stage of your research should be relatively brief, it is nevertheless extremely important to have a thorough grasp of the issues before you begin the substantive stages in the research process. During this stage, you will need to analyse the facts of the moot problem and identify the grounds of appeal and the legal context under which the appeal has been brought.

Stage 2 – Research the issues

Having identified 'what's what' in stage 1, you are now ready to commence your substantive research of the issues. During this stage, you will need to identify the legal issues that are relevant to the moot problem, consider the relevant material (cases, statutes, texts, etc.) that you will need to read in order to address these issues, and draw up a plan to identify the essential material that you will use during the moot. You will also need to understand the rules of the moot and, for present purposes, whether there are any limits placed on the number of authorities you may use during the moot.

Stage 3 – Construct your arguments

Having carried out your research, you are now at a stage when you can make a start in putting together your legal arguments (submissions). You should expect stages 2 and 3 to occupy the majority of your research time.

Stage 4 – Finalising your research and preparing your list of authorities, skeleton argument and bundle

Once you have put together your legal arguments, you should be ready to finalise your list of authorities and start drafting your skeleton argument. Once you have done this, you should begin to prepare your bundle in accordance with the rules of the moot.

Stage 5 – Final stages

Most moots require you to exchange your skeleton argument simultaneously with your opponent. Although you should attempt to anticipate your opponent's arguments throughout your own period of research, it is only upon sight of their skeleton argument that you will know for certain how they intend to argue their case. You should review your opponent's skeleton argument carefully and read the authorities upon which they seek to rely. Have they identified the relevant legal principles and applied them appropriately to their side of the appeal? Have they cited the appropriate authorities and interpreted them correctly? Are their cases distinguishable from the moot problem? Once you have considered these points, you will be in a good position to work out arguments to refute those of your opponent.

Additionally, during the final stages of your preparation you should make one final check with one of the online resources to make sure that none of your authorities has been judicially considered which would require you to amend your submissions in any way.

One final point to note: do not search endlessly for the 'correct answer' to the moot. Do not think that if you work hard enough, an answer will suddenly appear that will resolve the moot one way or the other. Thinking this way would be a fundamental misunderstanding of the entire purpose of mooting. A good moot, when taken as a whole, is one that does not have a 'correct answer' but instead has a number of points that can be argued either way.

Mooting tip
You should consider and analyse the moot problem from different angles so as to anticipate the case your opponent is likely to advance during the moot. With this in mind, you should also consider the likely consequences of your own submissions and be in a position to defend them from any questions the judge might ask.

Let us now consider the moot on page 242 in Chapter 10.

Moot problem	*Comments*
IN THE COURT OF APPEAL (CIVIL DIVISION)	This heading identifies the level of the court in which the moot will take place. This is crucially important when researching your arguments as it will influence the use of authorities in line with the doctrine of precedent. The doctrine of precedent is discussed in Chapter 2.
Davies v The Martial Arts Academy	This identifies the parties to the case. You will be told which party you will be representing although not necessarily by name. You may, for example, only be told that you are representing the 'appellant' or the 'respondent' in which case you will need to work out which party this is. The appellant is, of course, the party that is appealing the decision of the court below and has nothing to do with whether they were claimant or defendant[a] or the Crown or defendant,[b] etc. when the case was first heard. Nor is it always relevant which party appears first in the heading. In this case, the appellant is The Martial Arts Academy. With some moots, it will be necessary to consider the history of the case including the wording of the judgment to be appealed and the grounds of appeal to work out which party is which. In this moot, we can see that the Martial Arts Academy is the appellant because we are told that judgment was given against them by the trial judge, which decision they are now appealing to the Court of Appeal.

Moot problem	Comments

The Martial Arts Academy (MAA) is an academy that promotes martial arts at all levels. It employs a number of high-ranking martial arts instructors who have, over the years, trained students to an extremely high level, with many going on to represent their country in international competition.

Following a recent major competition in which students from the MAA won a number of medals, the instructors went out to celebrate. Unfortunately, the celebrations went on for longer than they had planned and as a result they missed their flight home that evening. This meant that the MAA was without any instructors for the following day's classes which, as it happened, were being filmed for promotional purposes. To avoid having to cancel classes, the MAA decided to engage the services of an external martial arts instructor, Mr Lee. Mr Lee had been used by the MAA a number of times over the past 12 months when the MAA needed cover for holiday-related absences. The MAA stressed to Mr Lee that, in accordance with MAA procedures, no students were to be allowed into the training hall (the Dojo) unless he was himself present and could therefore supervise them. It was also a requirement that Mr Lee only use MAA's equipment and attached MAA's badge/ emblem on his uniform. Mr Lee was also required to teach the classes himself and not delegate the work to anyone else.

The following morning, Mr Lee commenced the training and then gave the students a break. During the break, he left the Dojo unattended and a number of students stayed on the mats practising what he had taught them that morning. Unfortunately, one of the students, Sam Davies, suffered a broken arm when he was thrown to the ground by another student. It transpires that this other student used an advanced throwing technique on Sam for which he was not prepared. The throwing technique used was not one that had been taught. Mr Lee says that had he been there he would not have allowed this to have happened.

The facts of the case are set out here and you must read these very carefully. Although, sometimes, the facts can be somewhat unclear or ambiguous, they are not open to challenge. Nor is it permissible to adduce additional facts or further evidence. The whole idea of a moot is to argue points of law and you must, therefore, work within the factual parameters provided.

Moot problem	Comments
Sam Davies commenced proceedings against the MAA. At trial, Sensei J held that:	The basis of the claim, and the judgment at first instance, is set out here. It is this judgment that forms the subject of the moot. Where the moot is held in the Supreme Court, you are likely to be given the decisions of both trial judge and Court of Appeal. Moot problems differ in the extent of any judge's reasoning provided for their decision.
1. Mr Lee was negligent in leaving the students in the Dojo unsupervised.	
2. Mr Lee was an employee of the MAA.	
3. The MAA was vicariously liable for Mr Lee's actions.	
4. In disregarding the MAA's instructions, Mr Lee was acting in the course of his employment.	
The MAA appeals to the Court of Appeal on the following grounds:	These are the grounds of appeal. Some moots set out the grounds of appeal clearly while others leave the mooters to work them out from the reasoning and findings of the lower court.
1. Mr Lee was not an employee of the MAA but was an independent contractor.	
2. By disregarding the MAA's instructions, Mr Lee put himself outside of the course of his employment and the MAA cannot therefore be liable for his actions.	

a In a civil case
b In a criminal case

> **Mooting tip**
> You must ensure that you are clear which party you are representing. It is not unheard of for both parties to think they are representing the same side and prepare their submissions accordingly. As noted above, it is not always immediately apparent which party is which. Not only is it of paramount importance to know which party you are representing, but you must also appreciate what the appellant and respondent are seeking to argue.

The role of the team

You must always keep in mind that the party you are representing, whether appellant or respondent, is represented by a team, of which you are one of the members. The reason this is so important is that, *as a team*, your arguments must work seamlessly in support of your client's case. In other words, it is not enough that your arguments are well constructed if they don't also support those of your teammate. Make sure, therefore, that you are extremely familiar with your partner's arguments and that neither of you undermines the arguments of the other.

There is a strong convention in mooting that leading (or senior) counsel argues the first ground of the appeal, leaving the second ground to be argued by junior counsel. There is, of course, nothing 'senior' or 'junior' about either of you – these are just titles given for the purpose of the moot. Students will often look at the moot problem and decide which role they would prefer to take depending on their individual strengths and take the role appropriate to this.

Practical legal research

You should not underestimate the amount of detailed research and preparation that you will need to carry out if you are to succeed as a mooter. The following steps set out an effective way of researching and preparing your moot.

Read the moot problem and analyse the facts
Keep focused on what is relevant
Identify the questions that need to be considered
Research the law
Prepare your submissions (discussed in Chapters 4, 5 and 6)
Practise your submissions (discussed in Chapters 6 and 7)

We will now discuss these topics, using, where appropriate, the moot on page 242 in Chapter 10 as an example.

Read the moot problem and analyse the facts

Your first task should always be to read through the moot problem. Once you have done this, you will need to analyse the facts of the moot so that you have a thorough understanding of the issues. Do not disregard any part of the problem, even if you do not immediately appreciate its significance: this may only become apparent upon further reading of the problem.

In many moots, the legal merits of one of the grounds of appeal will often favour one side more than the other. However, this will often be balanced by the other ground of appeal favouring the other party. This might not always be the case, and the moot, when taken as a whole, might not favour your side at all. In such a case, you should bear the following in mind. First, winning the law has no bearing on the outcome of the moot. In other words, the party that succeeds on the law may lose the moot and vice versa. Second, many mooters actually prefer to be on the side with the weakest legal case. This is because having a weaker legal argument often forces the mooter to be more resourceful and creative when constructing their submissions. Third, it allows them to demonstrate their superior advocacy skills which, of course, remains one of the most important of the skills of mooting. Finally, the fact that the legal merits of the appeal weigh heavily in one team's favour will not have escaped the notice of the judge who will quite likely have been in the same position in his own professional practice and, as a consequence, may look more favourably at well-argued and resourceful submissions even if they don't actually succeed in law.

Mooting tip

Some moots are factually complex and lengthy. In such a case, you might find it helpful to prepare a 'time line' setting out the material events in chronological order. This doesn't need to be elaborate, but just enough to give you a clear picture of the key events in one easy-to-read place.

Keep focused on what is relevant

It is important to remain focused and not to distract yourself with matters that are not relevant to establishing your case. At this stage, don't worry about research-ing the legal issues; instead, you should concentrate on identifying what is legally relevant. If we consider the moot on page 242 in Chapter 10, you will see that the relevant points can be found in the judgment of Sensei J and in the grounds of appeal. It will be recalled that Sensei J held that:

1. Mr Lee was negligent in leaving the students in the Dojo unsupervised;
2. Mr Lee was an employee of the MAA;
3. the MAA was vicariously liable for Mr Lee's actions; and that
4. in disregarding the MAA's instructions, Mr Lee was acting in the course of his employment.

The grounds of appeal are stated as:

1. Mr Lee was not an employee of the MAA but was an independent contractor.
2. By disregarding the MAA's instructions, Mr Lee put himself outside of the course of his employment and the MAA cannot therefore be liable for his actions.

At the most basic level, you will need to consider:

- **For lead counsel:** whether Mr Lee was an employee of the MAA or alternatively was an independent contractor.
- **For junior counsel:** whether Mr Lee's conduct was such as to put himself outside of the course of his employment, meaning that the MAA is not liable for his actions.

Identify the questions that need to be considered

You will see from the above that the following questions need addressing:

- Is the 'employment test' the correct test to apply in these circumstances and, if so, what determines whether a person is an employee or an independent contractor?

- What amounts to conduct that puts an employee outside of the course of his employment?
- What is the relationship between the first and second grounds of appeal?

Research the law

As well as needing a good general knowledge of the subject area of the moot, you will now be in an ideal position to research the specific legal issues that are relevant to the appeal. The legal issues are those that you have identified in the above stage.

Although providing guidance on specific legal issues is beyond the scope of this book, it is important to bear in mind the relationship between the first and second grounds of appeal. Mooters often overlook the fact that the party they are representing, whether appellant or respondent, is being represented by a team, of which you are one of the members. The reason why this is so important is that, *as a team*, your arguments must work seamlessly in support of your client's case. In other words, it is not enough for your arguments to be well constructed if they contradict or otherwise damage those of your teammate. Make sure, therefore, that you are extremely familiar with your partner's arguments and that neither of you undermine the arguments of the other.

The alternative argument submission

An alternative argument submission is, as its name suggests, one where a subsequent argument is made in the alternative to an earlier argument rather than in furtherance of it. Alternative argument submissions feature frequently in legal practice as well as in mooting. An alternative argument arises in the following two situations:

- Where a subsequent submission is advanced as an alternative to an earlier submission within the same ground of appeal.
- Where the second ground of appeal is argued in the alternative to the first ground of appeal.

The appeal in *Davies v The Martial Arts Academy* provides a good example of a submission made in the alternative. You will see that Ground 1 raises the question as to whether or not Mr Lee was an employee of the MAA or alternatively was an independent contractor. Ground 2 then goes on to consider whether, by disregarding the MAA's instructions, he put himself outside of the course of his employment with the MAA, meaning that they are not liable for his actions. At first glance, it can be seen that the submissions made in Ground 2 follow seamlessly from those made in furtherance of Ground 1.

The alternative argument submission arises in the event that the court determines that Mr Lee is not an employee of the MAA and there exists no relationship that is capable of giving rise to vicarious liability. In such a case,

Ground 2 becomes futile because vicarious liability does not arise outside of the employer–employee relationship unless the relationship is such as to be capable to giving rise to vicarious liability.[1] Since the court will not determine the first ground of appeal until it delivers its judgment on the entirety of the appeal, you will need to argue fully the second ground of the appeal as set out in the moot problem.

The following draft submission places the above into a practical context which you may wish to adapt for your own submissions in an appropriate case. It assumes that you are junior counsel representing the MAA and are therefore arguing Ground 2 of the appeal.

> My Lord, I will now deal with Ground 2 of the appeal. If your Lordship accepts my learned senior's submissions and finds that Mr Lee was not an employee of the Martial Arts Academy and that no other relationship existed that was capable of giving rise to vicarious liability, then it follows that no question of vicarious liability can arise in this case. [This simply summarises the outcome of the arguments from Ground 1 made by leading counsel.]
>
> However, if your Lordship finds against us in Ground 1 and holds that Mr Lee was an employee of the MAA or that some other relationship existed that was capable of giving rise to vicarious liability, then, in our submission, Mr Lee's conduct in disregarding the MAA's instructions puts him outside of the course of that employment, and as there was no close connection between the employment and the tortious act it would not be just and reasonable for the court to impose liability against the MAA . . . [This is your argument advanced in the alternative to Ground 1.]

You will see from the above that the respondent will then have made submissions based on the judge accepting the respondent's submissions on Ground 1 as well as where he rejects them.

The different approaches to preparation: appellant and respondent

Before reading this section, you should briefly remind yourself of the different roles played by the four mooters. This is illustrated in the table on page 7 in Chapter 1.

Evaluating both sides of the argument is important. Irrespective of which side you represent in the moot, you will need to be able to advance arguments not only in support of your own client (the so-called 'positive' case) but also in refutation of your opponent's case (the so-called 'negative' case). As we will shortly see, there is a difference in the way the parties should deal with their positive and negative cases.

---

1 *Cox v Ministry of Justice* [2016] UKSC 10

APPELLANT

The appellant represents the unsuccessful party in the court below and, therefore, seeks to persuade the appeal court to change that decision. Although the appellant needs to argue that the reasoning of the court below was wrong, it is nevertheless important to consider carefully what was said in that court because it is likely to feature heavily in the respondent's submissions. Furthermore, the appellant needs to advance sufficiently robust arguments if it is to stand any chance of the appeal court reversing the earlier decision.

The majority (but by no means all) of the appellant's submissions should be spent developing their client's positive case. This is because, as the advocates to speak first,[2] all they will know about the respondent's case is what they will have read in their skeleton argument. Although the respondent's skeleton will have set out their arguments, they will only be in summary form and great care needs to be taken trying to anticipate how they will actually develop their arguments when addressing the court. The majority of the appellant's negative case should be left to the reply, by which time the respondent will have completed the entirety of their oral submissions.

RESPONDENT

The respondent succeeded in the court below and it is their task to persuade the appeal court that the decision of that earlier court was correct and should not be disturbed. As the respondent is content for that decision to stand, they should consider adopting the reasoning of that court as a starting point in their submissions.

As the appellant has initiated the appeal, it is the respondent's role to *respond* to the appellant's arguments. In general terms, the respondent does this by advancing arguments aimed at refuting the appellant's submissions as well as advancing their own positive case.

It can be seen, therefore, that the respondent has two separate but related tasks. Although the respondent has slightly more to do than the appellant, its task is not that much more difficult or burdensome. Whereas the appellant might just about be able to get away with giving little thought to how the respondent will advance their oral arguments,[3] by the time the respondent addresses the court they will have heard the entirety of the appellant's positive case (as well as some of its negative case) and will be in a good position to demonstrate a far wider range of mooting skills by including in their submissions a degree of refutation. Done well, this can often place a respondent at an advantage in terms of winning the moot.

2 The position in Scottish moots is slightly different – see page 8.
3 A lazy tactic and one not to be recommended.

Mooting tip
Although it is important for both parties to reflect carefully on the decision of the lower court, neither party should restrict their submissions to the issues raised in the reasoning of that court. Restricting the arguments to the grounds of appeal is, however, essential.

The law

The purpose of this section is to put the above into the context of your legal research rather than to provide a definitive summary of the law. Ground 1 of the appeal turns on whether Mr Lee was an employee of the MAA or alternatively was an independent contractor, while Ground 2 turns on whether Mr Lee's conduct was such as to put himself outside of the course of his employment with the result that the MAA is not liable for his actions.

GROUND 1

You will need to consider the statutory meaning of 'employee' and 'worker' which can be found in s 230(1) and s 230(3) of the Employment Rights Act 1996. You will then need to review the common law position as to whether a person is an employee. The courts use a 'multiple test' which looks at every aspect of the relationship and incorporates the older tests including those of personal service,[4] control,[5] mutuality of obligations[6] and economic reality.[7]

GROUND 2

The rules relating to vicarious liability have been the subject of recent significant change and this appeal is an example of where the law might have overtaken the language used in the moot.

As Lord Reed explained in the opening remarks of his judgment in *Cox v Ministry of Justice*:[8]

> The law of vicarious liability is on the move. . . . It has not yet come to a stop. This appeal, and the companion appeal in *Mohamud v WM Morrison*

---

4 Who performs the work? Must the individual complete the work themselves or can they select and send an appropriate substitute?
5 Who controls when, where and how the individual works: the business or the individual?
6 Is there an obligation to the other party? Is the business obliged to provide work and is the individual obliged to accept the work?
7 Was the individual 'in business on his own account'?
8 [2016] AC 660

Supermarkets plc . . . provide an opportunity to take stock of where it has got to so far. The scope of vicarious liability depends upon the answers to two questions. First, what sort of relationship has to exist between an individual and a defendant before the defendant can be made vicariously liable in tort for the conduct of that individual? Secondly, in what manner does the conduct of that individual have to be related to that relationship, in order for vicarious liability to be imposed on the defendant?[9]

You will, therefore, need to consider the two-stage test formulated in the separate, but complimentary, judgments in *Cox* and *Mohumud*:

1. Is there a relationship between the parties which is capable of giving rise to vicarious liability?[10]
2. Is there a close connection between the employment and the tortious act that means it would be just and reasonable for the court to impose liability?[11]

How to select your authorities

The first thing to note is the number of authorities that you are permitted to use. This will be set out in the rules that you will be provided with. Although you must not exceed this number, there is no reason why you should necessarily use the maximum number allowed. Remember that you are required to deliver your submissions in a very limited time, and some of this time will almost certainly be taken up dealing with judicial interventions. Therefore, it is important to consider carefully how many authorities you actually need to support your submissions.

Sometimes the moot question itself will refer to cases. When this happens, these cases are known as court authorities, which means that (unless the moot rules expressly state otherwise) either party may refer to them without them counting towards the allowed number of authorities.

Selecting your authorities is extremely important as this will determine the basis of your submissions. You should only select the key authority or authorities that support your proposition. There are bound to be other authorities that make ostensibly the same or similar points, but these are not necessary unless they make a point that goes beyond that in your primary authority. Addressing the court with a number of authorities that make the same (or largely the same) point will only eat into your valuable time without advancing your case much further. Notwithstanding this, you should still be familiar with these subsidiary authorities because they might be raised during argument either by your opponent or by the judge.

---

9 Ibid., 664
10 *Cox v Ministry of Justice* [2016] AC 660
11 *Mohamud v WM Morrison Supermarkets plc* [2016] AC 677

Although the following point might appear obvious, its importance cannot be overstated. When selecting your authorities, you must make sure that they are relevant. An authority will be relevant if it deals with the same legal principles that feature in the moot problem, even if the facts are not identical. An excellent example illustrating this point is the famous case of *Donoghue v Stevenson*.[12] This is the case involving the decomposed snail in the ginger-beer bottle. Although no case has yet presented itself with identical facts, as lawyers we are only concerned with the legal principle that was established in that case, which is that a manufacturer of a product owes a duty of care to the consumer of the product. This principle has since been applied in many situations outside of product manufacture, including personal injury and occupiers' liability as well as a number of other cases that have considered the question of duty of care in tort. By way of example, the Court of Appeal has very recently referred extensively to the *Donoghue* principles when considering an appeal by the owners of a factory which suffered fire damage.[13]

The law–fact distinction on the usefulness of authorities was explained by Sir Donald Nicholls VC in *Molnlycke AB and Another v Procter & Gamble Ltd and Others (No. 5)*[14] when he pointed out: 'Citing previous decisions on a question of fact is not a useful, nor is it a proper, exercise.'[15]

Do not use too many authorities

For the purpose of mooting, as well as in professional practice, you need to forget all that you have been taught about writing essays and answering exam questions whereby you are encouraged to cite as many relevant cases as you can possibly fit in with significant use of footnotes.

For advocacy to be effective, it needs to be to the point. Citing too many authorities runs the risk of losing focus. This is especially the case in mooting where the time allocated for your submissions is very limited. The overuse of authority has long been criticised. In 1939, concern expressed as to the increase in the number of law reports led to the establishment of a Committee under Simonds J which reported to the Lord Chancellor in 1940.[16] In *Lambert v Lewis*,[17] Lord Diplock spoke of his concerns about the 'superfluity of citation':

> [T]he respect which under the common law is paid to precedent makes it tempting to the appellate advocate to cite a plethora of authorities which do no more than illustrate the application to particular facts of a well-established

---

12 [1932] AC 562
13 *Howmet Ltd v Economy Devices Ltd & Ors* [2016] EWCA (Civ) 847
14 [1994] RPC 49
15 Ibid., 114
16 Discussed in *R v Erskine; R v Williams* [2010] 1 WLR 183, [68], Lord Judge CJ.
17 [1982] AC 225

principle of law that has been clearly stated . . . [I]n those cases that are no more than illustrative, however, there are likely to be found judicial statements of principle that do not follow the precise language in which the principle is expressed . . . but use some paraphrase of it that the judge thinks is specially apt to explain its application to the facts of a particular case. The citation of a plethora of illustrative authorities, apart from being time and cost-consuming, present the danger of so blinding the court with case law that it has difficulty in seeing the wood of legal principle for the trees of paraphrase.[18]

Lord Roskill made a similar observation in *Pioneer Shipping v BTP Trioxide*:[19]

I hope I shall not be thought discourteous or unappreciative of the industry involved in the preparation of counsel's arguments if I say that today massive citation of authority in cases where the relevant legal principles have been clearly and authoritatively determined is of little or no assistance, and should be firmly discouraged.[20]

The problems associated with excessive citation of authority grew with the ready availability on the various legal databases and the internet generally of most High Court and all Court of Appeal and Supreme Court decisions. Laddie J had this to say about the problem in *Michaels and another v Taylor Woodrow Development Ltd and others*:[21]

[T]he recent growth of computerised databases has made it an even more frequent and extensive occurrence. There are now significantly more judges, more cases and more databases than there were even two decades ago. Until comparatively recently, this was not a substantial problem . . . now there is no pre-selection. Large numbers of decisions, good and bad, reserved and unreserved, can be accessed . . . it seems to me that the common law system, which places such reliance on judicial authority, stands the risk of being swamped by a torrent of material . . .[22]

Not only is the overuse of authority unhelpful to your case, but it is likely to invoke the annoyance of the judge. This was the outcome in *Seagrove v Sullivan*[23] where Holman J explained that:

The whole topic of beneficial interests following cohabitation has been the subject of recent consideration by the Supreme Court, in particular in [two well known cases]. . . . It would be surprising, frankly, if it was necessary to

---

18 Ibid., 274
19 [1982] AC 724
20 Ibid., 751
21 [2001] Ch 493
22 Ibid., 520
23 [2014] EWHC 4110 (Fam)

look beyond those two authorities; but most certainly, when the Supreme Court has, on more than one recent occasion, traversed all the historic law in relation to this topic, it is quite ridiculous and completely disproportionate to produce bundles of no less than 32 authorities.[24]

We are, however, to some extent assisted by the pragmatic approach taken by some judges who take the trouble to explain that a particular judgment will add nothing to the case law on the subject in question. For example, in *Colborne v Colborne*[25] Black LJ stated at the outset of her judgment that '[this case] turns on its own facts and does not give rise to any issues of principle'.[26] Observations such as these indicate in the strongest terms that such a case is unlikely to be helpful in support of your appeal.

> **Mooting tip**
> You must select very carefully the cases that you wish to refer to. Only those cases which help establish the principle of law under consideration should be used. Conversely, authorities that merely illustrate a principle, or otherwise restate it, should not be used.

List of authorities

Some moots require mooters to prepare a list of authorities. Even where the rules do not stipulate this as a requirement, mooters often include a list of authorities immediately after their skeleton argument, starting on a new page.

We will consider how best to deal with your opponent's cases at pages 107 and 108.

Why are you citing that case?

Unlike an exam or piece of coursework where you will almost certainly impress the examiner by discussing a large number of cases and other sources including academic opinion, you should approach a moot differently. You must always have in mind the limited time you will have to present your arguments and you will simply not have the time to take the judge through too much material. It is also important not to be unnecessarily repetitive. Once you have made a point, it is rarely necessary to repeat it unless there is something that you later need to add. Again, unlike with an exam, you will rarely need to cite a case just because it exists and supports another case.

24 Ibid., [37]
25 [2014] EWCA Civ 1488
26 Ibid., [1]

You must always have in your mind the principal reason you are citing a particular case (or other material) and be able to articulate that reason succinctly by explaining how it supports your case. This is just one example of a question that is often asked by judges.

How and when to use cases that are not binding on the moot court

Just because a case is not binding on the moot court, it does not mean that you cannot or should not use it.

(A) IF A CASE IS BINDING

If a case is binding on the moot court, then it follows that you should use it. You should also be prepared to explain why the case is appropriate and was correctly decided.

(B) IF A CASE IS NOT BINDING

As noted above, just because a case is not binding on the moot court it does not mean that you cannot or should not use it. It may have a particular persuasive quality.

In the majority of cases, an authority will bind another court following the usual rules of precedent without there being any need for the judge in the earlier case to say anything further about it. However, you should be aware of the occasional case where the judge does make some reference to the binding nature of a case. For example, in the first instance decision of HHJ Moloney QC in *ParkingEye Ltd v Beavis and another*[27] the learned judge emphasised that 'since I am a Circuit Judge not a High Court Judge, this decision has only persuasive force'.[28] In other cases, the court might state the decision to be 'on its own particular facts'. For example, in *Gurmukh Singh Gahir v Gurdial Singh Bansal*[29] Sir David Eady observed: 'Ultimately, however, the authorities can only offer general guidance: each case turns on its own facts and the judge must take all those individual circumstances into account in arriving at what seems to be the just outcome.'[30]

Ratio decidendi and *obiter dicta*

It is, of course, only the *ratio decidendi* of a case that is binding. You must therefore be able to identify the *ratio decidendi* of the cases you wish to cite.

---

27 County Court at Cambridge, 19 May 2014. *ParkingEye* was subsequently determined by the Supreme Court ([2015] 3 WLR 1373).
28 Paragraph 1.2(a)
29 [2016] EWHC 2041 (QB)
30 Ibid., [3]

In *R (Kadhim) v Brent London Borough Council Housing Benefit Review Board*,[31] Buxton LJ reminded us that:

> Cases as such do not bind; their *rationes decidendi* do. While there has been much academic discussion of the proper way of determining the ratio of a case, we find the clearest and most persuasive guidance . . . to be that of Professor Cross in *Cross & Harris, Precedent in English Law*, 4th ed (1991), p 72: 'The *ratio decidendi* of a case is any rule of law expressly or impliedly treated by the judge as a necessary step in reaching his conclusion, having regard to the line of reasoning adopted by him'.[32]

But remember, even *obiter dicta* can, in appropriate circumstances, be extremely helpful to your argument as persuasive (rather than binding) authority and, in appropriate cases, it will be followed. This was explained recently by McCombe LJ in *R (on the application of Brooks) v The Independent Adjudicator & Anor*[33] where he stated:

> I was attracted by that . . . submission, having as it does the support of a number of powerful *obiter dicta* of a number of distinguished judges and opinions of authors. Had my decision in this case depended upon giving effect to such *dicta*, I would have been inclined to do so.[34]

Dissenting judgments

Just as *obiter dicta* can, in appropriate circumstances, be helpful in your moot, so, too, can a dissenting judgment. However, if you do cite a dissenting judgment, expect the judge to want to know why he should follow a judgment that did not gain the support of the majority in the case when it was decided. A good recent example where the Supreme Court cited with approval a dissenting Court of Appeal judgment is *Rainy Sky SA and Others v Kookmin Bank*[35] where Lord Clarke quoted with approval from the dissenting Court of Appeal judgment of Sir Simon Tuckey in relation to the correct approach to contract interpretation.

Cases from other jurisdictions

Although decisions from other jurisdictions are not binding on our courts, it does not mean that you should not cite them. Our courts often follow decisions from other jurisdictions, including decisions of the Privy Council. Such cases can be

---

31 [2001] QB 955
32 Ibid., 961
33 [2016] EWCA Civ 1033
34 Ibid., [39]
35 [2011] UKSC 50

extremely helpful where there are domestic cases that are extremely unhelpful to your submissions.

> **Mooting tip**
>
> A key part of your role as an advocate is to persuade the court that your submissions carry greater legal weight than those of your opponent. In appropriate circumstances, therefore, it might be helpful respectfully to remind the judge that you are presenting an authority that is binding on the court. This might be especially helpful if your opponent cites an authority on the same point that, for whatever reason, does not bind the particular court.

Hierarchy of law reports

When a case is reported, it will often appear in different series of law reports. It is important to appreciate that not all law reports are equal.

Let us consider the well-known case of *Caparo Industries Plc v Dickman & Others* which was decided by the House of Lords on 8 February 1990. There are numerous citations for the case including [1990] 2 AC 605; [1990] 2 WLR 358; [1990] 1 All ER 568; [1990] BCC 164; [1990] BCLC 273; [1990] ECC 313; [1955-95] PNLR 523; (1990) 87(12) LSG 42; (1990) 140 NLJ 248; (1990) 134 SJ 494; *Times*, 12 February 1990; *Independent*, 16 February 1990; *Financial Times*, 13 February 1990; *Guardian*, 15 February 1990; and *Daily Telegraph*, 15 February 1990.

Caparo was a case that considered whether or not a duty of care was owed by auditors to various parties when preparing their auditor's report, although for present purposes the facts and decision are unimportant. What is important is the difference between these reports and which one should be cited. The difference is of crucial importance in terms of both legal and practical consequences.

(a) Legal consequences

On 23 March 2012, Lord Judge CJ issued a Practice Direction on Citation of Authorities[36] the purpose of which was 'to clarify the practice and procedure governing the citation of authorities and applies throughout the Senior Courts of England and Wales, including the Crown Court, in county courts and in magistrates' courts'. The Practice Direction explains that when authority is cited (whether in written or in oral submissions), the following practice should be followed:

36 [2012] 1 WLR 780

- Where a judgment is reported in the official Law Reports (AC, QB/KB, Ch, Fam) published by the Incorporated Council of Law Reporting for England and Wales, that report must be cited. These are the most authoritative reports; they contain a summary of the argument. Other series of reports and official transcripts of judgment may only be used when a case is not reported in the official Law Reports.
- If a judgment is not (or not yet) reported in the official Law Reports but it is reported in the Weekly Law Reports (WLR) or the All England Law Reports (All ER), that report should be cited. If the case is reported in both the WLR and the All ER, either report may properly be cited.
- If a judgment is not reported in the official Law Reports, the WLR or the All ER, but it is reported in any of the authoritative specialist series of reports which contain a headnote and are made by individuals holding a Senior Courts qualification,[37] the specialist report should be cited.
- Where a judgment is not reported in any of the reports referred to above, but is reported in other reports, they may be cited.
- Where a judgment has not been reported, reference may be made to the official transcript if that is available, not the handed-down text of the judgment, as this may have been subject to late revision after the text was handed down. Official transcripts may be obtained from, for instance, BAILII (www.bailii.org). An unreported case should not usually be cited unless it contains a relevant statement of legal principle not found in reported authority.
- Occasions arise when one report is fuller than another, or when there are discrepancies between reports. On such occasions, the practice outlined above need not be followed, but the court should be given a brief explanation why this course is being taken, and the alternative references should be given.

Mooting tip

Quite understandably, mooters concentrate their efforts on perfecting their submissions and delivery, and it is correct to say that those factors are among the most important in determining the winner of a moot. However, it is equally the case that many moots are very close, which can present the judge with difficulties in determining the winner. It is with these evenly matched moots that the judge can be swayed by the small but important detail such as the overall presentation of the bundles and the use of the correct law reports.

Whenever you see reference to the 'Law Reports', as opposed to law reports in general, it refers to those reports published by the Incorporated Council of Law Reporting for England and Wales (ICLR) and which appear at the head of the table of hierarchy.

---

37 For the purposes of section 115 of the Courts and Legal Services Act 1990.

The figure below provides a useful summary of the hierarchy of law reports.

The Law Reports	AC, QB/KB, Ch, Fam published by the Incorporated Council of Law Reporting for England and Wales
Weekly Law Reports or All England Law Reports	WLR or All ER
Specialist series of reports	Authoritative specialist series of reports which contain a headnote and are made by individuals holding a Senior Courts qualification
Other reports	
Official transcript	Where a judgment has not (yet) been reported, reference may be made to the official transcript if that is available, not the handed-down text of the judgment, as this may have been subject to late revision after the text was handed down. Official transcripts may be obtained from, for instance, BAILII (www.bailii.org)
Unreported cases	An unreported case should not usually be cited unless it contains a relevant statement of legal principle not found in reported authority

(b) Practical consequences

Judgments reported in the official Law Reports also contain a summary of the legal arguments as used by counsel in the particular case. To read how some of the country's leading legal practitioners have argued the case should provide an invaluable inspiration to mooters, especially given that you are also seeking to rely on the same case in support of your own submissions. You will, of course, need to moderate your arguments to reflect any changes in the law since the case was first argued and any material differences between the case cited and the moot.

In addition, the Law Reports often include, in the same report, the judgments of the lower courts. This will enable you to see, in one report, the history of the case as it journeyed through its appeal process. The absence of this feature led the Court of Appeal to criticise one of the parties in *Governor and Company of the Bank of Scotland v Henry Butcher & Co*[38] for citing an authority from the All England Law Reports when the same case had also been reported in the Law Reports (Appeal Cases).

38 [2003] EWCA Civ 67, per Munby J at [79]

Using and citing unreported cases

As we have just seen, unreported cases should not usually be cited unless they contain relevant statements of legal principle not found in reported authority. Where a judgment has not (yet) been reported, reference may be made to the official transcript if that is available but not the handed-down text of the judgment as this may have been subject to late revision after it was handed down. An excellent source for finding official transcripts of cases is the British and Irish Legal Information Institute (BAILII) which can be found at www.bailii.org.

Case citations and neutral citations

The neutral citation system was introduced in January 2001 for all judgments in England and Wales that were handed down by the House of Lords, Privy Council, Court of Appeal and all divisions of the High Court. It was later extended to include the Supreme Court. The neutral citation is assigned to the case by the court. The principal aim of a neutral citation is to facilitate the easier retrieval of judgments that appear electronically on the internet. They are especially helpful where the case has not (yet) been reported in one of the series of law reports.

The diagram below shows an example of a UK case citation followed by a case using a neutral citation.

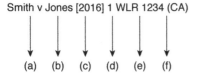

Smith v Jones [2016] 1 WLR 1234 (CA)

(a)   (b)   (c)   (d)   (e)   (f)

UK case citation

(a)   Names of the parties
(b)   Year of the report[39]
(c)   Volume number
(d)   Abbreviation for the law report series
(e)   Page number
(f)   Court[40]

---

39 You will see some reports with the year in square brackets while others use round brackets. Round brackets are only used if the year is not needed to identify the correct volume.
40 In this example, Court of Appeal. The Division is not noted.

Smith v Jones [2016] EWCA Civ 100

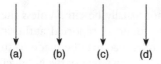

(a)   (b)   (c)   (d)

Neutral citation

(a) Names of the parties
(b) Year of the judgment
(c) Court[41]
(d) Judgment number

When referring to a case by its neutral citation, the court that heard the case forms part of the citation itself. You should not, therefore, add the name of the court in brackets at the end as you might do when not using a neutral citation.

> **Mooting tip**
> Where a case has been reported in one of the series of law reports, that citation should be used (utilising the hierarchy discussed above) rather than its neutral citation.

The use of headnotes

The first thing to remember about headnotes is that they do not form part of the judgment and therefore cannot form any part of the *ratio decidendi* of a case. As its name suggests, the headnote is merely a brief (albeit often very useful) summary of the case. Do not, therefore, cite from the headnote as you would from a passage in a judgment.

A quick scan of the headnote can save you an enormous amount of preparation time. Headnotes provide a succinct summary of the issues and procedural history of a case and the court's decision. At the very least, reading the headnote should give you a good indication of whether or not the case is relevant and needs to be read further.

In addition to the headnote, you should also look through the report's catchwords which summarise, in shortened form, the issues in the case and any words, phrases or legislative provisions that the court has considered and ruled upon. Unlike the headnote, the catchwords do not state the court's decision.

---

41 In this example, England and Wales Court of Appeal, Civil Division.

The figure below shows the headnote and catchwords section from *Southern Pacific Mortgages Ltd v Scott (Mortgage Business plc intervening).*[42]

385

A   Supreme Court

Southern Pacific Mortgages Ltd *v* Scott (Mortgage Business plc intervening)

[on appeal from **Mortgage Business plc *v* O'Shaughnessy**]

B   **[2014] UKSC 52**

2014 March 3, 4;   Baroness Hale of Richmond DPSC, Lord Wilson,
      Oct 22   Lord Sumption, Lord Reed JJSC, Lord Collins of Mapesbury

C *Land registration — Overriding interest — "Actual occupation" — Vendor prior to sale agreeing to pay back significant part of completion money to purchaser in return for right to continue in occupation — Exchange of contract of sale, completion and execution of mortgage all taking place on same day — Vendor remaining in occupation pursuant to tenancy granted by purchaser — Mortgagee's claim for possession — Whether vendor having overriding interest taking priority over mortgagee's charge — Land Registration Act 2002 (c 9), s 29, Sch 3, para 2*

> Catchwords

D   The vendor agreed to sell the freehold interest in her home to a purchaser acting as the nominee of N. The purchaser promised the vendor that she would be entitled to remain in occupation indefinitely after completion at a discounted rent, in return for which the vendor agreed to pay back to N a significant part of the completion money, although that arrangement was not referred to in the contract of sale. The purchaser obtained a buy to let mortgage from the claimant lender on the basis that the property was being purchased at full value with vacant possession. Exchange of
E contracts between the vendor and the purchaser, completion of the contract by execution of the transfer and execution of the mortgage all took place on the same day. Subsequently, in breach of the terms of the mortgage, N purported to grant a two-year assured shorthold tenancy at a discounted rent to the vendor. When the purchaser defaulted on the loan and disappeared, the lender brought proceedings for possession against the purchaser and the vendor. Following the trial of preliminary issues, the judge rejected the vendor's claim that she had had an equitable interest in
F the property from the moment of exchange of contracts which, by section 29(2)(a)(ii) of and paragraph 2 of Schedule 3 to the Land Registration Act 2002[1], was an unregistered interest which overrode the interests of the lender. He accordingly made the order for possession sought. The Court of Appeal dismissed the vendor's appeal.

> Headnote

On appeal by the vendor—
     Held, dismissing the appeal, that the unregistered interests which overrode registered dispositions by virtue of section 29(2) of, and paragraph 2 of Schedule 3 to,
G the Land Registration Act 2002 had to be proprietary in nature; that prior to acquisition of the legal estate a purchaser of property could not grant equitable rights of a proprietary character; that, therefore, the vendor had acquired no more than personal rights against the purchaser when she had agreed to sell her house on the basis of the purchaser's promise that she would be entitled to remain in occupation; that the vendor's rights had only become proprietary and capable of taking priority over a mortgage when they had been fed by the purchaser's acquisition of the legal
H estate; and that, since the acquisition of the legal estate and the grant of the lender's charge were one indivisible transaction, the vendor could not assert against the lender an interest which had only arisen on completion (post, paras 59–60, 71, 75, 77, 79, 90, 94, 95, 111–112, 122, 123).

¹ Land Registration Act 2002, s 29, Sch 3, para 2: see post, para 39.

Mooting tip

Even though the headnote carries no legal authority, you should nevertheless be familiar with its content and the terminology used. The table below lists the terminology used to note the effect of the case on the existing case law.

Headnote terminology	Meaning
Affirmed	The court agreed with the decision of the lower court in the same case.
Applied	The court considered itself to be bound by the precedent set in an earlier, different, case. Consequently, the court 'applied' that reasoning to the present case.
Approved	The court agreed with the decision of a lower court in a different case.
Considered	The court has considered the principles explained in a different case, often one that has been decided by another court of equal status.
Distinguished	The court either cannot or does not want to overrule a previous decision but also does not want to apply it. It therefore distinguishes the two cases and thereby avoids having to follow it.
Overruled	The court has overruled a decision in a different case, usually (but not always) a case decided by a court of lower status.
Reversed	The court has overturned ('reversed') the decision of the lower court in the same case after hearing the appeal.
Semble	The court has expressed its opinion on a point that is not directly at issue. This is, therefore, *obiter dictum*.

When to use policy arguments

The short answer to this question is 'sparingly and with great care'. Moots take place in courts of law where judges are mainly interested in submissions based on law rather than issues of policy. Different considerations apply depending on whether the moot is set in the Supreme Court or in the Court of Appeal.

Supreme Court

Where the moot is set in the Supreme Court, you may refer to policy arguments more freely than would be the case had the moot been set in the Court of Appeal. You will need to keep in mind the terms of the 1966 *Practice Statement (Judicial Precedent)*[43] which was discussed in Chapter 2 and, in particular, where the House

---

43 [1966] 1 WLR 1234, discussed at page 37.

of Lords and now the Supreme Court may decide 'to depart from a previous decision when it appears right to do so'. Where a House of Lords or Supreme Court decision is cited against you, you can advance policy arguments to explain why it appears right for the Supreme Court to depart from a previous decision. Even where you are not faced with an adverse House of Lords or Supreme Court decision, you may still decide to advance policy arguments to explain why the court should *not* depart from its previous decision.

Court of Appeal

Where the moot is set in the Court of Appeal, your ability to argue matters of policy are somewhat more limited. Rather than trying to fit policy arguments within the 1966 *Practice Statement* as we have just discussed, you should instead ensure that they satisfy the exceptions laid down in *Young v Bristol Aeroplane Co Ltd*[44] (for civil cases) or in *R v Taylor*[45] (for criminal cases), both of which were discussed in Chapter 2.

> **Mooting tip**
> Before even considering whether or not to deploy policy arguments you should first make sure that there is no authority that goes against you for which the particular court is bound. No argument of policy, no matter how powerful, will entitle a court to depart from an authority to which it finds itself bound.

For an excellent discussion on policy arguments, see John Bell's *Policy Arguments in Judicial Decisions* (Oxford University Press, 1983).

Legal journals and textbooks

Although there is no general rule against doing so,[46] quoting from legal journals and textbooks should be done with extreme care. First, they are secondary sources and have absolutely no binding force on any court. Given the absence of binding authority, you should consider whether it might be preferable to adapt or adopt the reasoning and arguments of the particular author and build them into your own submissions. If you are to consider this approach, you should check to make sure that doing so does not contravene any rules or regulations of the

---

44 [1944] KB 718 (CA)
45 [1950] 2 KB 368 (CCA)
46 Although you should check the rules of the particular moot to see if there is anything said about quoting from this kind of material.

particular moot or academic institution.[47] If you do decide to adapt or adopt an author's thoughts, you should consider mentioning that your submission is based on arguments that have been advocated by a legal academic and, where appropriate, provide their name and title/status.

However, where the author or text that you are considering quoting from is acknowledged as a leading legal writer, then, even though it will still not bind a court, you might wish to cite it as a specific source. A good example of this is *Smith & Hogan's Criminal Law* which has been referred to in a number of criminal cases. Similarly, with journal articles, you should select from the main journals (such as the *Law Quarterly Review* or *Modern Law Review*, or specialist subject journals such as the *Construction Law Journal*) rather than those that publish in newspaper or magazine format. The key is to understand which texts satisfy this 'superior legal writer' label. Although there is no list of such superior writers or texts, the following can be used as a guide. The most obvious category is where the author's name appears as part of the title of the text. These texts are typically the leading practitioner texts on the subject and are often referred to with approval in judgments. You should always make sure that you cite from the most up-to-date edition. These texts include:

Subject	Title
Agency	Bowstead and Reynolds on Agency
Company law	Gore-Browne on Companies
Conflict of laws	Dicey, Morris and Collins on the Conflict of Laws
Contract law	Chitty on Contracts
Criminal law	Archbold Criminal Pleading, Evidence and Practice
Damages	McGregor on Damages
Encyclopaedia of law	Halsbury's Laws of England
Equity	Snell's Equity
Land law/real property	Megarry and Wade: The Law of Real Property; Emmet and Farrand on Title
Negligence and nuisance	Charlesworth and Percy on Negligence
Private international law	Dicey, Morris and Collins on the Conflict of Laws
Restitution	Goff and Jones on Restitution
Tort law	Clerk and Lindsell on Torts
Trusts and Trustees	Underhill and Hayton, Law of Trusts and Trustees

47 In particular, where your moot forms part of an academic assessment, the regulations relating to plagiarism are likely to require you to disclose the source of the original author's work.

For a Scottish law moot, the relevant practitioner texts include the following:

Subject	Title
Company law	Gore-Browne on Companies
Contract law	McBryde, The Law of Contract in Scotland
Criminal law	Gordon, The Criminal Law of Scotland
Delict	Walker, The Law of Delict in Scotland
Encyclopaedia of law	The Laws of Scotland: Stair Memorial Encyclopaedia
Land law	Gordon and Wortley, Scottish Land Law
Private International Law	Anton and Beaumont, Private International Law
Trusts and succession	Meston, Scottish Trusts and Succession Service

Law Commission reports should also be cited with caution. They can be very illuminating in setting out the (then) current state of the law and its defects together with their proposals for reform. The difficulty with citing such material is that if the proposals for reform are substantial, the court is likely to say that any such changes are a matter for Parliament rather than the courts. As with any argument that you might advance, you will need to provide cogent reasons why the court should accede to your submissions.

Changes in the law – Parliament or the courts?

It was noted in Chapter 2 that cases remain good law unless and until they are overruled by a subsequent case or by an Act of Parliament. This reflects the declaratory theory of the common law which provides that judges do not create law but merely declare what the law is and has always been. Any changes to the law are matters for Parliament.

This presents something of a dilemma for mooters whose submissions may contain an argument that the law needs to change. How should a mooter deal with a judge who retorts that a change in the law is a matter for Parliament and not the courts? This is precisely what happened in *Government of the United States of America v Montgomery & Montgomery*[48] where Stuart-Smith LJ explained:

> I accept the submission of [Counsel] who appeared for the appellants, that if Parliament had thought [the case] was wrongly decided, it has had plenty of opportunity to put the matter right since then, but has declined to do so, for the obvious reason in my view that it is plainly right.[49]

The answer to this dilemma is that the declaratory theory of the common law is just that: a theory. And because it is a theory that some judges have followed more

48 [1998] EWCA Civ 1175
49 Ibid., [18]

stringently than others, it is a fertile ground for mooters and advocates alike. The way you will deal with this problem will depend on whether you are seeking to persuade the court to change the law or are resisting your opponent's attempts to do the same.

General guidance on the matter was set out in *C (A Minor) v DPP*[50] where Lord Lowry stated as important the following five factors when considering the appropriateness of judicial law-making by the House of Lords:[51]

(1) If the solution is doubtful, the judges should beware of imposing their own remedy.

(2) Caution should prevail if Parliament has rejected opportunities of clearing up a known difficulty or has legislated, while leaving the difficulty untouched.

(3) Disputed matters of social policy are less suitable areas for judicial intervention than purely legal problems.

(4) Fundamental legal doctrines should not be lightly set aside.

(5) Judges should not make a change unless they can achieve finality and certainty.

Despite the above guidance which clearly suggests that judges should adopt a cautious approach to changing the law, this has not always been followed. By way of example, in *R v Dica*[52] the Court of Appeal overruled the earlier authority of *R v Clarence*[53] and held that a defendant could be criminally liable for recklessly infecting another person with HIV. The Court of Appeal changed the law in this way despite the fact that the Home Office had previously decided not to introduce legislation which would have imposed criminal liability in such a situation. In declining to introduce such legislation, the Home Office observed that 'this issue had ramifications going beyond the criminal law into wider considerations of social and public health policy'.[54]

> **Mooting tip**
> Judges often ask mooters to explain why they are asking the court to change the law when this ought to be a matter left to Parliament. In addition to the above discussion, the following guidance should assist when answering this question.

---

50 [1996] AC 1
51 Ibid., 28
52 [2004] QB 1257 (CA)
53 (1888) 22 QBD 23 (CCCR)
54 Violence: Reforming the Offences Against the Person Act 1861, Home Office, London, 1998

Arguing for the court to change the law

If your submissions require the court (rather than Parliament) to change the law, the following arguments might assist:

- The case is before the court now and a decision is needed in order to do justice between the parties. This argument is particularly powerful if there is an absence of statutory provision or relevant case law (either because the point in issue is a novel one or the existing relevant case law is distinguishable).
- Leaving it for Parliament to make changes in the law is far too slow and cumbersome. With both of these points, you may wish to refer to the famous quote from William E Gladstone: 'Justice delayed is justice denied'; or the equivalent-meaning quote from William Penn: 'To delay justice is injustice.'
- The law must not remain static but should be flexible enough to reflect changes in social conditions. As Lord Scarman explained in *McLoughlin v O'Brian*:[55]

> The distinguishing feature of the common law is this judicial development and formulation of principle. Policy considerations will have to be weighed: but the objective of the judges is the formulation of principle. And, if principle inexorably requires a decision which entails a degree of policy risk, the court's function is to adjudicate according to principle, leaving policy curtailment to the judgment of Parliament. Here lies the true role of the two law-making institutions in our constitution. By concentrating on principle the judges can keep the common law alive, flexible and consistent, and can keep the legal system clear of policy problems which neither they, nor the forensic process which it is their duty to operate, are equipped to resolve.[56]

Lord Scarman went on to explain that if principle leads to results which are thought to be socially unacceptable, 'Parliament can legislate to draw a line or map out a new path'.[57]

A good modern-day example of a case where the House of Lords adapted the law to satisfy social change is *Fitzpatrick v Sterling Housing Association Ltd*.[58] Mr Fitzpatrick had lived with his partner, Mr Thompson, who was the original tenant of a flat of which the Housing Association were the freehold owners from 1976 until Mr Thompson's death in 1994. The couple had been partners in a long-standing, close, loving and monogamous homosexual relationship. After Mr Thompson's death, Mr Fitzpatrick sought a declaration that he had succeeded to the tenancy of the flat under the Rent Act 1977, as

---

55 [1983] 1 AC 410 (HL)
56 Ibid., 430
57 Ibid.
58 [2001] 1 AC 27 (HL)

amended by the Housing Act 1988. His case was that he was a 'spouse' of Mr Thompson within the terms of the Act in that he had been living with him 'as his wife or husband', or alternatively that he was a member of Mr Thompson's family. At first instance, the judge held that Mr Fitzpatrick could not succeed to the tenancy under either of the ways in which he put his claim and his appeal to the Court of Appeal was dismissed by a majority.

On further appeal to the House of Lords, Mr Fitzpatrick argued that 'spouse' should be interpreted in the present climate to include two persons of the same gender intimately linked in a relationship which was not merely transient and which had all the indicia of a marriage save that the parties could not have children, and further that the intimacy of the relationship of two persons living together as he and Mr Thompson had been was such that they should be regarded as constituting a family. Reversing the Court of Appeal, the House of Lords held by a majority that under the legislation a gay man was entitled to take over the tenancy formerly held by his long-term male partner, now deceased. Lord Slynn said that the legislation could not be interpreted to allow Mr Fitzpatrick's claim on the basis that he had been living 'as the husband or wife' of the deceased simply because if Parliament had intended such a relationship to include same-sex partners, it would have said so. However, Mr Fitzpatrick could claim as 'a member of the family' living with the deceased at the time of his death. Lord Slynn said that the word 'family' is used in many senses, some wider than others, and if Mr Fitzpatrick could show (as on the facts he could) the mutual interdependence, sharing of lives, caring and love, commitment and support that are rebuttably presumed to exist between married couples, that would be enough to establish a family relationship between the two men.

- Similarly, the law should be flexible enough to reflect changes in economic conditions.

Arguing against the court making a change in the law

If your submissions require Parliament (rather than the court) to effect changes in the law, the following arguments might assist:

- Parliament is in the unique position to consider the issues in their widest context. Conversely, judges are only able to determine the issues based on the arguments advanced by the parties in a particular case.
- If judges are allowed to depart from the well-established declaratory theory and thereby make new law, they might lose the powers they currently enjoy when exercising their judicial function. This was the concern advanced by Lord Scarman in *Duport Steels Ltd v Sirs*:[59]

---

59 [1980] 1 WLR 142 (HL)

For, if people and Parliament come to think that the judicial power is to be confined by nothing other than the judge's sense of what is right (or, as Selden put it, by the length of the Chancellor's foot), confidence in the judicial system will be replaced by fear of it becoming uncertain and arbitrary in its application. Society will then be ready for Parliament to cut the power of the judges. Their power to do justice will become more restricted by law than it need be, or is today.[60]

- Parliament has had the opportunity of correcting any common law decision that it considers was wrongly decided but has not done so.[61]
- Judges should refrain from making changes to the law in any case where it is reasonable to conclude that Parliament would not support such a change. For example, in *President of India v La Pintada Compania Navigacion SA (The La Pintada)*[62] a powerful argument was advanced for the House of Lords to overrule an earlier authority which had held that a party was not entitled to receive interest on a contractual debt. However, it was observed that the Law Commission had itself recommended that this rule should be abolished but Parliament decided not to do so. Lord Brandon explained that for the House to change the law in such circumstances could well be regarded as

> an unjustifiable usurpation by your Lordships' House of the functions which belong properly to Parliament, rather than as a judicial exercise in departing from an earlier decision on the ground that it has become obsolete and could still, in a limited class of cases, continue to cause some degree of injustice.[63]

- Judges should also refrain from making changes to the law in cases that involve public interest where such public interest issues are also being considered by Parliament at the same time. One reason that has been given to explain why judges need to be particularly circumspect in the use of their powers to declare the law in such cases is:

> not because the principles adopted by Parliament are more satisfactory or more enlightened, but because it is unacceptable constitutionally that there should be two independent sources of law-making at work at the same time.[64]

---

60 Ibid., 169
61 See *Government of the United States of America v Montgomery & Montgomery* [1998] EWCA Civ 1175, discussed at page 83.
62 [1985] AC 104 (HL)
63 Ibid., 130
64 Lord Radcliffe, *Not in Feather Beds* (Hamish Hamilton, London, 1968), 216

- Judge-made changes to the law can bring about practical difficulties because of their retrospective effect. This not only violates the presumption against retrospective changes in the law but could also mean that transactions that were considered settled under previous rules could be subject to reconsideration. Parliamentary changes to the law do not usually have retrospective effect.

Finding cases and other material

This section deals with the skills needed to identify current statute law, statutory instruments, case law and any other material that you will need to provide an accurate and up-to-date statement of the law.

Halsbury's Laws of England

A good starting point for any legal research is *Halsbury's Laws of England* which covers the whole spectrum of English law, including niche and esoteric areas of the law. *Halsbury's Laws* is an authoritative encyclopaedia of law organised according to subject area and is an invaluable resource both for areas of law with which you are not familiar as well as those areas where you are more familiar but need to ensure that your knowledge is up to date. It is particularly useful if you need to find the most important cases, legislation and commentary in any given area of law.

   Halsbury's Laws of England is available in print or online via LexisLibrary and is regarded as an authoritative work and used extensively by legal practitioners.

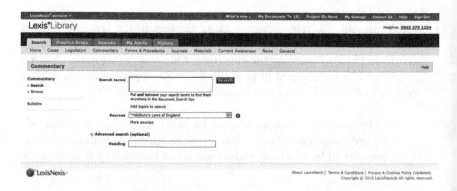

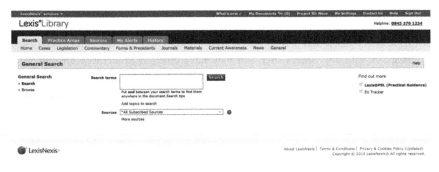

> **Mooting tip**
> The main paragraph within *Halsbury's Laws* summarises the key points of law and the footnotes list the key primary sources, including legislation, law reports and official publications. Do not forget to scroll to the bottom of the page to check for any relevant updates that you need to be aware of.

The Law of Scotland: Stair Memorial Encyclopaedia

The Scottish equivalent to *Halsbury's Laws of England* is *The Law of Scotland: Stair Memorial Encyclopaedia*.

Textbooks

A good subject-specific textbook will provide a broader and more detailed overview of the relevant areas of law with plentiful discussion and guidance for further reading. You may also be lucky and find some discussion in the textbooks of the problems and arguments that the moot you are researching demands answers to.

> **Mooting tip**
> The above note about textbooks in this part of the book is provided to assist you in gaining a more detailed understanding of the areas of law that are set out in the moot problem. Great care must be taken if you intend to quote from a textbook. Generally, only the leading heavyweight or practitioner texts should be cited in legal argument. This is discussed in more details at pages 81 and 82.

Case law

Your *Halsbury's Law* and textbook research will have identified a number of cases. These cases, and any others that you may have covered in lectures, should now form the basis of your next area of research and case preparation. You will need to read these cases very carefully and note the points that support your grounds of appeal as well as the points that go against you.

It is quite likely that during your research you will uncover a number of cases that deal with the same (or very similar) legal principle. When faced with such a situation, it is a good idea to read the most recent of these cases first. This can save you a lot of time because cases often summarise within the judgment the earlier cases dealing with the same legal principle.

Mooting tip

It is important for you to be fully aware of any points that go against your arguments because these can be fertile areas for judicial intervention. By considering these points at the research stage of your preparation, you will be in a much better position to be able to anticipate the kind of questions that you may be asked and be better prepared to answer them.

In order to persuade the court to follow the cases you are citing, there will need to be something in them that connects with your submissions. Clearly, the closer the factual matrix is between the two cases, the easier it will be to persuade the court that the case you are citing should be followed. As already noted, there is no need to find a case with identical facts to those in your moot. Instead, you should look for parallels or analogous situations to support your submissions. Conversely, when faced with an authority that appears to support your opponent's arguments rather than your own, you might wish to adopt the opposite approach and seek to persuade the court that the case is sufficiently different and should therefore be distinguished.

Finding cases

There are several ways to find cases, both online and manually, although for a number of good reasons the former is usually the preferred route for mooters as well as for practitioners. Online research has many advantages over library-based research including the ability to:

- search large numbers of cases and other material for key words
- save cases and other material for later use
- cut and paste text and other data
- research at any time of day or night from wherever you have internet access
- share material electronically between different people.

Mooting tip

Many electronic reports also contain direct links to other material, such as academic or professional commentary on the case as well as to other cases referred to in the judgment. These additional and easy-to-link resources can be enormously helpful in your research and can save a considerable amount of time.

Library research

Before looking at the various online resources, you should not dismiss the importance of the traditional library approach to finding cases and other legal resources. Not only are you likely to find a helpful librarian who can prove invaluable when things are not going exactly to plan, but you should also find that they can assist with online database queries. Law librarians can often help you to locate difficult-to-find cases and other legal resources.

Electronic databases and research

For the reasons discussed above, the use of electronic databases should form a vital part of your research and case preparation. We will now look at some of the more common and popular online resources.

Search engines

Search engines can be a very useful first-stage research tool. They are certainly helpful in identifying material that might aid your research, but the sheer number of results that are likely to be returned means that, unless you are careful, you could waste a lot of time sifting through them. The screen shot shown below shows the first page of results from Google when searching '*Donoghue v Stevenson*' which returned more than 80,000 results. There are, of course, other search engines available, although these, too, are likely to return a substantial number of results.

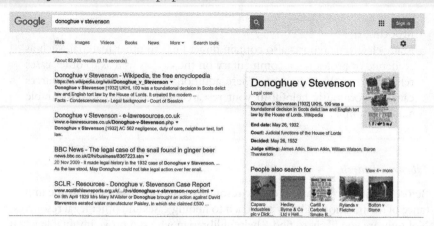

Let us now consider the first page of these results. You will see that the first match on the list is from Wikipedia. You might find this informative as background knowledge but you should not rely on it for your moot. An 'important note' to this effect is provided by Wikipedia itself:

> IMPORTANT NOTE: Most educators and professionals do not consider it appropriate to use tertiary sources such as encyclopedias as a sole source for any information – citing an encyclopedia as an important reference in footnotes or bibliographies may result in censure or a failing grade. Wikipedia articles should be used for background information, as a reference for correct terminology and search terms, and as a starting point for further research. As with any community-built reference, there is a possibility for error in Wikipedia's content – please check your facts against multiple sources and read our disclaimers for more information.[65]

Another problem that can arise when relying on sources other than the appropriate primary sources of law is that the references or citations may not be the correct ones to use. You will see from the above screenshot that the case reference listed for *Donoghue v Stevenson* on the Wikipedia page is [1932] UKHL 100. This is an unofficial neutral form of citation taken from BAILII and, while helpful, is not appropriate to be used in your skeleton argument or oral citation, and should not, therefore, be used for mooting. The formal system of neutral citations was not introduced until 2001 when it was used by the Court of Appeal and Administrative Court before being extended to all divisions of the High Court in England and Wales the following year. For the reasons discussed at pages 74 and 75, the correct case citation to use for *Donoghue v Stevenson* is [1932] AC 562.

---

65 https://en.wikipedia.org/w/index.php?title=Special:CiteThisPage&page=Law&id=387799726 (accessed 6 March 2017).

The second result from the Google search is from e-lawresources.co.uk, a private website. Although not comprehensive in its coverage, it does contain a number of useful law resources. It is not, of course, an appropriate resource to cite for mooting and does not contain copies of official law reports.

The third and fourth returned search results are links to a 2009 BBC news story about the case and to the Scottish Council for Law Reporting site, which is perhaps unsurprising given the Scottish origins of the case.

Although all of the above will provide some helpful background knowledge about a particular case, none takes you to the law report, which you will need if you intend to cite the case in your moot. You will find the law report itself either in hard copy in your law library or electronically from a variety of professionally recognised legal databases. These electronic databases also provide a host of additional invaluable features and greater functionality than you will achieve with a general internet search.

Being able to conduct a search by cases that have referred to a particular statutory provision can be invaluable where you need to know how a particular statutory provision has been applied by the courts. You will find this feature in some of the professionally recognised legal databases.

Before looking at these online legal databases, it should be noted that not all of them contain all the reports or other material that you might need. The following table provides a summary of some of the main materials and the databases in which they are held.

Resource	*Citation*	*Database (and dates)*
The Law Reports	AC, QB/KB, Ch, Fam	Westlaw (1865–) LexisLibrary (1865–) Justis
Weekly Law Reports	WLR	Westlaw Justis
All England Law Reports	All ER	LexisLibrary
English Reports	ER	Justis
All England Law Reports European Cases	All ER (EC)	LexisLibrary (1995–)
Butterworths Company Law Cases	BCLC	LexisLibrary (1983–)
Butterworths Medico-Legal Reports	BMLR	LexisLibrary (1986–)
Common Market Law Reports	CMLR	Westlaw (1962–)
Criminal Appeal Reports	Cr App R	Westlaw (1990–)
European Commercial Cases	ECC	Westlaw (1978–)
European Human Rights Reports	EHRR	Justis Westlaw (1979–)
Family Court Reporter	FCR	Lexis (1998–)
Human Rights Law Reports	HRLR	Westlaw (2000–)
Industrial Cases Reports	ICR	Justis Westlaw (1972–)
Industrial Relations Law Reports	IRLR	LexisLibrary (1972–)
Personal Injury & Quantum Reports	PIQR	Westlaw (1992–)
Tax Cases	TC	LexisLibrary

Westlaw UK

Westlaw UK is a subscription service to which most UK universities subscribe.

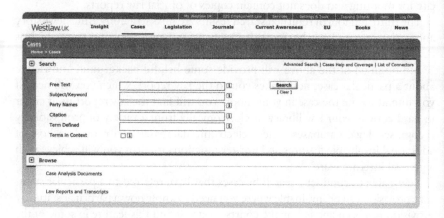

Westlaw UK covers digests of all UK cases back to 1865. Case law in general includes English Reports which go back to 1220. Coverage includes:

- The Law Reports
- The Weekly Law Reports
- Industrial Cases Reports
- Session Cases
- Sweet & Maxwell series of law reports
- Full-text transcripts covering the Supreme Court, House of Lords, Courts of Appeal, plus selected High Court and tribunal judgments back to 1999.

Westlaw also features a 'case analysis' button which is accessible from the judgment page of the case. This has a facility to see 'cases citing this case' which provides a judicial history of the case.

JOURNAL ARTICLES

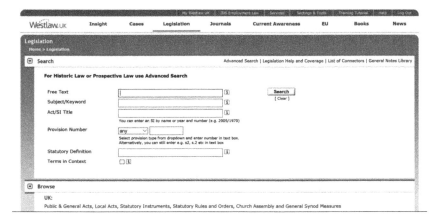

Westlaw UK Journals offers two services: full-text articles and article abstracts. The full-text articles service contains thousands of articles in full text from journal titles published by Sweet & Maxwell, Oxford University Press, Cambridge University Press, among others. The article abstracts service includes the Legal Journals Index (LJI) and contains over half a million abstracts of articles from English language legal journals published in the United Kingdom and Europe, providing users with seamless integration to full-text journal articles (where available) and direct links to relevant case law and legislation.

Both full-text articles and article abstracts are indexed and categorised with Sweet & Maxwell's Legal Taxonomy. LJI abstracts also provide access to publisher details for each journal.

LEGISLATION

Westlaw UK contains the fully consolidated full text of Acts since 1267 and Statutory Instruments since 1948. As with other content, the ability to link seamlessly to other pieces of legislation, cases citing that legislation and secondary material is also available.

CURRENT AWARENESS

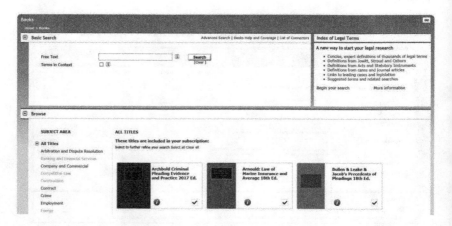

Westlaw UK Current Awareness contains daily updates and notices of cases, legislation and legal developments derived from official publications, press releases and legal news relating to the United Kingdom and is updated throughout the day. The information remains in Current Awareness for 90 days and then can be found by searching the Current Awareness Archive.

BOOKS

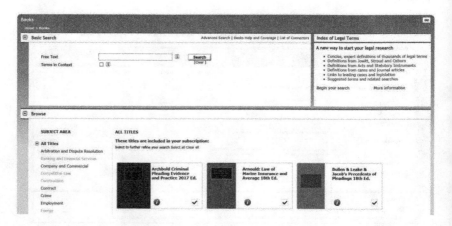

Under the Westlaw 'Books' tab, you will find all of the titles that are included in your institution's subscription.

INSIGHT

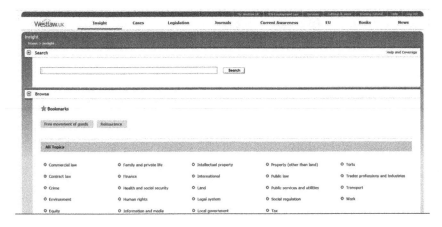

In 2012, Westlaw UK launched Insight, an online legal encyclopaedia that aims to provide a comprehensive statement of the law in the United Kingdom. Insight is made up of regularly updated articles written by subject-specific legal experts. You can search for articles using the general search box or browse through a list of topic headings that are each broken down into sub-headings.

LexisLibrary

LexisLibrary is another subscription service to which most UK universities subscribe. Its databases include both UK and EU law reports, UK legislation and legal journals published by a number of publishers including Butterworths, Oxford University Press and Cambridge University Press. Also included on LexisLibrary is a range of practitioner textbooks and *Halsbury's Laws of England*.

GENERAL SEARCH – 'FIND A TITLE'

CASES

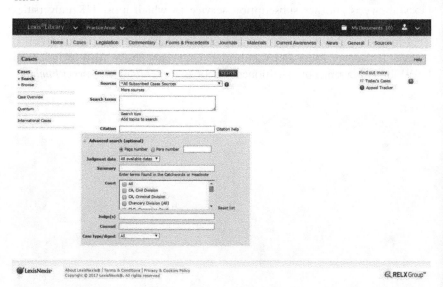

You will see from the above search boxes that LexisLibrary also enables a search to be carried out by judge(s) and counsel.

JOURNALS

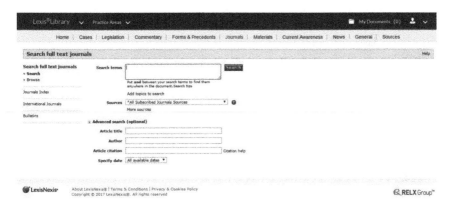

LEGISLATION

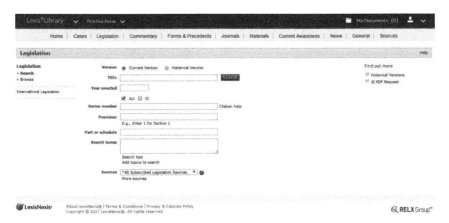

CURRENT AWARENESS

Similar to Westlaw, LexisLibrary also offers a judicial history analysis feature which can be accessed from the home page by searching for a case using the 'Case name or citation' box in the 'Find a Title' section of the Homepage. This includes, in the results page, a 'Cases Referring to this Case' which sets out the subsequent judicial history of the case originally searched.

BAILII

www.bailii.org

BAILII is the British and Irish Legal Information Institute. It is a non-profit making charitable trust which builds and operates an interactive database of full-text primary legal materials available without charge or subscription on the internet. BAILII provides a growing amount of primary and secondary legal material which can be browsed by the user and/or located by using the BAILII search engine.

BAILII contains key common law databases of all of the decisions of the Privy Council, many decisions of the Supreme Court, House of Lords and the Court of Appeal, important courts such as the Scottish Court of Session, the Irish Supreme Court, European Court of Human Rights and European Court of Justice and tribunals, and legislation from three jurisdictions (e.g. Northern Irish legislation goes back to 1495). It also contains recent reports and consultation papers from the Law Commission of England and Wales and the Scottish Law Reform Commission, in addition to the Irish Law Reform Commission materials which have been on the site for some time.

The website includes most of the recent British and Irish primary legal materials that are freely available to the public. Most of these materials are derived from published and unpublished CD ROMs or provided directly by courts, tribunals and government departments. In addition, it contains materials not available from any other free source. All of the data have been converted into a consistent format and a generalised set of search and hypertext facilities added; this, among other advantages, allows searching across all databases and all jurisdictions.

An extremely useful facility on BAILII is the series of buttons linking to:

- **New cases of interest:** These are cases that have been uploaded very recently and may not yet be accessible via the normal search functions. They will be in the system within two hours, but may remain on this list for a little longer.
- **Recent decisions:** Recent decisions lists contain the 20 most recently rendered court judgments for each BAILII court/tribunal database, in reverse chronological order.

- **Recent additions:** Recent additions lists contain decisions that have recently been added to BAILII (both recent decisions and older material that has newly come into BAILII's possession).

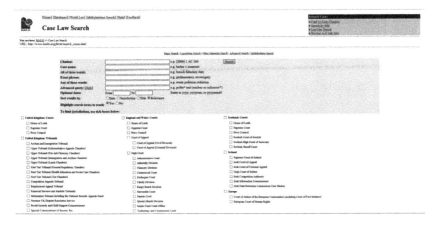

Casetrack

Casetrack is a subscription service with judgments listed as follows:

- Court of Appeal (Criminal and Civil Divisions) from April 1996 to present
- Administrative Court from April 1996 to present
- all divisions of the High Court from July 1998 to present
- searchable links to Supreme Court (formerly House of Lords) and Privy Council judgments from November 1996 to present
- selected judgments from the European Court of Human Rights and the European Court of Justice.

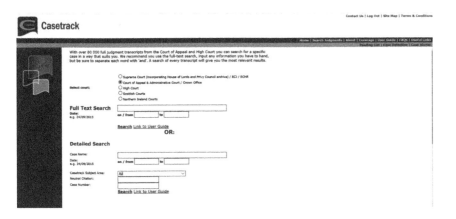

Justis

Justis is a subscription-based full-text online legal library of UK, Irish and EU case law dating back to 1163 and legislation from 1235.

Lawtel

Lawtel is a subscription-based site covering cases, legislation and articles. The cases are in summary and transcript format. The case summaries also provide links to the full case reports.

Lawtel is a resource that is often favoured by practitioners. It is updated daily and contains many recent cases which have not yet been reported.

The Supreme Court

Judgments of the Supreme Court are published on the Supreme Court's website (www.supremecourt.uk/decided-cases/index.html). Additionally, for each judgment there is also a Press Summary, the purpose of which is 'to assist in understanding the Court's decision'. The Press Summary 'does not form part of the reasons for the decision. The full judgment of the Court is the only authoritative document.'

Although not forming part of the judgment, the Press Summary contains a lot of helpful information setting out:

- the background to the appeal
- the judgment in summary
- the reasons for the judgment, referring to the specific paragraphs from the judgment.

Although not a substitute for reading the full judgment, the Press Summary can save a lot of time in helping you to understand the key legal issues and court's reasoning and directing you to the specific paragraphs from the judgments. The following Supreme Court Press Summary from *Woolway v Mazars* illustrates the succinct, yet extremely useful, information provided.

29 July 2015

PRESS SUMMARY
Woolway (Appellant) v Mazars (Respondent) [2015] UKSC 53
On appeal from [2013] EWCA Civ 368

JUSTICES: Lord Neuberger (President), Lord Sumption, Lord Carnwath, Lord Toulson, Lord Gill

BACKGROUND TO THE APPEAL Local authority rates are payable in respect of the rateable occupation of hereditaments. Rates are a tax on property and 'hereditaments' are the units of assessment. The statutory definition of 'hereditament' in section 115(1) of the General Rate Act 1967 states that it is 'such a unit of . . . property which is, or would fall to be, shown as a separate item in the valuation list.' Where different parts of an office building are occupied by the same occupier, the ordinary practice of the valuer is to enter them as a single hereditament if they are contiguous, but as separate hereditaments if they are not. The property in question in this appeal, Tower Bridge House, is an eight-storey office block in St Katherine's Way, London. Mazars, a firm of chartered accountants, occupies the second and sixth floors of the building under separate leases. These floors are separated by common areas in the building and were entered in the 2005 rating list as separate hereditaments. In February 2010 Mazars applied to the Valuation Tribunal for England ('VTE') to merge the two entries to form a single hereditament. The VTE agreed that the two entries should be merged. The Valuation Officer, Mr Woolway, appealed to the Upper Tribunal (Lands Chamber) on the grounds that the properties were two separate hereditaments. The Upper Tribunal confirmed that the premises could be treated as one hereditament. The Court of Appeal dismissed Mr Woolway's appeal. Mr Woolway appeals to the Supreme Court.

JUDGMENT The Supreme Court unanimously allows the appeal. Lord Sumption gives the leading judgment and Lord Neuberger, Lord Carnwath and Lord Gill give separate concurring judgments.

REASONS FOR THE JUDGMENT The question in this appeal is how different storeys under common occupation in the same block are to be entered in the rating list for the purpose of non-domestic rating [1]. Three broad principles apply in answering this question. The primary test is geographical, being based on visual or cartographic unity. Contiguous spaces will normally possess this characteristic, but unity is not simply a question of contiguity. If contiguous units do not intercommunicate and can be accessed via other property of which the common occupier is not in exclusive possession, this will be a strong indication that they are separate hereditaments. Second, where two spaces are geographically distinct, a functional test may nevertheless enable them to be treated as a single hereditament, but only where the use of the one is necessary to the effectual enjoyment of the other. Third, the question whether the use of one section is necessary to the effectual enjoyment of the other depends not on the business needs of the ratepayer but on the objectively ascertainable character of the premises. This calls for a factual judgment on the part of the valuer, exercising professional common sense [12]. In the present case neither a geographical nor a functional test was applied [20].

The appeal is allowed therefore. The orders of the Valuation Tribunal and Upper Tribunal are set aside and the Court makes a declaration that the premises demised to Mazars on the second and sixth storeys of Tower Bridge House are to be entered in the rating lists as separate hereditaments [22]. In his concurring judgment, Lord Gill emphasises that the reference to functionality in the tests articulated by Lord Sumption does not refer to the use which the ratepayer chooses to make of the premises. Rather, it is a reference to the necessary interdependence of the separate parts of the property that is objectively ascertainable [39]. The concept of fairness has no place in the application of the three principles laid down by Lord Sumption, which provide straightforward and workable guidance [40]. Contiguity is not the decisive criterion in the geographical tests. Properties that are discontiguous but geographically linked may constitute one hereditament if the occupation of one part would be pointless without the occupation of the other [41]. The discontiguity between the offices in question lies in the fact that the only access between them is through the public part of the building, not whether they are vertically or horizontally adjacent [43]. Lord Neuberger, concurring with Lord Sumption and Lord Gill, concludes that a hereditament is a self-contained piece of property, namely all parts of which are physically accessible from all other parts, without having to go onto other property [47]. Where premises consist of two self-contained pieces of property it would require relatively exceptional facts before they could be treated as a single hereditament. The mere fact that each property may have the same occupier should, normally, make no difference [51]. If, however, one property could not be sensible occupied or let other than with the other property, they should normally be treated as single hereditament [52]. In order to decide whether two separate self-contained units of property constitute a single hereditament the relationship between the two properties should be considered. The plant, machinery and other fixtures which form part of the property for rating purposes are relevant to this consideration [55]. Two separate self-contained floors in the same office building, whether or not they are contiguous, cannot be said to constitute a single hereditament, at least in the absence of very unusual facts. Once they cease to be self-contained, so that each floor is accessible from the other without going onto other property, then the two hereditaments will normally be treated as having been converted into one larger hereditament [56]. Lord Carnwath agrees with the judgment of Lord Sumption but does not express a concluded view on the treatment of contiguous floors [62].

References in square brackets are to paragraphs in the judgment.

NOTE This summary is provided to assist in understanding the Court's decision. It does not form part of the reasons for the decision. The full judgment of the Court is the only authoritative document. Judgments are public documents and are available at www.supremecourt.uk/decided-cases/index.html

Mooting tip
As the above 'note' makes clear, the Press Summary does not form part of the reasons for the Supreme Court's decision and is provided solely to assist a reader's understanding of the decision. Consequently, the Press Summary should never be cited as authority in any of your submissions

EUROPA/EUR-Lex

EUROPA is the main website of the EU. EUR-Lex provides free access, in the 24 official EU languages, to:

- the Official Journal of the European Union
- EU law (EU treaties, directives, regulations, decisions, consolidated legislation, etc.)
- preparatory acts (legislative proposals, reports, green and white papers, etc.)

- EU case law (judgments, orders, etc.)
- international agreements
- EFTA documents
- other public documents.

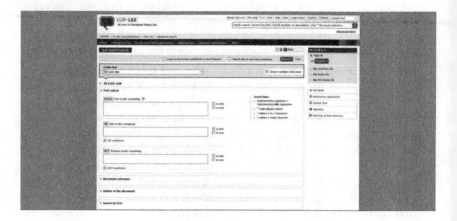

HUDOC

HUDOC is the official database of the European Court of Human Rights. The *Reports of Judgments and Decisions* is an official collection of the Court's leading judgments, decisions and advisory opinions since 1998.

Understanding the cases that you and your opponent is citing

You must have a thorough understanding of the cases that you and your opponent are citing. This includes:

- Was the decision unanimous or by a majority? Which judges were in each category?
- Who gave any dissenting judgment? A dissenting judgment given by a highly respected judge might carry greater weight than one given by a more junior judge.
- Has the case been cited in subsequent cases? The way in which a case has been subsequently considered can have an effect on its status as an authority. Checking the status of cases before your moot is important:

    o   To make sure that none have been overruled: it is difficult to imagine anything more damaging to your prospects of success than basing your submissions on a case or proposition that has been overruled.
    o   Even if a case has not been overruled, it may have been the subject of subsequent criticism, judicially or otherwise.
    o   A good understanding of a case's history may also alert you to additional authorities and other material which will add to your overall knowledge of the legal issues and might also assist your submissions.

Dealing with your opponent's skeleton argument

Although you will have completed most of your research by the time you exchange your skeleton argument with your opponent, further research will be necessary once you have received your opponent's skeleton. Although it is not possible to work out precisely what your opponent is going to say from their skeleton argument, it should give you enough information to be able to gain a reasonable understanding of their arguments and of their approach to the moot. Indeed, when carrying out your preparatory research you should also look to anticipate the kind of arguments that your opponent is likely to make so that you can counter them in your submissions.

You should read your opponent's skeleton argument and authorities carefully so that you are familiar with their arguments. Although with pressures on time it might be tempting to neglect this part of your research, you should make sure that you leave aside sufficient time for this important part of your case preparation. It could prove fatal to your prospects of success if you proceed with your planned submissions in total disregard of your opponent's arguments. Although you should follow your own skeleton, you might need to moderate your approach in view of your opponent's skeleton, especially if theirs discloses an approach that you hadn't previously anticipated. The judge will appreciate this position given the rule for simultaneous exchange of skeleton arguments.

The following checklist should prove helpful.

Once you have received your opponent's skeleton argument you should:

- Obtain a copy of their authorities and read them. (In many moots, both parties will use identical cases but will seek to apply their own interpretation on them.)

- Note the points in your opponent's authorities that:

  o support their arguments
  o might be useful to your own arguments.

- Identify any weaknesses in their authorities. For example, have they used cases that no longer represent good law?
- Try to identify ways to distinguish their authorities.

Once you have completed the above checklist, you should consider whether you need to modify your own approach and, if so, the best way of doing so.

Mooting tip

Once you have exchanged skeleton arguments with your opponent and researched their arguments, you can reasonably consider your research almost complete. As noted on page 58, you will need to make sure that, between exchanging skeleton arguments and the day of your moot, nothing has occurred that requires you to amend your submissions. If anything significant has occurred, such as a newly handed-down judgment, page 169 explains what you should do.

4 The skeleton argument and good legal writing

Introduction

Most moots require the participants to prepare skeleton arguments which are to be exchanged simultaneously with your opponent in advance of the moot. You should always check the rules of the moot carefully to see whether skeleton arguments are required and, if so, what rules apply to them. The rules should set out whether any word or page limits apply and the date by which you need to exchange them with your opponent and send them to the judge.

Skeleton arguments serve a number of purposes; the two most important being:

- To enable all parties to appreciate the arguments that will be run and to prepare appropriately for the moot. This helps to promote fairness between the parties by ensuring that they are aware of their opponent's arguments and therefore prevents either party from ambushing the other during the moot.
- To enable the judge to prepare more effectively for the moot and to identify the issues on which to focus the advocates' attention when they are making their submissions.

Mooting tip
A good skeleton argument must be user-friendly, clearly written and readable, properly structured, effective and punchy. You should use it to give structure and coherence to your oral submissions.

What is a skeleton argument?

Lord Neuberger has described skeleton arguments as the *hors d'oeuvre* to the main course of the oral submissions: they come first in time and they are normally less substantial than what follows, but they should be perfectly good if taken on their own, and anticipate and complement what follows.[1]

---

1 (2008) L.S. Gaz, 17 Jan, 30

A skeleton argument is a written document prepared in advance of the hearing which summarises the issues to be addressed and the authorities to be relied upon. Its purpose 'is to inform the court of the essential elements of the parties' submissions and thereby enable it to understand the issues and arguments arising on the appeal'.[2] This should be done by setting out as concisely as practicable the arguments upon which a party intends to rely. They should not only be concise but should both define and confine the areas of controversy without including extensive quotations from documents or authorities.[3] In *Tombstone Ltd v Raja*,[4] Mummery LJ reminded practitioners that:

> Skeleton arguments should not be prepared as verbatim scripts to be read out in public or as footnoted theses to be read in private. Good skeleton arguments are tools with practical uses: an agenda for the hearing, a summary of the main points, propositions and arguments to be developed orally, a useful way of noting citations and references, a convenient place for making cross-references, a time-saving means of avoiding unnecessary dictation to the court and laborious and pointless note-taking by the court.
>
> Skeleton arguments are aids to oral advocacy. They are not written briefs which are used in some jurisdictions as substitutes for oral advocacy. An unintended and unfortunate side effect of the growth in written advocacy (written opening and closing submissions and 'speaking notes', as well as skeleton arguments) has been that too many practitioners, at increased cost to their clients and diminishing assistance to the court, burden their opponents and the court with written briefs. They are anything but brief. The result is that there is no real saving of legal costs, or of precious hearing, reading and writing time. As has happened in this case, the opponent's skeleton argument becomes longer and the judgment reflecting the lengthy written submissions tends to be longer than is really necessary to explain to the parties why they have won or lost an appeal.[5]

Perfecting your skills at drafting skeleton arguments will be of enormous benefit to you in practice where poorly drafted skeleton arguments will not be tolerated. In a recent sharp rebuke to practitioners, Jackson LJ complained that:

> I have protested previously about the poor quality and excessive length of some skeleton arguments in this court. On occasion the Court of Appeal has deprived successful parties of the costs of preparing their skeletons. So far,

2 *Standard Bank plc v Via Mat International Ltd and another* [2013] EWCA Civ 490, per Moore-Bick LJ at [26]

3 See, for example, *Tchenguiz v Director of the Serious Fraud Office and others* [2014] EWCA Civ 1333, [2015] 1 WLR 838, per Jackson LJ.

4 [2009] 1 WLR 1143

5 Ibid., 1172

unfortunately, this message has failed to reach the profession. Mild rebukes to counsel and gentle comments in judgments have no effect whatsoever. Therefore, with regret, I must speak more bluntly.

The rules governing skeleton arguments . . . do not exist for the benefit of judges or lawyers. They exist for the benefit of litigants, namely (a) to ensure that their contentions are presented most effectively to the court and (b) to enable the court to deal with its caseload expeditiously, bearing in mind that there is always a queue of appellants and respondents waiting for their matters to be heard.

In essence an appellant's skeleton should provide a concise, user friendly introduction for the benefit of the three judges who will probably have had no previous involvement in the case. The skeleton should then set out the points to be argued clearly and concisely, with cross-references to relevant documents and authorities. . . . The skeleton should not normally exceed 25 pages. Usually it will be much shorter. In a straightforward case like this the skeleton argument would, or at least should, be much less than 25 pages.

As anyone who has drafted skeleton arguments knows, the task is not rocket science. It just requires a few minutes clear thought and planning before you start. A good skeleton argument (of which we receive many) is a real help to judges when they are pre-reading the (usually voluminous) bundles. A bad skeleton argument simply adds to the paper jungle through which judges must hack their way in an effort to identify the issues and the competing arguments. A good skeleton argument is a real aid to the court during and after the hearing. A bad skeleton argument may be so unhelpful that the court simply proceeds on the basis of the grounds of appeal and whatever counsel says on the day.

The appellant's skeleton argument in this case does not comply with the rules. It is 35 pages of rambling prolixity through which the reader must struggle to track down the relevant facts, issues and arguments.

Although the successful appellant in this case is entitled to his costs, he will not recover the costs of the skeleton argument against the respondents to the appeal.[6]

The rules governing skeleton arguments for the Court of Appeal are set out in paragraph 5 of Practice Direction 52A and in paragraph 31 of Practice Direction 52C.

Practice Direction 52A, para 5.1
(1) The purpose of a skeleton argument is to assist the court by setting out as concisely as practicable the arguments upon which a party intends to rely.

---

6 *Inplayer Ltd v Thorogood* [2014] EWCA Civ 1511, [52] – [57]

(2) A skeleton argument must –

- be concise;
- both define and confine the areas of controversy;
- be set out in numbered paragraphs;
- be cross-referenced to any relevant document in the bundle;
- be self-contained and not incorporate by reference material from previous skeleton arguments;
- not include extensive quotations from documents or authorities.

(3) Documents to be relied on must be identified.

(4) Where it is necessary to refer to an authority, a skeleton argument must –

(a) state the proposition of law the authority demonstrates; and
(b) identify the parts of the authority that support the proposition.

If more than one authority is cited in support of a given proposition, the skeleton argument must briefly state why.

(5) The cost of preparing a skeleton argument which –

(a) does not comply with the requirements set out in this paragraph; or
(b) was not filed within the time limits provided by this Practice Direction (or any further time granted by the court),

will not be allowed on assessment except as directed by the court.

Practice Direction 52c, para 31

(1) Any skeleton argument must comply with the provisions of Section 5 of Practice Direction 52A and must–

(a) not normally exceed 25 pages (excluding front sheets and back sheets);
(b) be printed on A4 paper in not less than 12 point font and 1.5 line spacing.

. . .

(3) At the hearing the court may refuse to hear argument on a point not included in a skeleton argument filed within the prescribed time.

In many mooting competitions, mooters are restricted in the length of their skeleton arguments, often being limited to a single page. Such restrictions do not apply where the skeleton argument is prepared as part of an assessment, although the principles of conciseness still apply.

In a professional court setting, the failure to heed the need for brevity in pleadings may well lead to strict adverse costs orders.[7] This kind of sanction against

---

7 See, for example, *Standard Bank plc v Via Mat International Ltd and another* [2013] EWCA Civ 490.

the use of overlong pleadings is rather tame compared with the kind of sanction that was imposed in the old days. In *Mylward v Weldon*,[8] Mylward's pleading consisted of 'six score sheets of paper' which the Lord Keeper deemed could have been 'well contrived' in 16 sheets. The result was that the Lord Keeper ordered that the miscreant be imprisoned in the Fleet until he paid a fine of £10 to Her Majesty and 20 nobles to the defendant. In addition, the Lord Keeper ordered

> that the Warden of the Fleet shall take the said Richard Mylward . . . and shall bring him into Westminster Hall on Saturday next, about ten of the clock in the forenoon and then and there shall cut a hole in the myddest of the same engrossed replication[9] . . . and put the said Richard's head through the same hole and so let the same replication hang about his shoulders with the written side outward; and then, the same so hanging, shall lead the same Richard, bare headed and bare faced, round about Westminster Hall, whilst the Courts are sitting and shall shew him at the bar of every of the three Courts within the Hall and shall then take him back to the Fleet . . .

How times have changed!

Mooting tip

Avoid the irritating use of padding in your skeleton argument. Don't use unnecessary words such as 'It is also of great importance for the Court to bear in mind the following issues' or 'The Court should give serious consideration to the possibility of carrying into effect the submissions which now follow'. Just make the point. The discipline of expressing the real issues succinctly will prove an aid to clearer thinking and expression.

When to start drafting your skeleton argument

Before considering *when* to start writing, you must know *what* you are going to say. This point is well made by Sir Ernest Gowers in *The Complete Plain Words* when he said:

> Clear thinking is hard work, but loose thinking is bound to produce loose writing. And although clear thinking takes time, the time that has to be given to a job to avoid making a mess of it not only cannot be time wasted but may in the end be time saved. It is wise therefore not to begin to write until you are quite certain what you want to say. That sounds elementary, but the

---

8 (1596) Tothill 102, 21 ER 136, [1595] ECHR Ch 1
9 A pleading made by a plaintiff in reply to the defendant's plea or answer.

elementary things are often the most neglected. Some people, it is true, can never be sure of clarifying their thoughts except by trying to put them on paper. If you are one of these, never be content with your first draft; always revise it.

Once your research is complete,[10] you should be ready to make a start in preparing your submissions. A submission is a strand of argument that you will use to advance your ground of appeal. Your speech will consist of a number of submissions, each one dealing with a different point of law. There is no such thing as the correct number of submissions that you should make because each moot will be different. However, you should bear in mind the limited time that you will have to make your submissions, some of which will be taken up with judicial interventions. Your submissions will help formulate your skeleton argument.

Composition and structure of a skeleton argument

A skeleton argument consists of four main parts which we will discuss in turn:

1. heading
2. introduction
3. main submissions
4. concluding submission.

The heading

The heading must follow a formal layout and style and is intended to inform the reader about the nature of the document and parties featuring therein. The heading identifies the court hearing the appeal, the names of the parties and on whose behalf the skeleton has been prepared.

(a) The identity of the moot court

The moot court is always identified in the top left-hand corner of the document. It should be in capital letters and underlined. Where the moot is heard in the Court of Appeal, you should also identify whether this is the Civil Division or the Criminal Division. The name of the Division also appears in capital letters, underlined, and appears in brackets. For example, a criminal appeal to the Court of Appeal will appear in the heading as:

IN THE COURT OF APPEAL (CRIMINAL DIVISION)

---

10 Apart from the final check that you will need to make in between exchanging skeleton arguments and the day of your moot to make sure that nothing has occurred that requires you to amend your submissions.

(b) The parties

The names of the parties appearing in the appeal are set out in full. Immediately before these names, you should add the word 'between' in capital letters, followed by a colon. The word 'between' appears at the left-hand side of the page. The names appear in capital letters and centred on the page. On the line below each party name, you should add the word 'Appellant' or 'Respondent' as the case may be. These words appear at the right-hand side of the page, underlined, with just the first letter in capitals. Where there are two or more parties either appealing or responding to the appeal, these words appear as 'Appellants' or 'Respondents'. There is no need to prefix individual names with Mr, Mrs, Ms, Dr or the like unless that party's first name does not appear in the moot problem. Where one or both parties is a body corporate, then the full name of the entity should be used, including the suffix 'Limited' or 'PLC', as the case may be.

The name of the appellant should precede that of the respondent. Between these names appears the word '-and-'. Do not use 'v', 'versus' or 'against'.

(c) On whose behalf the skeleton is served

Finally, the heading should identify the party on whose behalf the skeleton is to be served. This part of the heading should appear in capital letters, centred on the page, and appear between horizontal lines above and below.

The figure below illustrates a typical heading.

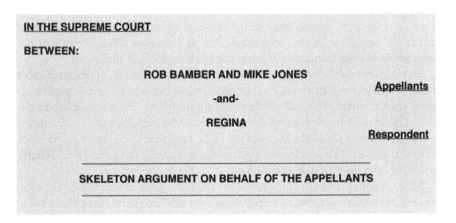

The introduction

Where space permits, both parties should provide a brief introduction to the appeal. This can be contrasted with a skeleton argument prepared in professional practice where the introductory section alone often runs to many pages. The introduction serves as a brief overview and statement of your client's position and should be brief and to the point. It should set out how the issues were decided below with an explanation setting out, if you are the appellant, why the court below was wrong or, if you are the respondent, why the court below was correct. The introduction should inform the reader what you want to achieve, why you want it and why the court should give it to you.

However, because most mooting competitions restrict, often to a single side of A4, the size of the skeleton that each party may serve, there may be no room for an introduction. In such a case, you should consider omitting the introduction and devote the available space to your substantive arguments.

Mooting tip

Any references you make in your skeleton argument to the facts of the case must be accurate. Although you should identify those facts that support your submissions, any attempt to misrepresent the case facts or to state them in a way that does not fairly set them out will likely invoke the wrath of the judge.

Main submissions

Immediately after the introduction (or after the heading if you choose to omit the introduction), you should proceed to your main submissions. These are the most important part of your skeleton argument.

In short, your submissions should summarise your side's positive arguments on each ground of the appeal. Because the skeleton argument is served on behalf of either the appellant or the respondent, the submissions should represent the arguments of your team, thereby covering both grounds of the appeal.

Your skeleton will benefit from arranging your submissions underneath short headings. These will make your submissions stand out and act as a helpful 'signpost' for the judge. You will see from the figure below that the first heading is noted as 'Should the defence of duress by threats be available where a defendant is threatened by a close relative, even where he only maintained minimal relations with that relative?' Depending on space, you can truncate this to 'the close relative point' or 'the close relative submissions'.

Most mooting competitions stipulate a simultaneous exchange of skeleton arguments which means that when drafting your side's skeleton you will not know the substance of your opponent's arguments. Therefore, you should say little, if anything, about rebutting your opponent's arguments when drafting your skeleton argument. You will have plenty of opportunity to rebut their arguments during your oral submissions.

Mooting tip

When researching your own arguments, you will have considered how your opponent is likely to deal with theirs. Although you are likely to be able to work out the general basis of their arguments, you should refrain from second-guessing its detail and attempting to rebut what they might eventually submit. Once you have exchanged your skeleton with your opponent, you will be able to reflect on the detail of their arguments and deal with them appropriately in your oral submissions. Further guidance on dealing with your opponent's skeleton argument is provided at page 107.

Make your submissions persuasive

To get the most out of your submissions, they will need to be persuasive, which in turn requires skilful drafting. Submissions need to be concise (even where the rules do not impose a strict page limit) and follow a logical format.

Concise

The word 'skeleton' should give this away. You should forget all that you have been taught about writing essays with a considerable amount of detail, citing as many relevant cases as you can fit in and footnoting your work at every opportunity.

The submissions for the purpose of your skeleton argument must be concise and pithy. You will have ample opportunity to elaborate when you are on your feet making your oral submissions but, for present purposes, brevity is key. Do not use lengthy, convoluted sentences or over-complicate what you need to say. Not only will this appear unprofessional and somewhat 'waffly', but it will also give too much away to your opponent. Furthermore, if you spell out each point in detail in your written skeleton, you will run the risk of being able to add very little when it comes to your oral arguments.

Logical

A persuasive argument is one that is logically made and easy to follow. It should explain what you are attempting to do and the legal basis for doing it. We discuss in Chapter 6 the PASA method for structuring your individual submissions from which you will see that there are four separate stages: **P**roposition, **A**rgument, **S**upport, **A**pply.

- **Proposition:** What is the point you are looking to make? What do you intend to demonstrate in your submission?
- **Argument:** How are you going to explain this?
- **Support:** Where is the legal support for your submission? You will need to identify the appropriate legal principle or rule of law that you intend to

advance in support of your submission. From there, you can then identify and apply the authority or authorities that underpin such legal principle or rule of law in support of the submission.

- **Apply:** How will you apply the above to the moot problem? You will need to apply the above principles/authorities to the facts of the moot problem and to the specific submission within the ground of appeal.

Mooting tip

It is important to appreciate that there are other ways of presenting your submissions, and your own style of advocacy might suggest an amalgamation of these steps or even taking them in a different order. What is important is that your submissions follow a logical format.

Since you will be referring back to your skeleton argument during the course of your oral submissions, your skeleton argument should be presented in the same order as you intend to advance your oral arguments during the moot.

The alternative argument submission

Advice on alternative argument submissions is provided in Chapter 3. When making an alternative argument submission, you must say so expressly in your skeleton argument.[11] Otherwise, the judge may not immediately appreciate what might at first glance appear to be two contradictory arguments.

There are two ways of explaining in your skeleton argument that the second submission is advanced in the alternative to the first. You should start your second submission with either:

- In the alternative, . . .; or
- Alternatively, . . .

A logical approach to preparing your skeleton argument applies equally to the order in which you deal with the stated grounds of appeal. Most moots have two distinct grounds of appeal which are dealt with by leading and junior counsel respectively. Unless there are cogent reasons for doing so (which is unlikely to be the case), you should deal with the grounds of appeal in the order that they appear in the moot problem. Many (but certainly not all) moots are drafted in such a way that the second ground of appeal follows naturally from the first and cannot sensibly be argued the other way round. Take, for example, a moot dealing with

---

11 As well as in your oral submissions.

duty of care. The first ground of appeal is likely to address whether or not a duty exists, while the second ground concerns whether any such duty that might be found to exist has in fact been breached. It would make no sense to argue these points the other way round since the whole question of breach will not arise unless a duty is held to exist.

You are likely to want to make a number of submissions in support of your ground of appeal. Often these submissions will vary in terms of their respective strengths and you should generally start with the strongest one as this is more likely to make a good first impression with the judge. Your subsequent (and possibly weaker or subsidiary) submissions will then have a solid base from which to build.

Concluding submission

Your skeleton argument should conclude with a final submission asking the court to allow (if you are acting for the appellant) or dismiss (if you are acting for the respondent) the appeal. The names of both mooters in your team should appear immediately below this concluding submission, followed by the date.

No footnotes

Although you are encouraged to make good use of footnotes in your written assessments, you should not use them in your skeleton argument. You should always bear in mind that a skeleton argument is only a summary (skeleton) of the issues to be addressed for the purpose of informing the court 'of the essential elements of the parties' submissions and thereby enabl[ing] it to understand the issues and arguments arising on the appeal'.[12] Therefore, if the point is worth making, it should be in the main body of the skeleton.

If you need to cross-reference something in your skeleton argument (which is unlikely given the space limits imposed in most moots), then you may use a footnote *but only* if bracketing the cross-reference in the main body of the skeleton is likely to interrupt the flow of the document and thereby reduce its readability.

Final check

Once you have completed your skeleton argument, you should read it over carefully to make sure that it reads well and does not contain spelling, grammatical or punctuation errors, as these signal a lack of attention to detail and do not inspire confidence. A good command of these important issues can make a significant difference to the way your team is perceived and, in a closely fought moot, could even be the deciding factor in determining the winner.

---

12 *Standard Bank plc v Via Mat International Ltd and another* [2013] EWCA Civ 490, per Moore-Bick LJ at [26]

If you refer to the facts of a case, check that you have referred to them accurately. Check that you have cited the cases correctly, including using the appropriate case citation.[13] You should not rely on the accuracy of case citations noted in textbooks or journal articles as these are sometimes wrong.

The completed skeleton argument

Putting all of the above together, you should now be in a position to start drafting your skeleton argument. The figure below shows an example of a skeleton argument prepared for the appellants in the *Bamber & Jones* case.[14]

> **Mooting tip**
> The skeleton argument shown above is provided as an example and is based on the skeleton argument used in a recent competition. You should note that as well as citing the relevant cases and other material you will be relying on in your oral submissions, you should also provide the paragraph or page number(s) as this will assist the court (and your opponent) in understanding the basis of your argument when reading your skeleton argument for the first time. Note the correct format and style for these references, including the difference between signposting a page number and a paragraph number.
>
> As with most moots, there are other ways of arguing the case. How would you have argued the appeal? It is a worthwhile exercise for you to consider the case yourself and draft your own skeleton argument.

Exchanging your skeleton argument with your opponent

The rules of the moot will set out the timetable and mechanism for exchanging skeleton arguments which are usually exchanged with your opponent simultaneously.[15] This might appear somewhat artificial if you are tasked with representing the respondent because it is the respondent's role to resist and to respond to the appellant's submissions. Simultaneous exchange, of course, means that the respondent will not have the benefit of knowing how the appellant will advance their appeal.

This is not a problem in professional practice simply because by the time the lawyers need to prepare their skeleton arguments they will already have considerable knowledge of their opponent's position, not least from the statements of case.

---

13 Which is discussed at pages 74 and 75.
14 The moot problem is set out in full on pages 236 and 237.
15 The rules will also set out if you need to send your skeleton argument (and any other material) to the judge, and, if so, when.

IN THE SUPREME COURT

BETWEEN:

ROB BAMBER AND MIKE JONES

<u>Appellants</u>

-and-

REGINA

<u>Respondent</u>

SKELETON ARGUMENT ON BEHALF OF THE APPELLANTS

Introduction
1. This is the appeal by the Appellants (Mr Bamber and Mr Jones) against the decision of the Court of Appeal (Criminal Division) dismissing their appeals against conviction under section 18 of the Offences Against the Person Act 1861 having unsuccessfully attempted to raise the defence of duress by threats.
2. The Appellants submit that the Court of Appeal erred in failing to recognise the situation of a defendant who is threatened by a close relative in circumstances where he only maintained minimal relations with that relative and further erred in denying a defence of duress in all circumstances where the defendant acts to avoid a threat of false imprisonment.
3. The Appellants ask the Court to allow the appeal for the reasons advanced below.

Ground One
Should the defence of duress by threats be available where a defendant is threatened by a close relative, even where he only maintained minimal relations with that relative?
4. It cannot be said that Rob Bamber 'voluntarily' allowed himself to be coerced into committing a crime or foresaw any material risk of being coerced, merely by spending time with his father. (*R v Graham* [1982] 1 WLR 294, 300; *R v Hasan* [2005] 2 AC 467, [37]–[38]).
5. A distinction must be made between voluntary association with a known violent criminal, and association with a relative who happens by the way to carry a criminal conviction relating to violence. A person will not easily dismiss a family member from their life for the purposes of being safe from a criminal conviction by association (*R v Hasan* [2005] 2 AC 467, [39] and [78]–[79]).

Ground Two
Should duress by threats be extended to cover situations where the defendant acts to avoid a threat of false imprisonment?
6. It is not contended that the defence of duress should be extended to cover situations where, without more, a defendant acts to avoid a threat of false imprisonment. It is, however, contended that the defence should not be denied where the threat of serious harm or death derives from the false imprisonment. It is entirely foreseeable that the false imprisonment of the 5-year-old girl will cause serious bodily harm and the father will carry the additional burden of guilt for failing to carry out the action he was threatened to do (*R v Ireland; Burstow* [1998] AC 147, 156–158; *R v Fernando Ortiz* (1986) 83 Cr. App. R. 173, 175–176; Janet Chiancone, 'Parental Abduction: A Review of the Literature' 2000, OJJDP).
7. *R v Dao* [2012] EWCA Crim 1717 is distinguishable on the facts. The accused in *Dao* had a key to the premises and their clothes as well as food were found inside the building. The threat in *Dao* was a threat to clean the premises.
8. Any concerns about having too wide a scope on the defence of duress have been addressed in *R v Dao* at [32]–[42].

Joe Smith
Sarah Brown
18 August 2016

When preparing your skeleton argument for your moot, especially in a case where you are acting for the respondent, you should proceed on the basis that you can anticipate how your opponent will likely argue their case and draft the skeleton accordingly.

> **Mooting tip**
> Although you will have completed most of your research by the time you exchange your skeleton argument with your opponent, further research will be necessary once you have received your opponent's written skeleton. It is only at this stage that you should consider your research almost complete. As noted on page 58, you will need to make sure that between exchanging skeleton arguments and the day of your moot nothing has occurred that requires you to amend your submissions.

Your opponent's skeleton argument

This chapter is concerned with the preparation of your own skeleton argument. You should also check the status of cases and other material cited by your opponent. Most moot rules require simultaneous exchange of skeleton arguments several days prior to the moot which should give you enough time to do this.

How to deal with errors in your skeleton argument after exchange

No matter how careful you have been in preparing and drafting your skeleton argument, it is possible that you will notice an error after you have exchanged it with your opponent. This section considers what options are available to you in these circumstances.

The appropriate way of dealing with drafting errors depends on the seriousness of the error as well as the rules of the moot. The most serious error is if your skeleton argument contains a submission that you now believe to be wrong or unarguable. You might spot this error when reading your opponent's skeleton argument and realising that they have referred to an authority that you either hadn't considered or, if you had considered it, hadn't appreciated its proper meaning. Having now read this authority, you might conclude that it effectively rebuts a key authority that you were seeking to rely on.

The first thing to do in such a case is not to panic. Just because your opponent seeks to rely on an authority that they say supports their case, it doesn't necessarily mean that they are correct. Don't forget that, just days earlier, you had done likewise. Take time to reflect on any authority that seems to be causing you concern and consider the following questions:

- Have they used an appropriate authority?
- Does it (still) represent good law?

- Have they interpreted the authority correctly?
- Do you have an authority on the same point that trumps theirs?
- Can their authority be distinguished?

If, after having reflected on the above points, you nevertheless conclude that you have indeed erred in your research and that as a result one of your submissions is no longer arguable, you should consider the follow two options:

- Consider whether you could reformulate your oral argument so as to avoid the fatal flaw while remaining within the general submission advanced in your skeleton argument. The fact that most moots restrict skeleton arguments to one side of A4 might well come to your assistance here. Don't forget, no one but you (and your teammate) knows how you intended to deliver your oral submissions, so fine-tuning them might work rather well.
- If you still conclude that your opponent has delivered a fatal blow and your original submission is no longer, even barely, arguable (which should happen extremely rarely), then you must inform the judge of this during your oral submissions. Rather than admitting that you have made a fatal mistake, there is still the possibility of salvaging something from the mess and turning it somewhat to your advantage. You should inform the judge that having reflected on your opponent's skeleton argument you will no longer be pursuing your submission on the point. If you are forced to adopt this approach, you should move forward to your next submission as quickly as possible.

Less serious errors include citation, spelling and grammatical errors. With straight-forward errors of this kind, the best option is just to live with them and not highlight them to the judge. The exception to this advice is where, during the course of your oral submissions, the error in your skeleton argument confuses the point you are trying to advance. In such a case, if necessary, correcting the error on your feet should not prove too disruptive. Where the error relates to an incorrect citation (for example, you have referred to the wrong report, volume, page or paragraph number), then if this is likely to cause confusion (for example, because the report mentioned in your skeleton argument does not match the one in the bundle), you can correct it, with a brief apology, when introducing the authority and then move on to your submission as quickly as you can.

A potentially more serious error is missing the deadline for exchanging skeleton arguments with your opponent, such deadline being set by the rules of the moot or competition. There is no hard and fast rule that sets out what will happen in such a situation and, unless the rules provide for this kind of breach, it is a matter for the judge on the day to decide on a solution. It is unlikely that the judge, or the organiser, will disqualify you from participating in the moot (although this is a possibility) and the most likely consequence is that, if the moot is close, a failure to abide by the rules might determine which side wins the moot.

Common mistakes with spelling, grammar, English usage and punctuation

Accuracy and the appropriate use of language are of fundamental importance to lawyers and mooters alike. Poor grammar and spelling will do nothing to impress the judge. Once you have prepared your skeleton argument, you should read it and check it again very carefully. This section discusses some of the main errors in English usage and how to avoid them.

The following mistakes often crop up in English writing and find their way into skeleton arguments.

Spelling and words

Affect and effect

'Affect' is typically used as a verb. 'Effect' is most commonly used as a noun but can also be used as verb.

'Affect' means 'to influence or make a difference to':

- The salary increase will greatly affect Fred's lifestyle.
- The poor weather will affect my plans for the weekend.

'Effect' is used both as a noun and a verb. As a noun it means 'a result' or 'an influence':

- You can add more red to the paint until you get the effect you want.
- The effects of smoking are well known.
- Over time the effect of loud music can damage your hearing.

When used as a verb 'effect' means 'to bring something about as a result':

- The new legislation did little to effect change.
- The Lord Chief Justice effected many policy changes.
- Growth in the economy can only be effected by tough economic controls.

Counsel and council

'Counsel' refers to a barrister or someone who counsels another. 'Council' refers to a local authority.

Fewer and less

'Fewer' means 'not as many'. 'Less' means 'not as much'. You should use the word 'fewer' when referring to items that you can count individually (such as books or judges) and the word 'less' when referring to anything that you cannot count individually (such as water or material). So, for example, 'After the fire in the library, there are fewer books on the shelves' and 'After spending the morning mopping up, there is now less water on the floor'. Another example is money: you might have 'less money', but never 'less five pound notes' (correctly, you would have 'fewer five pound notes').

Do not get confused by the supermarket checkout signs that read '10 items or less' which might sound right only because we are used to seeing them. Correctly, these signs should read '10 items or fewer' or 'Up to 10 items'.

Its and it's

'Its' is a possessive pronoun and means 'belonging to it'. 'It's' is a contraction of 'it is' or 'it has'.

Examples:

* It's in its box waiting to be repaired.
* It's ready for collection.
* It's arrived.

In formal English writing, you should not use contractions. Therefore, the above should be written as 'It is in its box waiting to be repaired', 'It is ready for collection' and 'It has arrived'.

Judgment and judgement

In legal English, the word is 'judgment'. The word 'judgement' should be used, for example, when referring to a person's ability to form an opinion about something or someone, as in 'she lacks proper judgement about . . .'.

Me, myself and I

How to refer to oneself can be problematic, especially when also referring to another person in the same sentence. In such a case, you should always place that other person's name before yours in the sentence. A good way of telling whether to refer to yourself as 'me' or 'I' is to remove that other person's name to see which sounds right. For example, 'David and I are leaving now for the moot' is correct. Following the above guidance and removing 'David' from the sentence, you wouldn't say 'me is leaving now for the moot' if you were going to the moot alone. If you were going alone, you would say 'I am leaving now for the moot'.

You should only use the word 'myself' if you have already used the word 'I', making you the subject of the sentence. For example, 'I'll deal with the respondent's skeleton argument myself' or 'I thought to myself that the respondent's skeleton argument was rather poor'. You would never say 'Pass the skeleton argument to myself'.

Practice and practise

If you remember the following general rule, you will never confuse these two entirely different words. When used with a 'c' the word is a noun and when used with an 's' it is a verb.

Examples:

- Debbie works in a law practice.
- Debbie practises law.

The same rule applies to many other words; for example:

- advice/advise: 'I need some advice and will let my solicitor advise me.'
- licence/license: 'I need to apply for a driving licence'. 'I need to license my car'.

Principal and principle

'Principal' is commonly used as an adjective in legal submissions and means something that is the 'most important', 'chief' or 'main' thing you are discussing: 'My principal submission is . . .'. 'Principal' can also be a noun as in 'the school's principal'.

'Principle' is always a noun and is an entirely different word to 'principal'. 'Principle' is an idea, belief, basis or rule as in 'as a matter of principle', 'in principle', 'the principles of law' and 'he is a man of principle'.

To and too

It is not too difficult to understand the difference.

'To' serves two functions. First, as a preposition, where it always precedes a noun:

- I am going to the shops.
- I am going to Llandudno.
- This computer belongs to Sue.

'To' is also used to indicate an infinitive when it precedes a verb:

- I need to study.
- Everyone wants to help people in need.
- Adam is going to study hard for his exams.

'Too' also serves two functions. Its first use is as a synonym for 'also':

- Can I go too?
- Dave went to France too.

'Too' also means 'excessively' when it precedes an adjective or adverb:

- You are walking too quickly.
- Adam ate too much for breakfast.
- I am too tired to go to the gym today.

Their, there and they're

These three different words have entirely different meanings.

- 'Their' indicates possession as in 'it is in their skeleton argument'. 'There' refers to a place other than here as in 'the bundle is over there'.
- 'There' is also used as part of saying something, such as 'there is not enough time to read that authority again'.
- 'They're' is a contraction of 'they are'. As noted above, in formal English writing, you should not use 'they're' as it is a contraction of 'they are' which should be used in its place.

Who or whom

'Who' refers to the subject of a sentence while 'whom' refers to its object. If you can rearrange the sentence and put a subject pronoun ('I' or 'he') in the space, you should use the word 'who'. Conversely, if you can put an object pronoun ('me' or 'him') in the space, then the word you need is 'whom'. The following examples illustrate the correct usage of the words:

- Whom shall I invite to the moot?
- To whom did you send the skeleton argument?
- Who is responsible for organising the judge?
- Mr Justice Jones was the only judge who offered to judge the moot.

Whose or who's

'Whose' is a possessive form that means 'belonging to who' or 'of whom':

- Whose skeleton argument is this?
- The appellant, whose claim was dismissed by the trial judge, now appeals to the Court of Appeal.

'Who's' is a contraction of 'who is' or 'who has':

- Who's judging the moot today? (who is)
- Who's got the bundles? (who has)

As already noted, in formal English writing, you should not use 'who's' as it is a contraction of 'who is' or 'who has' which should be used in its place.

Your or you're

'Your' indicates possession and 'you're' is a contraction for 'you are':

- Since you have been using your new beauty cream you're really beautiful.
- Since you have been using your new beauty cream your skin is really beautiful.

Again, as already noted, in formal English writing, you should not use 'you're' as it is a contraction of 'you are' which should be used in its place.

Grammar and English usage

Subject–verb agreement

A verb must always agree with its subject in number. This means that if you have a singular subject, then you will need a singular verb. Conversely, if you have a plural subject, then you will need a plural verb.

- The skeleton argument was served on the respondent.
- The skeleton arguments were served on the respondent.

Pronoun–antecedent agreement

In much the same way as subject and verb must agree in number, a pronoun must also agree with its antecedent in number. A pronoun is a word that substitutes for a previously mentioned noun. If that noun (known as the antecedent) is plural, then the pronoun standing in for it must also be plural. Conversely, if the antecedent is singular, the pronoun must also be singular.

A common mistake made by mooters is to use a plural pronoun ('their') when they should have used a singular pronoun ('its', 'his' or 'her'). For example, 'The appellant submits that the court should allow their appeal' should be 'The appellant submits that the court should allow its/his/her appeal'. This is because the word 'appellant' is a singular noun.

Modifiers

A modifier is a word or phrase which modifies the meaning of another word or phrase. An example of a modifier can be seen in the following sentence:

- All barristers who are in private practice must be members of a circuit.

The words 'in private practice' modify the application of the rule applying to 'all barristers' with the result that a barrister only has to be a member of a circuit if they are in private practice.

Care needs to be taken with modifiers to ensure that they relate *only* to the word or phrase to be modified. The following example illustrates the problem:

- Only solicitors and barristers in private practice may appear as advocates in the higher courts.

Does this sentence mean that appearing as an advocate in the higher courts is restricted to all solicitors and barristers if they are in private practice or does it mean that appearance is restricted to all solicitors but only barristers who are in private practice? In other words, the phrase 'in private practice' could modify either 'barristers' or 'solicitors and barristers'.

To remove this ambiguity, the sentence needs to be rewritten. If the modifier ('in private practice') is intended to apply only to barristers, the sentence should be written as:

- Only solicitors, and barristers in private practice, may appear as advocates in the higher courts.

If, on the other hand, the modifier is intended to apply both to solicitors *and* to barristers, the sentence should be rewritten in the following way:

- Solicitors and barristers may only appear as advocates in the higher courts if they are in private practice.

Split infinitives

The following are all infinitives: 'to laugh', 'to cry', 'to read', 'to write', 'to eat'. An infinitive will usually begin with the word 'to' followed by a verb. A split infinitive occurs when the word 'to' is separated from its verb by another word or words. An example of a split infinitive is:

- The judge told me that I had to quickly finish my sentence as I had run out of time.

To unsplit this infinitive, the sentence would read:

- The judge told me that I had to finish my sentence quickly as I had run out of time.

The general rule is that no word should separate (split) the 'to' of an infinitive from the simple form of the verb that follows.

Some people regard the splitting of the infinitive as something that must always be avoided in formal written English even though it is commonplace in spoken language. To avoid a split infinitive, you should move the 'offending' word so that it appears either before or after the infinitive as noted in the above example.

Occasionally, splitting the infinitive makes the sentence clearer and easier to understand. A good example of this is:

- My financial advisor told me that his advice represented the only way to more than double my money.

Trying to separate the infinitive would make this sentence rather clumsy and is best left as it is.

'Should of'

When people say or write 'should of' (as in 'I should of finished my skeleton argument last night'), they should have said 'I should have finished my skeleton argument last night'. 'Should of' is extremely poor English and should not be used.

Punctuation

Apostrophe

Misusing the apostrophe is a very common mistake but one that is easily avoided. The apostrophe can be used for different purposes:

- **Possession:** An apostrophe is used to indicate possession – i.e. something belonging to someone or something else. When using an apostrophe to indicate something belonging to one person, place it before the 's' as in 'it is the student's skeleton argument'. To indicate that the skeleton argument belongs to more than one student, place the apostrophe after the 's' as in 'it is the students' skeleton argument'.
- **Contraction:** Apostrophes are also used to indicate a contracted word. These were discussed above and should be avoided in formal English writing.
- **Plural words:** You should never use an apostrophe to signify that what you are describing is plural. The plural of 'book' is 'books' and not 'book's'. The same applies to numbers. You should never refer to a case that was decided in the 1980's – the correct form is, of course, the 1980s.

Question mark

A question mark should only be used at the end of a direct question: 'Shall I prepare the bundle?'

In the case of an indirect question, you should use a full stop: 'The judge asked who prepared the bundle.'

Quotation marks

Quotation marks can be either double (". . .") or single ('. . .'). They are also known as 'inverted commas'. There is no rule which dictates which type of quotation marks you should use.

A text will often use both double and single quotation marks. For example, double quotation marks could be used for directly quoted speech while single quotation marks could be used for titles of documents or other texts. Whichever way you decide to use them, you must remain consistent in their use.

You should never use quotation marks for indirect quotations as this merely describes or sets out what another person has said rather than using their exact words. For example, 'the appellant said that the judge was incorrect' does not require quotation marks to indicate what the appellant said.

Comma

The comma can be used in several different situations:

TO CLARIFY THE MEANING OF A SENTENCE

Consider the sentence: 'Fred too often interrupted'. It could have two different meanings which the insertion of a comma will determine:

* 'Fred too often interrupted' (Fred interrupted too often).
* 'Fred, too, often interrupted' (Fred also interrupted).

Similarly, the comma makes the world of difference in these two pairs of sentences:

* 'Let's eat grandma' and 'Let's eat, grandma'.
* 'Fred enjoys cooking his family and his pets' and 'Fred enjoys cooking, his family and his pets'.

BEFORE CERTAIN CONJUNCTIONS

You should use a comma before these conjunctions: 'and', 'but', 'for', 'nor', 'yet' and 'or', so as to separate two independent clauses. They are known as 'coordinating conjunctions'. For example: 'Jenna is a good lawyer, but will never be as good as Sue.' You should not generally use a comma with the conjunction 'because': 'David didn't need to prepare the bundles because they had already been prepared by his teammate.'

TO SEPARATE THE ELEMENTS IN A LIST OF THREE OR MORE ITEMS

'The bundle contained cases, statutes, articles and an index.' The general rule is that you should not place a comma before the final 'and' unless there is a danger that the last two items in the list will become blurred and confused without it. This might occur, for example, where the last item in the list contains two parts and itself contains the word 'and' (such as 'bread and butter' or 'fish and chips'). In this case, you should insert a comma before the final 'and' to indicate that the last item in the list constitutes a single item: 'Sue's favourite foods include chicken, steak, lobster, and fish and chips.'

TO SEPARATE, IN THE SAME SENTENCE, AN INTRODUCTORY OR MODIFYING
ELEMENT FROM THE MAIN PART

- Given the amount of work she put into the preparation, Helen is confident that she will win the moot.
- After a good night's sleep, Laura is looking forward to the moot.
- Unfortunately, the lack of assistance from my teammate damaged our chances of success. On the other hand, our opponent does not seem that well organised.

TO SEPARATE, IN THE SAME SENTENCE, ELEMENTS THAT EXPRESS CONTRAST

- The respondent's bundle is thorough, but untidy.
- Jenny is intelligent, not quick.

TO SEPARATE A PARENTHETICAL ELEMENT IN A SENTENCE

A parenthetical element is a word or group of words that interrupts the flow of a sentence to add additional, but non-essential, information to the sentence. A parenthetical element can be removed from the sentence without changing its overall meaning. You should use a pair of commas (never one) to set off the parenthetical element from the remainder of the sentence.

- The opponent's skeleton argument, although untidy, contained everything that was needed.
- Judge Smith, a very pleasant man, always judges our internal moots.

TO SEPARATE, IN THE SAME SENTENCE, A NUMBER OF ADJECTIVES

- The old, dusty, stained law report is all that is available.
- The bad-tempered, ill-mannered, badly dressed judge was the only one available to judge the moot.

The general rule with commas and parenthetical elements is that if you can place the word 'and' or 'or' between the various adjectives, then a pair of commas is appropriate. Otherwise, commas should not be used. An example showing where commas should not be used is: 'That little old book contains all you will need to know on the subject.'

TO SEPARATE DIRECT SPEECH OR QUOTATIONS FROM THE REMAINDER OF
THE SENTENCE

You should use commas to separate direct speech or quotations from the remainder of the sentence. For example:

- As Lord Denning explained in *Bratty v A-G of Northern Ireland* [1963] AC 386, 'the requirement that it should be a voluntary act is essential . . . in every criminal case'.

Note, however, that you could also use a colon for this purpose (although you will need to alter the structure of the sentence):

- In *Bratty v A-G of Northern Ireland* [1963] AC 386 Lord Denning stated: 'The requirement that it should be a voluntary act is essential . . . in every criminal case.' If using a colon in this way, you should begin the quotation with a capital letter.

Comma splice

A comma splice is an incorrect use of a comma and occurs when it is used to connect two independent clauses. The following example illustrates two clauses that make perfect sense on their own and should not be connected with a comma: 'The judge is liked by everyone, he is a lovely person.' This error can be corrected in one of two ways. The first is to replace the comma with a semicolon: 'The judge is liked by everyone; he is a lovely person.' Alternatively, you could use a coordinating conjunction to connect the two clauses. This would then read: 'The judge is liked by everyone as he is a lovely person.' Where the two clauses are longer, you should add a comma before the conjunction.

Colon

The colon acts as a pause to introduce *related* information. This information could be a list, an explanation or some quoted material. You will see from the examples below that the words that precede the colon are capable of making perfect sense on their own. If, on the other hand, the initial words do not make sense alone, you should not use a colon.

TO INTRODUCE ITEMS IN A LIST

- Topics to be discussed in today's lecture: *mens rea* and *actus reus*.

TO INTRODUCE AN EXPLANATION OR AMPLIFICATION OF AN EARLIER STATEMENT

- After careful deliberation, the judges have reached their decision: the appellant is this year's winner of the moot.

TO INTRODUCE QUOTED MATERIAL

- In *Bratty v A-G of Northern Ireland* [1963] AC 386 Lord Denning stated: 'The requirement that it should be a voluntary act is essential . . . in every criminal case.' If using a colon in this way, you should begin the quotation with a capital letter.

Semicolon

Whereas the colon acts as a pause to introduce the reader to related information, the semicolon represents a break within a sentence that is more powerful than a comma but less final than a full stop. The semicolon is used to separate certain items in a list as well as to link closely related sentences.

TO SEPARATE CERTAIN ITEMS IN A LIST

We discussed above the use of the comma to separate items in a list. Here, we are concerned with the situation where you need to separate items in a list when one or more of them already contains a comma.

- The judges for the mooting final are: Lord Dyson, Master of the Rolls; Lady Justice Hallett; and Professor Cooke, Liverpool John Moores University.

TO LINK CLOSELY RELATED CLAUSES

Linking clauses that are closely related can emphasise their relationship to each other.

- I read the case that I thought would support our proposition; it was not very helpful.

When linking sentences using a conjunctive verb as the connector ('however', 'therefore', 'otherwise', 'accordingly', 'consequently', 'nevertheless', etc.), you should add a comma immediately after the connector:

- I read the case that I thought would support our proposition; however, it was not very helpful.

Legal writing conventions

Lawyers adopt a rather formal method of writing that follows certain conventions. Insofar as preparing your skeleton argument is concerned, the following conventions should be followed:

Do not write in the first person

Your role as a mooter is identical to that of a practitioner in court, which is to advance arguments on behalf of your client. As a consequence, you should not make your submissions in the first person. You should, therefore, avoid expressing personal opinions, such as 'In my opinion . . .', or 'I think . . .'. Instead, advance your arguments using words such as 'It is submitted that . . .', 'The appellant (or respondent) submits that . . .'. Alternately, you could say: 'In my (or our) submission . . .'.

Do not use over-complicated sentences

Consider section 1 of the Road Transport Lighting Act 1967 ('Application of principal Act to reflecting material') which provides:

> It is hereby declared for the avoidance of doubt that material designed primarily to reflect white light as light of that or another colour is, when reflecting light, to be treated for the purposes of the principal Act as showing a light, and material capable of reflecting an image is not, when reflecting the image of a light, to be so treated.

Legal writing is necessarily formal but you should avoid using sentence structures that are over-complicated and difficult to follow. Remember that as the judge is the ultimate consumer of the skeleton argument, it must be in a form that he finds helpful and straightforward. You should avoid obscuring your meaning by using unnecessary or pompous words or indeed anything that makes your document difficult to comprehend. If you can say something using straightforward language, then do so.

Avoid inflammatory language

There is no place for inflammatory language in your skeleton argument. You should, therefore, avoid expressions that complain how 'outrageous' your opponent's client's conduct has been or any submissions that tell the court that your opponent's arguments are 'utterly hopeless'. Even if this is the case, the judge will not require your assistance in forming these views for himself!

Type fonts, margins and line-spacing

Unless the rules of the moot tell you otherwise, you should use a plain type font (Times New Roman or Arial are ideal) in 11- or 12-point font size.

Allow generous margins on both edges of the page and, where space permits, you should use one-and-a-half or double line spacing.

5 The bundle

Introduction

A bundle is the file of materials that you will be using in support of your arguments. Although the question of court bundles may not be the most enthralling of subjects, you should not overlook their importance. For mooting purposes, a well-prepared bundle will:

- put in a single place all the relevant written material to which reference will be made during the moot
- enable speedy access to your authorities and other material. This benefits the court and the mooters
- (where bundles are required to be filed or exchanged in advance of the moot) assist with pre-moot reading
- make a favourable impression on the court.

> **Mooting tip**
> Your bundle is part of your overall case presentation. It is likely to be the first thing the judge sees. First impressions are very important: you don't have a second chance to make a first impression. Although a well-prepared bundle cannot win a bad moot, a poorly prepared bundle can damage your chances in a good moot. Even where the moot rules do not insist on the production of bundles, it is a good idea to provide them.

It is likely that you will need to prepare several bundles: one for the judge (or one for each of the judges), one that you will use yourself, and possibly one for your opponent.[1] Make sure that all bundles are identical, and if you need to update

---

1 But check the moot rules for specific requirements.

the bundles, make sure that you update all of them. Any discrepancies between the bundles can eat into the already short time that you have to make your submissions, so it is important that when you direct the court to a particular 'tab' in the bundle,[2] the material behind that tab is identical in all of the bundles.

The consequences of a poorly prepared bundle

A poorly produced bundle can have significant consequences for the offending party in the moot. In professional practice, inadequate bundles can lead to adverse costs consequences as well as invoking the wrath of the judge. In *Pawar v JSD Haulage Ltd*,[3] the Court of Appeal criticised the appellant's bundles with significant costs consequences. Delivering the judgment of the court, Thirlwall J stated that 'the appeal bundles prepared by the appellant's solicitors were chaotic. Alternative bundles were prepared by the respondents for use by the parties and the court. Accordingly the costs of preparing the appeal bundles are to be the respondents' in any event.'[4] Further, in *PM Project Services Ltd v Dairy Crest Ltd*,[5] the claimant had brought three applications for summary judgment in connection with three separate claims, two of which were supported by a witness statement containing 750 pages of exhibits. The judge criticised the lack of pagination and the fact that many of the exhibits were not placed in the bundle where they were stated to be in the witness statements. The inadequate pagination meant that the time estimates for pre-reading and for the hearing were inadequate. Edwards-Stuart J found the claimant to be in breach of the Civil Procedure Rules' Overriding Objective in relation to the obligation to manage the courts' resources proportionately. As a consequence, he directed that

> the bundles are to be returned to [the claimant's] solicitors in order that the witness statement . . . can have the correct bundle references inserted. The costs of that exercise and any costs thrown away by the necessity to adjourn the second and third limbs of the application must be borne by [the claimant].[6]

How to prepare your bundle

You must prepare your bundle professionally. This includes making sure that the pages are neat and tidy, clean and carefully hole-punched so that the edges of each

---

2 For which see later.
3 [2016] EWCA Civ 551
4 Ibid., [47]
5 [2016] EWHC 1235 (TCC)
6 Ibid., [4]

page are in line. Do not place any of the pages inside plastic sleeves as they will need to be removed in order to read them.

The most appropriate kind of binder for your papers is a ring binder or lever arch file. This will enable you to present your bundle in a professional manner and enable the judge, and you yourselves, to access the relevant pages quickly and easily. Other methods of binding, such as comb or wire spiral binding, should not be used as they are much less user-friendly than either of the binders just recommended.

It is likely that both sides in the moot will prepare their own bundles. Therefore, in order to assist the judge in identifying which bundle belongs to which team it would be helpful to label them, on the spine and front cover, with 'Appellant's Bundle' or 'Respondent's Bundle' as the case might be. The label should also identify the name of the parties.

Contents of the bundle

Unless the moot rules provide otherwise, a good bundle will consist of the following, each separated by a labelled 'tab' (divider).

Numbering each page sequentially will also be helpful as it will help speed up accessing the relevant pages during your submissions.

> **Mooting tip**
> When referring the judge to a case, or other material, you should do so in the following way:
>
> May I refer your Lordship to Caparo Industries Plc and Dickman & Others reported in the second volume of the Appeal Cases reports for 1990 at page 605 which your Lordship will find behind Tab 3 of the Appellant's bundle at page 200 . . .

Index

The index is placed at the front of the bundle and lists, in the order they appear, every document contained in the bundle, identifying under which tab and on what page it can be found. Full citations must be used. The index should be headed with the name of the parties and should identify on whose behalf the bundle has been prepared. Figure 5.1 shows a Bundle index.

IN THE SUPREME COURT

BETWEEN:

ROB BAMBER AND MIKE JONES

Appellants

-and-

REGINA

Respondent

APPELLANTS' BUNDLE INDEX

Content	Tab	Page
Moot problem	A	1
Skeleton Argument	B	2–5
[name of case/report/article, etc.]	C	6–37
[name of case/report/article, etc.]	D	38–56
[name of case/report/article, etc.]	E	57–82
[name of case/report/article, etc.]	F	83–115
[name of case/report/article, etc.]	G	116–130

Moot problem

You should include a clean, unmarked and unedited copy of the moot problem.

Skeleton argument

Your skeleton argument appears next in the bundle.

Authorities and other material

Immediately after your skeleton argument, you should include a copy of every authority and any other material that you intend to refer to in your submissions. The authorities should be arranged in the order that they appear in your skeleton argument. In the rare case where you have not produced a skeleton argument, you should arrange the authorities in the order that they will be argued during your oral submissions. We discussed in Chapter 3 the hierarchy of law reports, and it is important that you adhere to this before finalising bundles.

Even though you will only be quoting from a small section of any given authority, you must nevertheless provide in your bundle full copies of all of your authorities. This will enable the judge to put the quoted passages into their correct context. Furthermore, the judge might want to take you to a different part of a judgment to the one you seek to rely on, possibly (but by no means certainly) because of something raised by your opponent. The requirement to provide full copies does not apply to textbooks where you will only need to provide a sufficient number of pages (say, a few pages before and after the passages you are quoting from) to enable the judge to appreciate the context of the passages you will be quoting from. In addition, you should also copy the title page of the book which should be inserted in front of the page(s) to be quoted.

You should not fasten any of the pages together with staples or any other form of fastener, such as paperclips.

Finally, you should mark the relevant passages with a vertical line in the page margin.[7] This will assist the judge to find the passage when you refer to it.

> **Mooting tip**
> Make sure that the cases you place in your bundle are the same as those referred to in your skeleton argument. Do not, for example, provide in your bundle a copy of a case from the All England or Weekly Law Reports if your skeleton argument refers to the case from the official Law Reports. Finally, once you have prepared your bundle, review it carefully to make sure that all of your materials are present, have been properly copied on the page, and are in the correct place. Spending time doing this now might save you from embarrassment if errors are discovered during the moot. The best way of doing this is to use your finalised bundle for practice run-throughs with a colleague playing the role of the judge.

---

7 See Practice Direction 52C, as amended by the Practice Direction: Citation of Authorities (2012).

6 Lawyers' skills

Preparation, presentation and personal skills

Introduction

A good advocate is someone who is well organised and able to present their arguments effectively in a clear, logical and persuasive manner. Good advocacy skills are essential, not just for mooting, but also for later when appearing in court in your professional life.

Advocacy is also an excellent life skill as it provides confidence in one's ability to communicate skilfully and effectively, and thereby extends beyond the moot court and professional practice.

In short, your role as an advocate is to structure your client's case to form cogent legal arguments and to make persuasive representations to obtain the best possible outcome.

Preparation

> **Mooting tip**
> The three golden rules of advocacy are preparation, preparation and preparation.

Preparation is essential. To be an effective advocate, you must prepare your case thoroughly. Thorough preparation will ensure that you know your material inside out. You will not be able to persuade a court of the merits of your case unless you have a substantial grasp of the material.

You should keep in mind the words of Benjamin Franklin who said: 'By failing to prepare, you are preparing to fail.' Winning or losing a case – or a moot – often turns on the extent and quality of the preparation. In terms of advocacy, the noted American trial lawyer, Louis Nizer, explained: 'Preparation is the be-all of good trial work. Everything else – felicity of expression, improvisational brilliance – is a satellite around the sun. Thorough preparation is that sun.'

Your preparation should start as soon as you receive the moot problem (although you should make sure that you are familiar with the moot rules even before the moot problem has been published).

You should discuss the moot problem with your teammate at the earliest possible opportunity. This will help identify the relevant issues and ensure that you work seamlessly as a team. This is an extremely important point as a moot could be lost simply because one of the mooter's submissions contradicts or otherwise damages those of their teammate.

Practising your submissions is an excellent way of preparing for your moot and will also help to identify any weaknesses which you will then be able to address. You should practise your moot submissions out loud and preferably in front of an audience. Doing this several times will help familiarise yourself with your arguments. You should also get your audience to ask questions and critique your submissions. You may also find it helpful to record your submissions, preferably with video as well as audio, as watching and listening to your own performance can be helpful in eradicating annoying habits such as littering your speech with 'you know' or 'erm' or twiddling with your hair.

Mooting tip

When reading cases, and other material, you will come across words or expressions that you are unfamiliar with. For example, in *Koufos v Czarnikow Ltd (the Heron II)*[1] the House of Lords observed that certain facts were found by the 'umpire';[2] in *Hadley v Baxendale*,[3] Alderson B stated that the maxim *'dolus circuitu non purgatur'*[4] did not apply; and in *Liesbosch Dredger v SS Edison*[5] it was stated that 'the wrongdoer must take his victim *talem qualem*'.[6] Whenever you come across something that you don't understand, it is good practice to look it up. Not only will this give you a far better understanding of the law in general terms, but the judge might just ask you a question which in some way touches upon the meaning of such a term.

Be extremely conversant with both the facts of the case and grounds of the appeal

It ought to go without saying that you must be thoroughly conversant with every aspect of your case. One of the most common mistakes made by mooters is not reading the moot problem with sufficient care or not understanding the

---

1 [1969] 1 AC 350
2 Ibid., 352
3 (1854) 9 Ex. 341
4 Ibid., 353
5 [1933] AC 449
6 Ibid., 452

key issues. There are four main aspects to any moot that you must thoroughly understand:

- the factual matrix
- the parties
- the legal issues and the grounds of appeal
- the strengths and weaknesses of the case.

The factual matrix

Unless you have a thorough grasp of the facts of the moot, you will not be able to argue your ground of appeal. Sometimes the facts can be very complicated and it might be beneficial for you to write them down in a different order to the way in which they are presented in the moot problem. This is often helpful where there are several events that took place over a period of time; seeing them in chronological order might make it easier to see precisely what happened, and when. Similarly, the facts may refer to numerous parties who may, in some way, be connected. In such a case, you might find it helpful to present the parties diagrammatically to illustrate how they might be connected, and the relevance, if any, of any association.

Whichever way you decide to analyse the facts, one thing is clear: they are absolutely sacrosanct. They may be unhelpful or extremely inconvenient to your case, but there is nothing you can do about them. You should treat the facts as though they have been determined by the court below: they are the facts you have been given and you must present your case based on them.

You must also avoid speculation. It might be tempting to speculate so as to present the factual matrix in a way that lends greater support to your case, but you must refrain from doing so. It is highly likely that any attempt at speculation will open a line of questioning from the judge that will not be helpful to you. Nor should you invite the court to speculate on the facts as that is not the purpose of a moot. You must remain faithful to the facts of the case, and apply the law to them.

Mooting tip
Although you must never misrepresent any aspect of your case, you should craft your submissions in such a way that you put them over in the most attractive and persuasive way possible.

Do not expect an appellate court to overturn findings of fact from the first instance court. As already noted, not only are the facts of the case not subject to the appeal, but an appellate court will exercise the greatest restraint before overturning findings of fact made at first instance. This was explained by Lord Hoffmann in *Piglowska v Piglowski*:[7]

> First the appellate court must bear in mind the advantage which the first instance judge had in seeing the parties and the other witnesses. This is well understood on questions of credibility and findings of primary fact. But it goes further than that. It applies also to the judge's evaluation of those facts. If I may quote what I said in *Biogen Inc v Medeva plc* [1997] RPC 1:
>
> > 'The need for appellate caution in reversing the trial judge's evaluation of the facts is based upon much more solid grounds than professional courtesy. It is because specific findings of fact, even by the most meticulous judge, are inherently an incomplete statement of the impression which was made upon him by the primary evidence. His expressed findings are always surrounded by a penumbra of imprecision as to emphasis, relative weight, minor qualification and nuance . . . of which time and language do not permit exact expression, but which may play an important part in the judge's overall evaluation.'
>
> The second point follows from the first. The exigencies of daily courtroom life are such that reasons for judgment will always be capable of having been better expressed.[8]

The parties

You must first identify the parties and understand which side you are representing. It is not unheard of for students to prepare the wrong side's case. Once you have identified which party you are representing, you will then need to decide which person takes which ground of appeal.

The legal issues and the grounds of appeal

Before considering the grounds of appeal, you must identify in which court the moot is to take place. This is usually stated in the heading. If it isn't, then you should be able to work it out from the procedural history of the case. For example, if you are told that the appeal relates to directions given by the trial judge to the jury in a criminal case, you can assume with confidence that the appeal will be heard in the Criminal Division of the Court of Appeal.

In England and Wales, it is usual for the moot court to be either the Court of Appeal (either Civil or Criminal Division) or the Supreme Court. To reflect the different legal system and court structure in Scotland, the moot court in a

---

7 [1999] 1 WLR 1360
8 Ibid., 1372

Scottish moot is either the Inner House of the Court of Session, the High Court of Justiciary or the UK Supreme Court.

Moot problems typically end by listing the grounds of appeal. If the problem does not specifically spell them out, they should be apparent from the findings and judgment of the lower court from which the appeal is brought. It is of paramount importance that you do not deviate from the grounds of the appeal or attempt to argue anything that is outside of these grounds.

The strengths and weaknesses of the case

You will get a much better understanding of the case if you are able to identify its weaknesses as well as its strengths. This will enable you to see the case from the position of your opponent.

You should also consider how you would argue the case if you were on the other side as this will help you to identify the kind of questions a judge is likely to ask. We will consider how to anticipate and deal with judicial interventions in Chapter 7.

The use of scripts and notes to aid your submissions

One of the main concerns of students when preparing for their moot is what they should have in front of them when they get to their feet to address the court. Everyone will have their own preferred way of preparing for the moot, although it is worth bearing in mind from the outset that a good advocate does not make his submissions reading word for word from pre-prepared notes.

Few people are able to stand up and speak for 15 or 20 minutes without any notes in front of them, and this is not an approach that is recommended for mooting. Even those people who are blessed with good memories will be assisted by having some notes in front of them even if those notes just contain case names, citations, page and paragraph numbers, and the like. Whichever approach you take, it should go without saying that the more prepared you are, the better you will be able to present your submissions without being over-reliant on a script.

Using a script, especially for those who have little experience of mooting or public speaking, might appear attractive. This is because you will have in front of you a prepared script that you can refer to without the risk of 'drying up'. You will not have to worry about forgetting any part of your submissions or getting the order wrong. Any awkward phrases or expressions will be right in front of you in a script which you will have spent a lot of time preparing and agonising over each word.

Avoid reading from a prepared script

Although writing out your speech word for word might *appear* to provide you with the greatest level of comfort, you should not do it. Having a prepared script in front of you runs the risk of shackling you to a rigid speech and will result in you reading it out. Mooting requires flexibility and a prepared script doesn't allow you to adapt your submissions as events unfold during the moot. Reading from a script is always frowned upon by judges and will adversely affect your mark, and ultimately your team's chance of winning the moot.

Even if you have a very good memory and feel confident in your ability to memorise your speech word for word, having it in front of you will present too much of a temptation to read from it. This is bound to lead to problems and often results in a dull and stilted performance.

Put yourself in the position of the judge or indeed anyone who has to listen to a speaker who hardly looks at anything other than the pages of a script they are holding. This hardly inspires confidence in their ability as an effective advocate or someone who is in control of their brief.

> **Mooting tip**
> You should not try to memorise every word of your submissions. Attempting to do so will only increase your stress and nervousness, especially if the sequence of the words you had planned to use goes wrong or, as is highly likely, the judge asks you a question which interrupts the flow of your prepared speech. It is far more important to know your submissions than your speech.

Being over-reliant on a script will also make it more likely that you will struggle if the judge asks you to address him on a point that you had intended to deal with later in your submissions. Taking a mooter away from their prepared script is a tactic often used by judges. You can, of course, inform the judge that you were intending to deal with the point he has raised later on in your submissions, and you might be fortunate enough for the judge to allow you to do so. But, and this often happens, the judge might want you to deal with the point there and then. Flicking through your prepared script to find the appropriate place is awkward and gives a very poor impression of your ability to deal appropriately with judicial interventions as and when they arise. Even if you find the correct place in your script, you will still be tied to reading from it, which, although it may be in the same area as the question you have been asked, is unlikely to hit the question square on.

Another problem with a prepared script is that it puts you at a disadvantage if the judge wants you to move on. There could be many reasons why a judge wants you to do this; for example, he may indicate that he is happy with your submissions on a particular point and would rather you address him on something else, or, conversely, he might indicate that he cannot accept your submission and, given the limited time available to you, suggests that you move on to your next point. Being tied to a script will significantly impair your ability to do this.

Mooting tip

The exception to the above is when you are quoting from a passage in a judgment or other text. In these circumstances, you should read the passage rather than trying to commit it to memory. Doing this has the following advantages. First, it will ensure that you recite the passage accurately. Second, it will help distinguish your oral submissions from text that you are quoting. Finally, it will also give you a moment or two to gather your thoughts, especially while the judge is finding the text referred to.

In summary, the problems with reading from a prepared script are numerous and cannot be over-emphasised. They include:

- lack of eye contact with the judge
- appearing 'wooden', unnatural, flat or monotonous
- speaking too quickly
- appearing to speak *at* the judge rather than *to* him
- difficulty in responding smoothly to judicial interventions
- losing your place when taking your eyes away from the script
- difficulty in moving to different parts of your argument if directed to do so by the judge
- difficulty in adapting your submissions to suit any situation that might arise
- a lack of flexibility in your approach
- adopting language and a style more suited to written rather than spoken work.

Mooting tip

Think about a subject that you are really interested in and knowledgeable about. This could be anything from football to the works of Shakespeare. Now, imagine meeting someone and telling them about it, and that other person asking you some probing questions about the subject. You would soon lose that person's interest if what you were telling them was read from a sheet of paper and you referred to that same sheet of paper when responding to their questions. Now, imagine how more engaging you would be if you had a decent conversation about the subject, perhaps referring, when necessary, to some notes, but without reading from a pre-prepared script. There is little difference between this example and doing the same during a moot. Spontaneity and flexibility are extremely powerful tools in oral argument.

Having explained the pitfalls of preparing a speech word for word, there are certain tactics you can deploy if this remains your preferred choice. First, do not read the script when addressing the judge. Instead, memorise key sections of it so you can recite them unaided. You might find it helpful to highlight the key sections in your notes. Whether you use a script or not, you will need a thorough grasp of the material so that when questions come from the Bench you are familiar enough with the material to be able to respond seamlessly and competently. You will also need to be able to find your way back to the part you had reached in your speech should your answer necessitate you moving to a different page. A good way of doing this is to keep a highlighter pen or small post-it note on your desk so you can mark the place you were at and return to it easily.

Although the prepared speech route is not one that many people would recommend, it is certainly not without its followers. For example, John Kelsey-Fry QC, an eminent barrister with a reputation for meticulous preparation, has described his method of preparing advocacy as follows:

> I type out every single word of my speeches including the apparent ad libs and asides. You write in the spontaneity. The first rule is that you've got to go into court knowing the case better than anyone else . . . I avoid lawyers' words at all costs and will rewrite a speech ten times until it fits.[9]

Notes – a better, more professional approach

Students who moot with notes in front of them perform consistently better than those who have prepared a full script, even if they don't intend to read from it. How you plan your notes is very much a personal choice and with experience you will soon find what works best for you.

The benefits of using notes are numerous:

- You will have a prepared outline of your submissions in front of you, leaving you to make your submissions with the flexibility needed as the arguments develop.
- Your notes will be your plan and running order, containing key subheadings and whatever other outline material you might find helpful.
- You will not be tied rigidly to a prepared script. Notes give you the greatest amount of flexibility when developing your arguments, and this flexibility can be especially helpful when dealing with judicial interventions.
- You will have much less material in front of you, which will assist considerably when locating a specific point in response to a question from the Bench.

How you prepare your notes is a matter of personal choice and experience. You can include anything that will assist you when you are on your feet. This might include:

9 *The Times* (Law pages), London, 29 November 2005, page 4

- outline running order
- key issues
- case names and citations
- brief facts of cases
- names of judges and decisions
- any preferred form of words or expressions.

You should treat your notes as an aide memoire to remind you of the running order and the key points you wish to make. When practising, you should try to reduce your notes to a minimum so that you do not have too much scripted paper in front of you.

Counsel's notebooks

Counsel's notebooks are ideal for preparing your notes. A counsel's notebook is a blue-covered book containing bound, white ruled and margined micro-perforated paper for easy removal of pages. They are the preferred choice for lawyers and are inexpensive and widely available from larger stationers.

Cards as notes

Some mooters prefer to write their notes on postcard-sized cards which they hold in their hands when addressing the court. The cards are placed in running order and the mooter moves through each one in turn until they have completed the pile. If this works for you, then that is good, but it is not an efficient way of dealing with your notes and not something you would expect to see advocates using. Cards are too easily dropped, thereby losing their running order, but even if you manage to keep hold of them, it can be rather clumsy and distracting continually having to turn them over.

If, however, cards are your preferred choice, it would be far better to place them on the lectern and turn them over as discretely as possible.

Skeleton argument with notes

Many mooters prefer to use an enhanced version of their skeleton argument as their notes. This is typically done by copying the text of your skeleton to which you can add your notes. Highlighting the words from your skeleton will help distinguish this text from the remainder of your notes.

Other methods of preparing notes

It is important for you to find a method of preparing your notes that you feel comfortable with and are able to use. There is no such thing as the 'best approach': it is just a matter of finding what works best for you.

Some mooters find flow diagrams and mind maps particularly helpful, especially during their research and preparation stage, as they can help identify the relationship that the different points or submissions have to each other. They also have the advantage of providing a visual image of the issues, which some people find helpful. If you find that flow diagrams or mind maps don't work for you, then consider making a numbered or bulleted list of points which you can follow and expand upon during your submissions.

> **Mooting tip**
> Whichever way you decide to organise your notes, you must practise your submissions. The more you are able to practise, the more fluent you will become and the less reliant you will be on notes. You should also see a marked improvement in your confidence.

Structuring your submissions

The skilful structuring of your submissions is key to a successful moot. Your submissions should contain the following elements which we will now consider in turn:

- introduction
- individual submissions
- concluding submissions.

Introduction

Before addressing the court with your individual submissions, it will be helpful for you to explain how you will be dealing with the appeal. This provides the court with a helpful roadmap of your submissions.

The following example is based on the cross-respondent's submissions from the moot on pages 254–256:

> My Lord, I will be making three submissions which are set out in the skeleton argument and which your Lordship will find behind Tab x of the bundle. First, damages are the primary remedy for a breach of contract, and specific performance should not be awarded where an award of damages will suffice. Second, the software and tablet designs are not unique for the purposes of specific performance. Third, it is not practicable for the court to grant specific performance in relation to the software and tablet designs, as this would require constant oversight to ensure the order was enforced.

The above introduction lays down a helpful and solid base from which you can now build your submissions.

Individual submissions

Once you have provided the court with the roadmap of your overall submissions, you can then move on to your individual submissions. A useful way to structure these submissions is to use the following plan which can conveniently be referred to by the mnemonic 'PASA' (**P**roposition, **A**rgument, **S**upport, **A**pply).

- **Proposition:** What is the point you are looking to make? What do you intend to demonstrate in your submission?
- **Argument:** How are you going to explain this?
- **Support:** Where is the legal support for your submission? You will need to identify the appropriate legal principle or rule of law that you intend to advance in support of your submission. From there, you can then identify and apply the authority or authorities that underpin such legal principle or rule of law in support of the submission.
- **Apply:** How will you apply the above to the moot problem? You will need to apply the above principles/authorities to the facts of the moot problem and to the specific submission within the ground of appeal.

> **Mooting tip**
> It is important to appreciate that there are other ways of presenting your submissions, and your own style of advocacy might suggest an amalgamation of these steps or even taking them in a different order. What is important is that your submissions follow a logical format.

We discussed PASA in brief in Chapter 4 in relation to preparing your skeleton argument. We will now consider its application in more detail. Using the PASA method, let us now consider the cross-respondent's submissions again from the moot on pages 254–256. Please refer to this moot when considering the following submissions.

> **Mooting tip**
> Before doing so, however, you must understand the *legal* basis for your appeal as well as the grounds of the appeal itself. By way of example, if your moot is based on criminal law, you should know that the sole ground for appeal against conviction by the defendant is that the conviction is 'unsafe'.[10] Therefore, when preparing for a criminal law moot, you should

---

10 Section 2 of the Criminal Appeal Act 1968 as amended by the Criminal Appeal Act 1995

keep in mind the meaning of 'unsafe' for this purpose. This will avoid any embarrassing silences if, for example, the moot judge were to ask you whether, notwithstanding your submissions, the conviction is nevertheless safe. You should also note that the titles of the parties change from how they were referred to at first instance. In a civil case, the parties start out as claimant and defendant (or, in Scotland, pursuer and defender), but on appeal the party seeking to challenge the lower court's ruling is known as the appellant and the party who is responding to the appeal and seeking to maintain the decision of the court below is known as the respondent. In a criminal case, the prosecution is brought in the name of the Crown (or occasionally by bodies authorised to commence proceedings) and the accused is known as the defendant. As with civil cases, the titles of the parties on appeal are appellant and respondent.

The cross-appeal states:

> Whether Pear Ltd should be entitled to specific performance of the new software and tablet designs.

Using the PASA method:

Proposition: What is the point you are looking to make? What do you intend to demonstrate in your submission?

Immediately before setting out your **Proposition**, you should provide a brief outline of where you are going with it. For example:

> My Lord, the appellant submits that an award of damages is the appropriate remedy for a breach of contract. The test for triggering the exceptional award of specific performance is not satisfied in this case for the following reasons. First, specific performance should not be awarded where an award of damages would be sufficient. Second, the software and tablet designs are not unique for the purposes of specific performance. Third, it is not practicable for the court to grant specific performance in relation to the software and tablet designs, as this would require constant oversight to ensure the order was enforced.

The above sets out your argument in a nutshell and leads nicely to the main substance of your argument.

Argument: How are you going to explain this?

The explanation is an amplification of the above. For example:

1. The remedy for a breach of contract is an award of damages. Specific performance is an exceptional remedy and will only be considered where an award of damages is not an adequate remedy. In the instant appeal, damages will be an adequate (and therefore appropriate) remedy.
2. A court will not make an order for specific performance unless the goods are unique. There is nothing in either the software or tablet designs that is unique for the purposes of specific performance.
3. A court will be reluctant to make an order for specific performance where supervision or oversight is needed. The specific features in the contract are likely to require judicial supervision and oversight.

Support: Where is the legal support for your submission?

This is where you take the judge through the authorities that you say support your arguments. Whenever you refer to an authority, you should explain to the judge its relevance to the ground of appeal. You can introduce this part of your submission as follows:

> My Lord, the relevant test was set out in the case of . . .

You can then follow on with the specific details. For example (following the three points outlined above):

1. In *Cohen v Roche*,[11] McCardie J explained that where the goods were ordinary articles of commerce, possessing no special value or interest, and no grounds exist for any special order for delivery, the judgment should be limited to damages for breach of contract as this constitutes an adequate remedy.
2. Just as the Hepplewhite chairs in *Cohen v Roche* were held to be ordinary Hepplewhite furniture with no specific unique properties, so too are the software and tablet designs. Similarly, in *Whiteley Ltd v Hilt*,[12] Swinfen Eady MR explained that the power vested in the court to order the delivery up of a particular chattel is discretionary and ought not to be exercised when the chattel is an ordinary article of commerce and of no special value or interest, is not alleged to be of any special value to the claimant, and where damages would fully compensate.
3. In *Co-operative Insurance Society Ltd v Argyll Stores (Holdings) Ltd*,[13] Lord Hoffmann explained that specific performance is not appropriate when the

---

11 [1927] 1 KB 169
12 [1918] 2 KB 808
13 [1998] AC 1

continued supervision of the court is necessary in order to ensure the fulfilment of the contract. His Lordship went on to explain that 'continued supervision' does not mean a judge or other officer of the court literally supervising the execution of the order, but rather takes the form of rulings by the court, on applications made by the parties, as to whether there had been a breach of the order such that there is a possibility that the court will have to give an indefinite series of such rulings in order to ensure the execution of the order. This is undesirable. Accordingly, it is not appropriate for the court to grant specific performance in relation to the software and tablet designs.

Finally, once you have properly introduced the authority and explained its relevance to your argument, you are then ready to take the judge to the specific passage or passages in that authority upon which you seek to rely. The following examples demonstrate how to do this:

> A: 'Would your Lordship please turn to Tab x of the bundle where, at page y, your Lordship will find the judgment of Lord Justice Jones. The relevant passage can be found half way down the page, starting with the words . . .'

or

> B: 'May I refer your Lordship to the judgment of Lord Smith, which can be found behind Tab x of the bundle, at page y. The relevant passage can be found on page z of the judgment, about half way down the page, starting with the words . . .'

Mooting tip

You must wait until the judge has found the relevant passage before you start to read from it. If the passage to which you wish to refer is lengthy – for example, more than eight lines in length – you should ask the judge whether he would like you to read it out aloud. If the judge indicates that he would prefer to read it for himself, you should remain silent while he does so. The judge might ask you to point out any specific parts of the passage that you wish him to concentrate on.

The advantage of reading out the passage to the judge is that you can place your own emphasis on the parts that are especially important.

Apply: How will you apply the above to the moot problem?

You should tie in the principles to which you have just referred to the specific facts of the appeal or to the specific point you were addressing. Using the

Cohen v Roche case from the above moot as an example, you might do this by explaining:

> My Lord, just as the Hepplewhite chairs in *Cohen v Roche* were held to be ordinary Hepplewhite furniture with no specific unique properties, so too are the software and tablet designs in the instant appeal . . .

Concluding submissions

Depending on the amount of time you have available to you, you should draw your submissions together with a conclusion. This might just be a few concluding sentences that draw together the key points of your case.

There remain two final matters to deal with:

1. Each speaker should conclude their individual speeches by asking whether the judge needs any further assistance from them. You can do this by saying: 'Unless I can be of any further assistance to your Lordship, those are my submissions.'
2. The final member of each team to speak should also close that team's submissions by informing the judge of the remedy you are seeking. For example: 'For the reasons explained in our submissions, we invite your Lordship to allow[14]/dismiss[15] the appeal.'

PASA and individual authorities

Using *Cohen v Roche* as an example, this is how to use the PASA method when dealing with the individual authorities that you wish to rely on during your submissions.

Proposition

> My Lord, specific performance should not be awarded where an award of damages would be sufficient.

Argument

> The remedy for a breach of contract is an award of damages. Specific performance is an exceptional remedy and will only be considered where an award of damages is not an adequate remedy. In the instant appeal, damages will be an adequate (and therefore appropriate) remedy.

14 If you are representing the appellant.
15 If you are representing the respondent.

Support

In support of this submission, I refer your Lordship to the case of Cohen and Roche reported in the first volume of the 1927 Kings Bench law reports at page 169.[16] In this case, McCardie J explained that where the goods were ordinary articles of commerce possessing no special value or interest, and no grounds exist for any special order for delivery, the judgment should be limited to damages for breach of contract as this constitutes an adequate remedy.

At this point, you should refer the court to any specific passages from the case that supports your argument.

Apply

My Lord, just as the Hepplewhite chairs in *Cohen v Roche* were held to be ordinary Hepplewhite furniture with no specific unique properties, so too are the software and tablet designs in the instant appeal . . .

Signposting or road-mapping

We discussed above the benefits of providing the judge with a so-called roadmap at the outset of your submissions. Signposting (or road-mapping) is a technique that helps judges follow your submissions more easily and should start at the very beginning of your submissions by explaining how you intend to structure them. An example of a good roadmap is as follows:

As your Lordship will see from the appellant's skeleton argument, I have [three] submissions to make in support of the first ground of the appeal. First, that . . . ; second . . . ; and third . . . Turning now to my first submission . . .

There are two further signposting techniques that you should be aware of: these are 'linking' and 'separating'.

Linking

Linking is where you tie two or more points together. The most obvious points you will want to tie together will be a rule or principle of law and an authority from which you contend that rule or principle derives. Having stated the rule or principle of law, you can then proceed to link it to the authority. For example: 'In my submission, this rule [or principle] derives from [state the authority].'

---

16 At this point, you should ask the judge whether he wishes to be reminded of the facts of this case. This is discussed at page 184.

Alternatively, you might prefer: 'In support of this submission, I will refer your Lordship to [state the authority].'

Separating

Although the point at which you end one submission and start the next one is usually clear, it is often helpful to state expressly that this is what you are doing. A typical way of doing this is to pause once you have completed one submission and say: 'My Lord, my next submission/point concerns . . .' or 'My Lord, I now turn to my next submission . . .'.

> **Mooting tip**
> An argument will be much more persuasive if you explicitly state what you intend to achieve rather than leaving it to the judge to draw his own conclusions. This is usually best dealt with under the proposition stage in PASA.

Persuasion

One of the best ways of persuading a judge of the correctness of your submissions is to gain his confidence. In order to do this, you must be able to demonstrate that you are both credible and reliable. In simple terms, if the judge is unable to trust your judgement, he is unlikely to be filled with much confidence in your submissions to the court. As to reliability, you must know your case inside out and know your way around the bundle.

Guidance on matters that will help you put your case over in an effective and persuasive manner is provided throughout this book and it is worth reminding yourself that there is little more certain to infuriate a judge, which in turn will damage your credibility and ability to persuade the court, than misrepresenting any aspect of your case.

Making your submissions persuasive

A persuasive argument is one that is logically made and easy to follow. It should explain what you are attempting to do and the legal basis for doing it. It is often said that first impressions are important, and this applies equally to mooting. It is, therefore, important that the judge forms a good impression of you from the start. Not only is the court more likely to find your submissions persuasive if you come across well, but you will also score more highly on style and presentation.

You will find a sample judge's score sheet on page 223. This will give you a good indication of what judges look for when marking a mooter's performance and determining the winner of the moot. It is important that your submissions are well structured and follow a logical path of progression.

Mooting tip

Although many legal concepts can be quite complex, the art of a good advocate is to explain them in as straightforward and simple a manner as possible. With simplicity comes persuasion.

In Chapter 4, we discussed, for the purpose of preparing your skeleton argument, how to make your written submissions persuasive. Very similar principles apply in making your *oral* submissions persuasive. We also explained that you should use your skeleton argument to give structure and coherence to your oral submissions. Referring back to your skeleton argument as you progress through your oral submissions is generally helpful as it assists the judge in following your overall approach and progress. Your skeleton argument and oral submissions must work seamlessly together; any discordance between the two is likely to be picked up by the judge. In order to avoid such discordance, it is important not to prepare your skeleton argument and oral submissions in isolation from each other.

Mooting tip

You will have seen from the above that there are four stages to the PASA method. It is important to appreciate that there are other ways of presenting your submissions, and your own style of advocacy might suggest an amalgamation of these steps or even taking them in a different order. What is important is that your submissions follow a logical format.

Effective speaking – 'connecting' rather than 'presenting'

To be an effective speaker, you will need to focus on the points and themes of your submissions rather than the specific words you may wish to use. We have already discussed this above, and it is important to re-emphasise that mooters who are tied to a prepared script will find it extremely difficult to persuade a judge that they have an adequate grasp of their brief.

Mooting tip

Rather than focusing on 'presenting' your submissions to the judge, you should instead focus on 'connecting' with him. This will make your submissions far more natural and persuasive. At best, 'rules will carry [judges] into the neighbourhood of a problem and then [they] must get off and walk'.[17] By connecting with the judge, you will stand a far greater chance of taking him with you on your journey.

Adaptability

You must remain ready to adapt your style to the specific circumstances as they unfold during the course of the moot. There are many aspects to this, including:

- Find out what you can about the judge and his approach to judging moots. Do you know anyone who has seen your judge judging a moot? Where possible, try to adapt your style to reflect any particular known preferences of your judge.
- When a judge indicates a preference in respect of submissions generally, you should adapt your presentation and style accordingly. For example, if the judge indicates at the start of the moot that he has read the papers and is familiar with the facts of the various cases that the parties will be referring to, then, subject to the exception noted on pages 186–187, you should not ask whether you should provide a summary of the case facts.
- If you are the respondent, you will have had the benefit of witnessing how the judge interacts with the appellant. You can then adapt your own style to what you have learned.
- Always keep the word 'adaptability' in mind. Listen for any cues from the judge and adapt accordingly.

Eye contact

Your eyes can be very powerful as a means of non-verbal communication. We discussed above that one of the benefits of not reading from a pre-prepared speech is that you will be able to make appropriate eye contact with the judge(s). A mooter who hardly lifts his eyes from the papers makes it virtually impossible to engage properly with the judge. This has a significant knock-on effect in terms of reducing the quality and effectiveness of the arguments. This is no different to lecturers trying to engage their students if they do no more than read from their notes with their heads down instead of interacting with the group.

One of the benefits of making appropriate eye contact with the judge was noted in the previous paragraph. But what does 'appropriate' mean in this context? First and foremost, your level of eye contact, as well as your general demeanour, should be enough to demonstrate to the judge that you are not reading from a script.

17 Professor Leon Green, *Judge and Jury*, p. 214, quoted in Hart and Honore, *Causation in the Law*, 2nd edn, Clarendon Press, Oxford, 1985, p. 98

This will also help you to pick up any facial or other expressions that might indicate that the judge is either with you or against you on a point and enable you to moderate your argument accordingly. Appropriate eye contact will also enable you to identify when the judge is about to intervene – something that you are unlikely to notice if your head is buried in your papers. This is little different to any other kind of conversation, where the other person's body language and general demeanour will indicate when they are going to speak. The difference here is that when the judge speaks, you don't: you should never speak over the judge as you might do in ordinary conversation. Finally, it is worth reminding yourself that staring is rude, and this is no different if your stare is fixed on a moot judge or anyone else.

Overall, it is important for you to engage the judge and to carry him with you as your submissions progress, something that you will find difficult to do unless you maintain appropriate eye contact. Maintaining appropriate eye contact will also make it very difficult for the judge not to concentrate on what you are saying.

Maintaining appropriate eye contact will also enable you to see when the judge is making notes. Two points arise from this. First, you should ordinarily wait for the judge to finish writing before starting your next point. Second, knowing that the judge has made a note of something you have said indicates that he found the point worthy of note. Together with his body language and especially any questions he asks, this might help you to work out whether he is with you or not on the particular point. Experienced mooters will appreciate how important it is to gain some insight into a judge's thinking and to moderate their approach accordingly.

Finally, where there is more than one judge on the Bench you will need to maintain appropriate eye contact with all of them, remembering that each one of them will have a say when it comes to deciding the winner.

Mooting tip

Another advantage of maintaining appropriate eye contact with the judge is that you will be able to see what he is doing and gauge whether he is following your submissions. The judge's own body language will often give away whether he is following you or whether he appears to be lost, in which case you might need to repeat or rephrase your point. Any reactions from the Bench, such as affirmatory comments, nods or other gestures, will enable you to maintain or amend your submissions accordingly.

Your voice

It is important to remember that you will need to be heard by a number of people which will require you to project your voice appropriately. The volume of your voice will depend to a large extent on the size of the moot room. Some moots take place in real courtrooms which can be quite considerable in size. Whatever you do, you must appreciate the difference between projecting your voice and shouting; the latter is something you must avoid doing!

No matter where the moot is held, moot rooms vary in size and it is likely that the Bench will be some distance away from you. It should go without saying that your voice needs to be heard clearly by the judge(s). Again, you should practise this with your colleagues, in rooms of varying sizes, to make sure that you are able to adapt to different settings. Getting to the venue in plenty of time will enable you to get a good feel for the room and its layout, and will assist you in judging how loudly you will need to speak in order to be heard.

It is important that the judge finds your submissions attractive and persuasive, which is virtually impossible if he has difficulty hearing them. It is also important for your opponent to be able to hear you; otherwise, they will have difficulty in responding to your submissions.

Intonation

Intonation refers to the way a person alters their voice as they speak, typically by the tone of their voice rising and falling and in varying the volume of their speech. Intonation is not used to distinguish the meaning of words per se but it can serve to indicate differing attitudes and emotions and to distinguish different aspects of speech, such as statements and questions. It is also useful for focusing the listener's attention on important elements of the spoken message as well as helping to regulate conversational interaction.

Most importantly, it puts feeling into your words and makes what you say more interesting, expressive and compelling. Without it, your voice can be monotonic, making it very difficult to engender any kind of enthusiasm. Reading from a pre-prepared script will often result in this kind of boring presentation that lacks any kind of feeling or genuine enthusiasm.

It can be a good exercise to listen to different people being interviewed on television to hear the difference between a good speaker and a poor one. See what you can pick up from this to improve your own speaking style.

> **Mooting tip**
> Although variation in your tone can be very engaging, you should avoid being over-theatrical as this can be distracting as well as annoying.

Accents

Do not worry if you have a regional accent. Whether or not you have one, make sure that you speak clearly and in a manner that is appropriate and shows respect to the court. Do not be put off if your opponent has so-called posh accents. Speaking with a posh accent and being able to moot well are not the same.

Dialects and slang

The UK has a rich landscape of regional dialects. It is, however, important to avoid them unless they form part of the moot and need to be repeated during your submissions. Consider the following sentence: 'Happen the appellant was suffering from an abnormality of the mind.' In this example, the word 'happen' is used to mean 'perhaps' or 'maybe' and might be heard in certain parts of Yorkshire or Lancashire. Its use is inappropriate in a courtroom. The same applies to the use of slang expressions.

Politeness

In any courtroom setting, the aim of the advocate is to win the case for their client. The same applies to mooting. Although our process is adversarial in nature, you must remain polite and respectful at all times both to the judge and to your opponent. You might feel irritated by something the judge or your opponent says, but you must remain calm and composed. You should never interrupt your opponent during their submissions, no matter what they do. Instead, take a note of anything you wish to bring to the court's attention and do so when it is your turn to speak. If the judge wishes you to speak out of turn, he will invite you to do so.

Non-verbal communication, body language, posture and gestures

Your body language is an important part of your overall communication process. Entire books have been written about body language, which you might wish to read, but, for present purposes, the key to an effective advocate's body language is congruence: an advocate must match their body language to the rest of their communication so that there is no imbalance between the two. Consider the following points:

- If you display a lack of confidence in your body language, you will find it very hard to be persuasive.
- If you slouch in your chair or stand unattractively, you will give the impression of sloppiness and inattention.
- Take care when employing gestures. You should use gestures to emphasise key points of your submissions. Any overuse of gestures will have the effect of making those that are really important less effective. Gestures should be purposeful without being over-theatrical.

Mooting tip
Always remember that you are in full view of the judge whenever you are in the moot room, whether you are speaking or not. Do not make a poor impression.

It is important that you make a good impression and hold and present yourself professionally.

When seated

- Do not fidget or play with anything on the desk.
- Do not slouch in your seat or do anything annoying such as kicking your feet.
- Look as though you are interested in the proceedings and are following the case as it advances.
- Ensure that your phone is turned off. Do not use it to text, no matter how discreet you think you are being.
- If you need a drink, water is the only acceptable refreshment. When drinking, sip from a glass rather than gulp from a bottle.

When standing and making your submissions

- Do not fidget.
- Do not slouch over the lectern.
- Do not stand so rigidly that you look like a soldier on parade.
- Stand in front of the lectern and do not move around the moot room as you often see advocates doing in the movies.
- Do not fiddle with pens, paperwork or hair, or do anything that might be considered annoying.
- Although some hand and arm gestures can often make submissions appear more effective and expressive, do not overuse them or act in an over-theatrical manner.
- As noted above, if you need a drink, water is the only acceptable refreshment. When drinking, sip from a glass rather than gulp from a bottle.

Remember that the judge can see you. You want to make a good impression at all times.

The pace of speaking

Many mooters, especially when mooting for the first time, speak far too quickly. Not only does this make it more difficult to present your case clearly and effectively, but it also makes it more difficult for the judge to keep up with your submissions. As noted above in relation to your voice, it is important for the judge to find your submissions attractive and persuasive, and this is virtually impossible if he has difficulty following them. In short, speaking too quickly is not appropriate in a courtroom setting and gives a poor impression of your performance as a mooter.

Good speakers speak at a pace that enables them to pause for breath whenever needed and to make effective use of these pauses. Pausing can serve a number of useful purposes, including:

- enabling you to catch your breath
- to give emphasis to a particular point
- to provide a natural pause between the end of one point and the start of the next
- to allow the judge to find the passages that you are referring to
- to allow the judge to take notes.

The best way to judge whether your pace is appropriate is to ask someone to listen to your submissions – preferably one of your tutors or someone who is experienced in mooting or public speaking.

Mooting tip

If you think that speaking quickly will discourage the judge from intervening and asking you questions, think again. Mooting is all about dealing with judicial interventions, and no moot judge will be deterred from asking questions because of the speed of your submissions.

Speaking fluently

You must avoid using 'fillers' such as 'er' and 'um' during your submissions. The odd one now and then might go unnoticed, but not when they are littered throughout your submissions. Speaking more slowly, and taking more pauses when you speak, can help you avoid these annoying fillers and will make your submissions more professional.

You should also avoid the annoyingly growing trend of starting your sentences with the word 'so', and never respond with 'no worries' or 'cool'. Similarly, you should never litter your speech with words like 'I mean', 'like' and 'you know'.

Appropriate and inappropriate language

You should avoid the unnecessary use of slang or jargon, unless, of course, these feature directly in the text you are dealing with.

You should also avoid the use of obscene language, again, unless it features in the text you are dealing with and it becomes necessary to repeat it verbatim.

Your demeanour

You must remember that you are representing your client in a court of law and must act appropriately at all times, whether you are speaking or not. You should avoid doing anything that is distracting and disrespectful to the court. The following points should be noted:

- You should stand when the judge enters the court and when he (or the court clerk) indicates that he is ready to leave the court.

- You should bow your head when the judge takes his place on the Bench and when he stands to leave the court.
- You should stand whenever addressing the court.
- You should keep your hands out of your pockets when addressing the court.
- You should stand still when addressing the court and should not fiddle.
- You should avoid fiddling even when seated. Avoid swivelling or leaning back on your chair or placing your hands behind you head.
- You should not do anything while seated that shows disrespect to the court, including texting, fiddling with rings or pens, playing with your hair, picking your nose or ears, biting or cleaning your fingernails or cracking your knuckles. Remember, the judge can see you from the Bench.

By all means, take notes while others are speaking and, if it is absolutely necessary to communicate with your partner, do so discreetly, preferably by way of a short note. Never communicate, or attempt to communicate, with anyone else during the moot.

Controlling your nerves

According to Mark Twain, 'There are two types of speakers: those that are nervous and those that are liars'. So, you are not alone in feeling apprehensive about having to moot.

Mooting, as with any kind of public speaking, can be a nerve-racking experience, especially for those doing it for the first time. However, despite actor and comedian George Albert Jessel's assertion that 'the human brain starts working the moment you're born and never stops until you stand up to speak in public', there are many things you can do to make your presentation less unnerving. The majority of mooters will confirm that their nerves disappear as soon as they get to their feet and start making their submissions. Most even enjoy it!

There are several things that you can do to help you to relax and remain calm during your moot. One of the best ways to overcome your nerves is to try to identify what it is that is causing the stress and then try to deal with it.

The most common fear is getting it wrong. It is perfectly understandable that you should not want to appear foolish when presenting your moot, but this concern is easily addressed. You should remember that you are making your submissions in response to the case that you have been presented with. The law may, or may not, be on your side, but at least it will be arguable. Provided that you don't ask the court to do something that the law does not permit it to do, or simply misunderstand the moot problem or the law, there is little that you can do that is 'wrong'.

Examples of these basic errors would include:

- asking the Court of Appeal to overturn a decision of the House of Lords or Supreme Court
- asking the court to consider points that are clearly outwith your grounds of appeal

- addressing the court on a point of law that is no longer current or otherwise misinterpreting the law
- failing to deal with a case or statutory provision that is relevant to your argument
- misunderstanding the moot problem or grounds of appeal
- failing to deal with the grounds of appeal that you are required to argue
- running your arguments in such a way that they cause damage to your team-mate's arguments

With most moots and mooting competitions, you will be given sufficient time to research and prepare your arguments, and therefore you should not fall down on any of these points. Thorough preparation is the key to success.

Avoid being nervous about your nervousness! Unless you openly display your nervousness, no one need know. Nervousness is not something that people can see unless you advertise it.

Mooting tip
Don't kick yourself if you make a mistake. Many people magnify their imperfections yet at the same time diminish all that is good. Most of us make mistakes, and when we do, we recover and proceed gracefully. Your 'mistake' may be nothing more than deviating from what you had intended to say. It may not be wrong: just different and unlikely to be noticed by anyone else unless you make a 'mistake' by emphasising it. Move on with poise. Allow yourself not to be 'perfect'.

Breathing

Controlling your breathing will help control your nerves. Even if you are not feeling particularly nervous, practising the following breathing exercises before your moot will help relax your body and mind.

- Stand upright with your feet shoulder width apart. Think about the ground beneath your feet. Feel how secure the ground feels.
- Close your eyes and relax. Now, imagine that you are precariously suspended from the ceiling by a fine strand of thread.
- Pay attention to your breathing. Concentrate on inhaling and exhaling. Inhale through your nose and exhale through your mouth.
- Remind yourself that there is no rush. This is your time to relax and to take control.
- Now, make an effort to slow down your breathing. Take 5–6 seconds to inhale through your nose and then 5–6 seconds to exhale through your mouth.
- Take another deep breath and you should be better prepared to moot in a relaxed and confident manner.

> **Mooting tip**
> You will benefit more from these exercises if you practise them regularly.
> Try practising them daily or at any time you feel under stress.

Listening skills

The first thing you must learn to do is listen. Do not answer any questions until the judge has finished asking them. Not only might this appear to be rude, but it is far too easy to anticipate a question that the judge hasn't in fact asked.

Projecting confidence

Good lawyers exude confidence. They always appear to be in control of their brief and in command of the courtroom. A good advocate is often likened to a swan: perfectly calm and unruffled on the surface yet paddling furiously under the surface. Thorough preparation is an excellent way to develop confidence.

> **Mooting tip**
> Stand tall, upright, shoulders back, chest out. Although this is not a military exercise, this will help you to exude confidence. And smile. Giving the impression of calmness and confidence goes a long way to being calm and confident.

Tone and pace of speech

You should deliver your submissions in a balanced and well-modulated manner. Your delivery should be neither quiet, dull and monotone nor loud and over-excited. Do not rush your submissions, and make sure that you emphasise the parts that are especially important. Make effective use of pauses which can help you to think about your next point before you start it.

> **Mooting tip**
> Do not think that you have to speak continuously. Pausing between one point and the next can be a very effective way of breaking up your submissions. It can also help you to gather your thoughts and compose yourself rather than waffle and say the first thing that comes into your head. Making effective use of pausing can also be invaluable when dealing with questions from the Bench as it can give you valuable thinking time. If you need a bit of time to

consider a point, then rather than stand there in silence, you might want to say something like 'My Lord, may I please have a moment?' This is what happens in professional practice and, provided these pauses are not too frequent or lengthy, no judge should take offence at it.

When should you start to practise your submissions?

Once you are reasonably happy with your submissions, you should start to practise them. Practising will help identify any weaknesses as well as make you more familiar with your submissions.

How to anticipate questions from the Bench

During your research, you will have given thought to how well your submissions will stand up to judicial scrutiny. This will have involved testing your submissions against hypothetical objections. These are likely to be some of the questions that will also be on a judge's mind and could well result in questions during your moot.

Another way of anticipating judicial questions is to put yourself in the position of a judge and consider what questions you would ask the mooter.

By anticipating possible questions, you will be able to give thought to how you would answer them. Thinking about possible questions is an excellent way of preparing for your moot.

You should also practise your moot in front of as many different people acting as judges as time allows. This will give you the experience of working with different judging styles and being able to practise responding to different questions, often put in different ways.

In Chapter 7, we will analyse a range of different questions that a judge might ask and consider how best to answer them in different kinds of situations.

Understanding the rules of the moot

Just as a practitioner needs to understand the rules of the court, a mooter needs to understand the rules of the moot. Most moots are governed by a number of rules in common and a sample set of rules is provided in Chapter 9.

Among the most important rules of any moot, and ones that every participating mooter needs to know, are:

- the length each speaker has to deliver their submissions
- whether or not the clock stops during judicial interventions
- the timescales and rules relating to the various stages leading up to the moot, including the exchange of skeleton arguments and the production of bundles
- the order of the speakers
- whether or not there is a right of reply and any rules relating to this.

Practise, practise, practise

No matter how much experience you have in public speaking, you must practise your submissions. Practising will improve your performance. You should take every opportunity to practise your submissions in front of as many people as possible. Include fellow students, tutors, friends and even family. Ask for critical feedback and reflect on it. You should also learn to be self-critical. Listen carefully to your own submissions and think about ways to improve them. Put yourself in the position of the judge or your opponent and think about how they might attack your submissions, either in content or clarity. Success is the product of a considerable number of hours of very hard work.

Filming yourself practising your submissions can be very helpful as it enables you, and others, to observe your performance. You may well be surprised about how you come across to others. We are often totally unaware of our own annoying habits until we can actually see them for ourselves. The advantages of reviewing a recording of yourself cannot be overstated as it enables you to observe your performance 'warts and all'. The kind of annoying habits to watch out for are those which we have considered above and include:

- speaking too quietly or too quickly
- speaking in a monotone voice and without passion or feeling
- excessive hand or arm gestures
- using fillers such as 'er' and 'um' during your submissions
- starting your sentences with 'so' or using words such as 'like', 'I mean' and 'you know'
- using regional dialect or slang (unless required for the purpose of your submission)
- acting in any way that might appear to be rude or impolite
- fidgeting or fiddling with pens, paper, hair, etc.
- slouching in your seat or over the lectern
- doing anything else annoying such as kicking your feet
- drinking from a bottle.

The final check

You must remain alert to any recent developments or any late changes in the law that might affect your moot. As a final check, it is a good idea to run your cases through one or more of the electronic databases. If you have read widely enough around the subject area of the moot, you should be aware of any cases that are pending a decision of an appellate court. Newly introduced statutes are not such a problem as they do not usually have retrospective effect.

7 Oral submissions

Introduction

We are now at the stage of considering your oral submissions. This is almost certainly the most important (and potentially daunting) part of the mooting process, and a good performance on the day will go a long way to winning the moot. No matter how good your research, preparation and skeleton arguments are, it is correct say that most moots are won by the quality and competence of the oral submissions. This is because most mooters can be expected to have researched and prepared their case thoroughly and produced a competent skeleton argument in accordance with the rules of the moot. In fact, in the majority of moots, there is not a great deal to distinguish the quality of the skeleton arguments, with most being perfectly adequate for the job. It is, as already observed, the quality and competence of the oral submissions that usually determines the overall outcome of the moot.

In short, a successful mooter is someone who is able to persuade the court of the superiority of their legal submissions and that they are up to the job as an advocate. In the main, this is done by making sure that your submissions are made concisely and clearly with well-reasoned and logical argument, and, insofar as possible, are supported by appropriate authority.

To achieve this, a good mooter will:

- address the judge(s) correctly
- avoid speculation
- understand what they need to achieve to persuade the court of the superiority of their legal arguments
- refer to appropriate authorities to support their submissions
- appreciate the weight a court is likely to give to each authority
- do not take authorities and quotations out of context
- deal appropriately and effectively with judicial interventions
- keep to the allotted time
- be extremely conversant with both the facts of the case and grounds of the appeal
- understand the strengths and weaknesses of the case
- provide clear and well-structured submissions
- cite authorities correctly
- avoid lengthy quotations and too many quotations
- avoid reading from a pre-prepared script
- work seamlessly with their partner as a team
- make good use of the time available

Order of the speakers

(a) The traditional approach

The traditional approach in mooting is that the appellant opens the appeal and presents their case, followed by the respondent. Each team consists of two speakers: a leader and a junior. The leader takes the first ground of appeal and the junior takes the second. The four speakers will be heard in the following order:

Speaker No.	
1	Lead/senior counsel for the appellant
2	Junior counsel for the appellant
3	Lead/senior counsel for the respondent
4	Junior counsel for the respondent
5	Appellant in reply

(b) The alternating approach

Where the 'alternating approach' is used, the first ground of appeal is heard in full before the mooters address the court on the second ground. Some moots stipulate that this approach should be adopted, whereas in other moots some judges might prefer this approach and direct the mooters accordingly.

Speaker No.	
1	Lead/senior counsel for the appellant
2	Lead/senior counsel for the respondent
3	Junior counsel for the appellant
4	Junior counsel for the respondent
5	Appellant in reply

(c) Appeal and cross-appeal

Where the moot takes the form of an appeal and cross-appeal, the order is as follows:

Speaker No.	
1	Lead/senior counsel for the appellant
2	Lead/senior counsel for the respondent
3	Junior counsel for the cross-appellant
4	Junior counsel for the cross-respondent
5	Appellant in reply
6	Cross-appellant in reply

Sometimes, either the rules of the moot, or the judges, will vary the above order of speaking and require the appellant's reply to follow straight after the appeal, and the cross-appellant's reply to follow straight after the cross-appeal. In such a case, the order will be as follows:

Speaker No.	
1	Lead/senior counsel for the appellant
2	Lead/senior counsel for the respondent
3	Appellant in reply
4	Junior counsel for the cross-appellant
5	Junior counsel for the cross-respondent
6	Cross-appellant in reply

In Scotland, the order (and titles) of the speakers are slightly different:

Speaker No.	
1	Junior counsel for the appellant/reclaimer
2	Junior counsel for the respondent
3	Senior counsel for the appellant/reclaimer
4	Senior counsel for the respondent

The right to reply

Not all moots include a right to reply. Where they do, the rules will explain whether this is obligatory or optional. Even where a right to reply is not obligatory, it is a right that you ought to exercise as doing so will give you a final opportunity to impress the judge with your rebuttal of the respondent's submissions.

No right to reply is given to the respondent because they will already have had the opportunity of rebutting the appellant's arguments as part of their submissions.

It is important to appreciate that the reply is a reply to your opponent's submissions (on both grounds of the appeal) and not an opportunity to repeat or rehash any of your own submissions or to make any further submissions.

The time allocated to the reply is usually very short, typically five minutes. You will, therefore, need to keep any introductions to a bare minimum, or even proceed straight to the substance of your reply. A good way of starting your reply is to say: 'My Lord, I have [three] points to make in reply. First, . . . Second, . . . Finally, . . .'

Once you have introduced your reply in this way, you can then proceed to deal with the substantive points you wish to make.

If time permits, you should also start each point with a very brief outline of the argument to which your point in reply relates.

Finally, you should end your reply with similar words to those used when concluding your own submissions: 'Unless I can be of any further assistance to your Lordship, that concludes the appellant's reply.'

> **Mooting tip**
> In order to prepare an appropriate reply, you should make notes of the points you wish to deal with while your opponent is speaking. As the reply will deal with both grounds of the appeal, your mooting partner should assist you in making notes referable to their ground of the appeal.

In the rare case where you do not wish to exercise your right of reply, you should indicate this to the judge by explaining: 'My Lord, the appellant is content to rest its case on the earlier submissions made.' As with all guidance provided about what to say in any given situation, it is not necessary to use the specific words noted.

Length of the speeches

The rules of the moot will set out the time available to each of the mooters and will also state whether or not the clock is paused during judicial interventions. In many competitions, mooters have 15 or 20 minutes to deliver their submissions.

Since it is not usual for the clock to be paused when questions are raised from the Bench or when you respond to them, the 'free' time that you will have to make your submissions will be less than the overall time allocated to you. Some judges are more interventionist than others, which makes it very difficult to determine how much time you will actually have to develop your submissions, especially if you are the first speaker and have no experience of the judging style of the judge. This is yet another reason why reading from a prepared script is unwise as doing so makes it very difficult to moderate your submissions to the time available.

> **Mooting tip**
> Although there is no strict formula for working out how long you will have to make your submissions once judicial interventions have been taken into account, you should aim to prepare your submissions to last around 60–70 per cent of the time stipulated by the rules. Thus, if the rules stipulate that a mooter has 20 minutes' speaking time, you should prepare your submissions to last between 12 and 14 minutes. In other words, you should plan for 30–40 per cent of your allowed time to be taken up by judicial interventions. Flexibility is, however, paramount. You may find that your judge asks very few questions or that he continually interrupts you. A useful tip is to mark your notes in such a way that you can identify which points are of fundamental importance to your case and which could be omitted should you be pressed for time.

Delivering your submissions

The delivery of your moot will differ depending on whether you represent the appellant or the respondent and whether you are leading or junior counsel. This is shown in the table below.

	Appellant		Respondent	
	Senior	Junior	Senior	Junior
Introduces all mooters	√			
Introduces the moot	√			
Individual submissions	√	√	√	√
Reply	√ or	√		

As you will see from the table above, the appellant opens the appeal. This is because it is the appellant that is unhappy with the decision of the court below and seeks a remedy. Mooters must stand when addressing the court. You will see throughout that you will be addressing the court in a formal manner observing general mooting conventions.

Working as a team

Before considering your own submissions, you must make sure that you and your partner are working seamlessly as a team.

Although there are four mooters in a moot, there are only two sides: the appellant and the respondent. Each side is usually presented with two grounds of appeal which are dealt with by leading and junior counsel respectively. During your preparations – and the moot itself – you must not lose sight of the fact that you and your teammate must present the case for your client in such a way that they complement each other and that neither of your arguments undermines the other.

Your moot speech will generally be divided into the following sections and delivered seamlessly:

Introductions – mooters

Your introductions must be made formally in a rather stylised format, observing general mooting and court conventions. The introductions will differ between mooters and the sides they represent; this reflects the different roles they have to play.

The appellant always opens the appeal. Mooters must stand whenever they address the court.

Appellant – leader

May it please your Lordship, my name is Miss Smith and I appear in this case for the appellant, Bloggs plc, with my learned junior, Mr Jones. My learned friends, Mr Peters and Miss Lee, appear for the respondent, Abacus Ltd. I will be addressing your Lordship on the first ground of the appeal.

> **Mooting tip**
> A brief glance towards your fellow mooters as you introduce them to the judge will assist the judge to note who is who.

Appellant – junior

> If it pleases your Lordship, I am Mr Jones and I will be dealing with the appellant's second ground of the appeal.

Respondent – leader

> If it pleases your Lordship, I am Mr Peters and I appear for the respondent with my learned junior, Miss Lee. I will be addressing your Lordship on the first ground of the appeal.

Respondent – junior

> May it please your Lordship, my name is Miss Lee and I will be dealing with the respondent's second ground of the appeal.

> **Mooting tip**
> As already observed, you do not have to use exactly the same words as noted above. You will see, for example, two slightly different ways of 'pleasing your Lordship', both of which have the same meaning and are entirely interchangeable. Similarly, there is absolutely no difference between 'my name is' and 'I am'.

Instead of beginning with 'May it please your Lordship(s)', another, perfectly appropriate, way of introducing your case is to start with 'May it please the Court'. Naturally, using this form of introduction does away with the need for distinguishing between single or multiple judges or an all-male, all-female or mixed Bench of judges. In this context, 'Lordships' and 'Court' are in any event interchangeable.

> **Mooting tip**
> If the judge calls you by name to start your submissions, you should omit your own name from your introduction.

At the end of your submissions, you should hand over to the next mooter. By way of example, if you are lead counsel for the appellant, you can do this by saying:

> Unless I can assist your Lordship any further, these are my submissions for the first ground of the appeal and my learned junior will now address your Lordship on the second ground of the appeal.

Introductions – background to the appeal

Once the first speaker has made the necessary introductions, the next stage is to explain what the appeal is about. This only needs to be brief, not least because it can be assumed that the judge has already read the moot problem when preparing for the moot.

By way of example, let us consider the moot on page 236. An appropriate introduction would be something like this:

> My Lord, this is the appeal by Mr Bamber and Mr Jones against the decision of the Court of Appeal which dismissed their appeals against conviction under section 18 of the Offences Against the Person Act 1861 having unsuccessfully attempted to raise the defence of duress by threats. The two grounds of appeal concern, first, whether the defence of duress by threats should be available where a defendant is threatened by a close relative, even where he only maintained minimal relations with that relative, and, second, whether the said defence should be extended to cover situations where the defendant acts to avoid a threat of false imprisonment.

Mooting tip
There will be no need to provide the above case introduction if the judge indicates that he has read the papers and that you should proceed straight away to your submissions.

Using appropriate language

Formality is extremely important when addressing a court. Some of the conventions may, at least initially, appear rather odd, but it is important that they are followed. The most important of these conventions are:

Addressing the judge(s) correctly

The majority of moots are set in either the Court of Appeal (Civil or Criminal Division) or the Supreme Court. The correct form of address in these courts when addressing an individual judge is 'my Lord' or 'my Lady' as the case may be.[1] When addressing a Bench consisting of more than one judge, the correct form is 'my Lords' if they are all male or 'my Ladies' if they are all female. In the case of a mixed-sex Bench, the traditional approach was to refer to the Bench as 'my Lords' even though at least one of their number was female. In such a case, you would still refer to the female judge as 'my Lady' when addressing her directly. More recently, the trend has been to refer to a mixed-sex Bench as 'the Court' (i.e. 'may it please the Court . . .' or '. . . which the Court will find at page . . .') or 'my Lady, my Lords' or 'my Lord(s) and my Lady(ies)'. It is certainly permissible to use both of these forms of address during the same case, especially where using the latter might become a little cumbersome if used too frequently.

My Lord or your Lordship/my Lady or your Ladyship

You must refer to judges as 'my Lord/Lady' or 'your Lordship/Ladyship' but never by their name or by using the word 'you'. Two examples will assist in working out whether 'my Lord' or 'your Lordship' and 'my Lady' or 'your Ladyship' are the correct forms of address:

- If, in ordinary speech, you would use the person's name, you should instead say 'my Lord/Lady'. Thus: 'Helen, these are our submissions' would become 'My Lady, these are our submissions'.
- If, in ordinary speech, you would say 'you' or 'your', you should instead say 'your Lordship/Ladyship'. Thus: 'If you could turn to Tab A of the Appellant's bundle' would become 'If your Lordship could turn to Tab A of the Appellant's bundle'.

The following examples further illustrate the above:

'My Lord, I appear on behalf of the respondent' (addressing a single male judge).

'In my submission, my Ladies, the case referred to by my learned friends has no relevance to this appeal' (addressing more than one female judge).

---

1 In 1994, Sir Thomas Bingham, MR, issued a Practice Note, [1994] 1 FLR 866, [1994] EW Misc 1 (Practice Note) 'Mode of Address: Dame Elizabeth Butler-Sloss'. This provides: 'Since 1988, the Court of Appeal has enjoyed the great benefit of including among its members Dame Elizabeth Butler-Sloss. Formally, she has been a Lord Justice of Appeal and is required to be so styled by s 2(3) of the Supreme Court Act 1981 unless and until that section can be amended. But she has, when sitting in court, been addressed as "My Lady", as she was when sitting as a puisne judge, and as other female puisne judges are addressed. This has led counsel, when referring to her in court, to adopt the usage "My Lady, Lord Justice Butler-Sloss". This usage is plainly absurd. Nothing can for the time being be done to alter the formal position, but for informal purposes it is desirable that reference should be made to Lady Justice Butler-Sloss, so that she will be referred to in court as "My Lady, Lady Justice Butler-Sloss".'

'My Lady, if I may have a brief moment to consider your Ladyship's question' (addressing a single female judge).

'My Lord, if I may now deal with the point your Lordship raised earlier' (addressing a single male judge).

'If I have understood your Lordship's point correctly . . .' (addressing a single male judge).

'My Lords, my Lady, I will now turn to the second ground of appeal' (addressing a mixed-sex Bench with one female judge and more than one male judge).

'My Lord, my Ladies, I will now turn to the second ground of appeal' (addressing a mixed-sex Bench with one male judge and more than one female judge).

'If I may now address the Court on the second ground of appeal' (an alternative to the above two lines).

The following table provides a useful summary of the above:

| | Single judge | | More than one judge[a] | | |
	Male	Female	All male	All female	Mixed sex
Direct	My Lord	My Lady	My Lords	My Ladies	My Lords, my Lord(s) and my Lady(ies), or the Court
	My Lord, I appear on behalf of the Respondent	*My Lady, I appear on behalf of the Respondent*	*My Lords, I appear on behalf of the Respondent*	*My Ladies, I appear on behalf of the Respondent*	*My Lords, I appear on behalf of the Respondent;* or
					My Lords, my Lady, I appear on behalf of the Respondent; or
					I appear before the Court on behalf of the Respondent
In place of 'you'	Your Lordship	Your Ladyship	Your Lordships	Your Ladyships	Your Lordships, your Lordship(s) and your Ladyship(s), or the Court
	May it please your Lordship	*May it please your Ladyship*	*May it please your Lordships*	*May it please your Ladyships*	*May it please your Lordships;* or
					May it please your Lordship(s) and your Ladyship(s); or
					May it please the Court

	Single judge		More than one judge[a]		
	Male	*Female*	*All male*	*All female*	*Mixed sex*
In place of 'your'	Your Lordship's	Your Ladyship's	Your Lordships'	Your Ladyships'	Your Lordships', your Lordships' and your Ladyships', or the Court's
	The case can be found at Tab 3 of your Lordship's bundle	*The case can be found at Tab 3 of your Ladyship's bundle*	*The case can found at Tab 3 of your Lordships' bundle*	*The case can be found at Tab 3 of your Ladyships' bundle*	*The case can be found at Tab 3 of your Lordships' bundle; or*
					The case can be found at Tab 3 of your Lordships' and your Ladyship's bundle;[b] or
					The case can be found at Tab 3 of the Court's bundle

a The table refers to addressing the Bench collectively. When addressing one member of the Bench directly, the appropriate singular form should be used.

b The positioning of the apostrophes assumes one female judge and more than one male judge. There is, of course, no difference in the way one would pronounce this if there was one male judge and more than one female judge.

Mooting tip

You may find the above terms of address somewhat awkward and they might take a bit of getting used to. This is where practising your moot will prove invaluable and, with experience, you will find that this becomes second nature. If you realise that you have used an incorrect form of address, you should correct it provided that you have noticed it straight away and move on. Do not make an issue out of it as this will only highlight the mistake.

Referring to judges from the authorities

During your submissions, you will invariably need to refer to specific passages from the authorities you have selected to support your case. To do this, you will need to refer to the judge from whose judgment you wish to quote. You may also need to quote from the judgment of the (fictitious) judge whose decision is the very subject of the moot. Once you have referred to these judges by name, you may thereafter shorten it to 'the learned judge' or 'the learned Lord Chancellor', and so on.

The following table provides a useful summary of the above:

Written form	Spoken form
Mr/Mrs Recorder Smith	Mr/Mrs Recorder Smith
HHJ Smith	His/Her Honour Judge Smith
Smith J	Mr/Mrs Justice Smith
Smith and Jones JJ	Mr/Mrs Justice Smith and Mr/Mrs Justice Jones
Smith LJ	Lord/Lady Justice Smith
Smith and Jones LJJ	Lord/Lady Justice Smith and Lord/Lady Justice Jones
Lord/Lady Smith of Whitecare	Lord/Lady Smith
Lord/Lady Smith CJ	Lord/Lady Smith, the (then) Lord Chief Justice
Lord/Lady Smith MR	Lord/Lady Smith, the (then) Master of the Rolls
Lord/Lady Smith VC	Lord/Lady Smith, the (then) Vice Chancellor

There are six further points to note. First, when referring to a female judge of the High Court you should always use the prefix 'Mrs', regardless of her marital status; the prefix 'Miss' is always incorrect. Second, where the judge you have referred to has subsequently been elevated, you should use the words 'as he (or she) then was'. Third, do not use honorifics such as 'the Honourable' or 'the Right Honourable' when referring to judges. Fourth, unless the omission causes ambiguity, you should not refer to a judge by his territorial qualification (i.e. Lord Smith of Whiteacre should simply be referred to as Lord Smith). Fifth, in the case of a judge who shares a surname with another judge of equal rank, to avoid ambiguity it is customary to add his first name before his surname (i.e. Mr Justice Peter Smith). Finally, in the same way as you would not address the moot judge as 'you', you should not refer to a judge in a case you are citing as 'him' or 'her' but as 'his Lordship' or 'her Honour', as the case may be, or even simply as 'the learned judge'.

> **Mooting tip**
> A judge is addressed by reference to the capacity in which he is sitting. This means that a Circuit Judge sitting as a High Court Judge is addressed as 'my Lord', and not 'your Honour'.

Referring to your opponent

It is likely that you will need to refer to your opponent during the course of your own submissions. You are likely to do this for a number of different reasons. First, if you are the lead mooter for the appellant (and thereby the first mooter to speak), it is your task to introduce all other mooters, including your opponent. Here, you should introduce your opponent by their title and surname (i.e. Mr Smith or

Miss Jones). Second, when refuting a point made by your opponent, you can refer to them as follows:

- If the point you are refuting relates to a point made by your opponent generally, say, for example, in their skeleton argument, you should refer to them as 'my learned friends opposite'.
- If the point you are refuting relates to a point made by one of the mooters on the other side during the course of their submissions, you can refer to them as 'my learned friend, Miss Smith'.

Referring to your mooting partner

Similarly, you may need to refer to your teammate during your own submissions. This may be in the course of introducing the mooters to the judge (as noted above) or for any other reason (for example, when stating that a particular point will be dealt with in detail by them). In such a situation, you can refer to them as 'my learned friend, Miss Smith', 'my learned friend', 'my learned junior/leader', or just by their name (Miss Smith).

> **Mooting tip**
> Consider glancing briefly towards the person when referring to them during your own submissions. You should never use the first names of any of the mooters during the moot.

Gender

You need to take care when referring to judges of the High Court and Court of Appeal to ensure that you refer to them according to their correct gender. This is because they are often referred to simply by their surname followed by J or LJ. For example, Arden J or Arden LJ refers to Mrs Justice Arden, later to become Lady Justice Arden. Unless you know the gender of these judges, you can easily make an embarrassing mistake and refer to them incorrectly as Mr Justice or Lord Justice. To avoid making such an embarrassing faux pas, you should look up any judge where you are unsure of their gender.

Do not express your own thoughts, beliefs or opinions

When you address the Bench, you make submissions. You should never express your thoughts, beliefs or opinions. Therefore, you should never say 'I think . . .' or 'I believe . . .' or 'in my opinion . . .'. The correct form of words to use is 'I submit . . .' or 'in my submission . . .' or 'it is submitted that . . .'.

Express your gratitude for any judicial observations or guidance

It is likely that during the course of your submissions the judge will make some observations or provide some kind of guidance to you – for example, by informing you that he has read the particular authority and doesn't need to be reminded of its facts or that he doesn't require you to address him on a particular point. Whether or not you welcome such guidance, you should respond along the following lines:

- 'My Lord/Lady, I am grateful/obliged.'
- 'My Lord/Lady, I am grateful/obliged for that indication.'

There is no need to over-egg your gratitude and you should avoid appearing to be too gushing or sycophantic with your thanks!

Remain respectful even if you disagree with the judge

The judge might say something with which you fundamentally disagree or otherwise take issue. It hardly needs saying that you must never argue with the judge or tell him he is wrong. You should remember that the judge might only be testing your submissions or your ability to challenge his views appropriately.

You might consider starting your response with 'with respect . . .', but you should avoid 'with the greatest of respect . . .' as this often comes across as though you are annoyed or frustrated with the judge and, despite the words uttered, actually have no respect for the judge whatsoever.

Citing authorities

It is important to cite cases properly to the court.

Case names

Case names should be cited in full. The following protocol should be used:

- The 'v' in between the parties' names is cited orally as 'and'. '*Donoghue v Stephenson*' is therefore read out as '*Donoghue and Stephenson*'.
- Where there is more than one party either side of the 'v', you should use 'against' rather than say another 'and'. Thus, '*Smith v Jones & Peters*' is more eloquently cited orally as '*Smith against Jones and Peters*' rather than '*Smith and Jones and Peters*'.
- The 'R' in a criminal case is cited orally as 'the Crown'. If referring to a case from the Privy Council, the 'R' becomes 'the Queen' or 'the King', depending on whether the Queen or the King was the Sovereign when the case was decided.

Citations

Case citations need reading out in full without using their abbreviations. Thus, [1966] 1 WLR 1234 is read out as: 'reported in the first volume of the 1966 Weekly Law Reports at page 1234'; or 'reported in the first volume of the Weekly Law Reports for 1966 at page 1234'.

You only need to provide the full case name and citation the first time the case is mentioned. Subsequent mentions of the same case only need referring to by their short name and without the citation. For example, subsequent mentions of *Caparo Industries Plc and Dickman & Others* [1990] 2 AC 605 can be abbreviated to '*Caparo*' or 'the *Caparo* case'. If you are the respondent and the case has already been cited by the appellant, then you can shorten it to '*Caparo Industries*, as cited by my learned friends opposite'.

> **Mooting tip**
> When directing the judge to a specific passage in a case you should do so as follows:
>
> > May I refer your Lordship to *Caparo Industries Plc and Dickman & Others* reported in the second volume of the Appeal Cases reports for 1990 at page 605 which your Lordship will find behind Tab 3 of the Appellant's bundle at page 200. I would like to direct your Lordship to the speech of Lord Bridge at page 616 of the judgment . . .

Where the judgment has marginal letters or other marginal identification, you should refer to these.

As already noted, you do not need to keep rigidly to these words.

Alternatively, you could give the tab number before providing the case reference. This has the time-saving advantage of enabling the Bench to turn to the case while you are giving its citation.

When (and how) to provide the facts of cases

There are two situations in which you might need to provide the facts of cases. These relate to the facts of the moot problem itself and the facts of cases cited in support of your arguments.

The facts of the moot problem

The lead appellant opens the appeal and provides an outline of the case. He or she should ask the judge whether it would be helpful to provide a brief summary of the facts of the case and the issues of the appeal. If the judge answers this in the affirmative, then the lead appellant should do so as briefly as possible. There is no need to read the moot problem word for word as this will eat into your valuable time; instead, you should provide a brief summary of the main facts and the grounds of appeal.

> **Mooting tip**
>
> When summarising the main facts of the case, it would be helpful to emphasise those that are especially important. You can do this by pausing briefly at these points to give them particular emphasis. Remember, though, that your task in summarising the main facts of the case is to assist the court and you should not, therefore, selectively emphasise only those facts that support your own submissions.

The facts of cases cited in support of your arguments

The factual background of a case often provides the context to the legal principles involved. The reason why the facts are often important is that the legal principles might not sit too easily (or at all) in cases with materially different factual backgrounds.

Therefore, once you have cited an authority to the judge, you should enquire whether he would like you to summarise the facts. This should be done before you deal with the legal issues that you intend to deal with. You can do this in a number of ways, such as:

- Would it assist your Lordship to be reminded of the facts of the case?
- Would your Lordship like a brief summary of the facts of the case?

> **Mooting tip**
>
> Although the exact form of words is unimportant, you should not ask whether the judge is familiar with the case. This is because some judges might consider such a question to be impertinent, and, in any event, their reply might not be particularly helpful. For example, the judge might be 'familiar' with the case but would still appreciate a brief summary of the facts and decision. Conversely, the judge might not be familiar with the case, but, for any number of reasons, might not want a summary from you.

You should be prepared to provide a case summary in respect of every case that will be presented to the court, whether by your own team, your opponent or any of the court authorities. If the judge requires a summary of any of the cases, then you must provide it succinctly – not least because the time spent summarising the case will eat into your allocated time.

You should familiarise yourself with the following information about the cases:

- The facts of the case.
- The legal principles involved.
- The status of the court which made the decision.
- Whether the decision was unanimous or by a majority. If it was by a majority, who dissented and why? What was the view of the minority?
- Has the case been considered since and, if so, with what result? Has it, for example, been followed?

You will see from the above that the first bullet point refers to the facts of the case. Although it will be a matter for the judge to decide, you may have taken the view that the facts are not remotely relevant to the moot problem and have no bearing on the issues. Even so, you will still need to know the facts as the judge might ask you about them. Two situations might arise:

(a) Where the facts are relevant

The facts will be relevant where you intend to draw factual parallels between the case you are citing and the facts in the moot. In this situation, you will be referring to these factual similarities so as to persuade the court to reach the same conclusions as the court did in the case you have cited. Conversely, you may seek to persuade the court to distinguish the facts of a case and not follow it.

(b) Where the facts are not relevant

It may be that the facts of a case are not remotely relevant to the moot problem and that it is the legal principle alone that is important. We have already discussed this on page 69 in relation to *Donoghue v Stevenson*.[2] By way of further example, if you are dealing with a criminal law moot where the issue is one of dishonesty, you will almost certainly wish to refer to the decision in *R v Ghosh*,[3] where the Court of Appeal (Criminal Division) laid down the correct test to be applied when considering the meaning of dishonesty.[4] The specific facts in *Ghosh* will probably be of no interest.

However, just because the facts of a case are wildly different to the points raised in the moot problem, it does not mean that you should not refer to them. For

---

2 [1932] AC 562
3 [1982] QB 1053
4 *R v Ghosh* outlined a two-part test in determining dishonesty. First, whether according to the ordinary standards of reasonable and honest people what was done was dishonest. If it was dishonest by those standards then, second, whether the defendant knew what he was doing was, by those standards, dishonest.

example, as we have seen from *Donoghue v Stevenson*[5] and *R v Ghosh*,[6] the legal principles have been applied to cases with different factual backgrounds. Conversely, you may wish to refer to the facts of a case solely to illustrate that they are so dissimilar to the instant appeal that the court should distinguish that case and not follow it.

Mooting tip

A situation might arise where the facts of a case are hugely significant and you don't want to risk the judge declining your offer to be reminded of the facts. In such a case, instead of asking the judge whether he would benefit from a brief reminder of the facts, you could instead explain that they are extremely important to the appeal and then provide them. You can do this in a number of ways, such as:

- 'My Lord, the facts of the case are hugely significant and can be stated shortly . . . [provide brief summary]';
- or more simply: 'My Lord, this case concerned . . .'

As already noted, whenever you provide any information to the judge about a case, you must do so honestly and without attempting to omit or alter anything that might appear unhelpful to your own case.

Referring to the legal principles

Once you have introduced a case and dealt with the facts as outlined above, you are then ready to deal with the legal principles involved. This will usually involve referring to a passage or passages from one or more of the judgments handed down in that case.

Mooting tip

In the vast majority of cases, you will be expected to (and will wish to) refer to a passage or passages from one or more of the judgments handed down in the case that you are citing as giving authority to your proposition. There may be the rare occasion where you do not intend to refer to a particular passage from a case, but instead simply refer to the case itself and,

---

5 [1932] AC 562
6 [1982] QB 1053

presumably, the legal principle laid down therein. In such a situation, you should inform the judge immediately you refer to the case that you do not intend to cite a passage from it. You should have ready a good reason for not wishing to follow the conventional approach in referring to a part of the judgment as it is more than possible that you will be asked to justify your decision.

Quoting passages from a case

As noted above, you will almost certainly need to take the judge to a particular passage of a judgment or other material that you seek to rely on. After citing the material correctly, you should then signpost the text to which you intend to refer. You can do this by saying:

> May I refer your Lordship to the speech of Lord Hoffmann at page [x] of the judgment where at paragraph [y] his Lordship explained that . . .

Once you have referred the judge to the particular passage you want to deal with, you must then wait until he has found it. The judge will usually indicate that he has found the passage by looking up or otherwise confirming that he has the particular passage in front of him. If you are unsure whether or not the judge has the correct passage in front of him, you could ask: 'Does your Lordship have sight?'

Once you have finished quoting from the passage, you should pause briefly before proceeding with your submissions. The judge may well ask you to explain how the passage to which you have just referred relates to the moot problem and in particular to the issues he has to decide. It is good practice, therefore, to anticipate that such a question will be asked and have prepared a good answer to it.

Mooting tip
You will recall that the headnote does not form part of the *ratio decidendi* of the case and you should not, therefore, quote from it as representing the court's judgment. Even though some reports are approved by the judges, you are expected to quote from what the judge actually said in the case rather than from what the law reporter has reported him as having said. Some reports include a summary of the submissions made by counsel; these, too, should not be cited in support of your proposition.

Avoid lengthy quotations and too many quotations

Given the very short amount of time you are given to make your submissions, it is important to make every minute count. You must resist the temptation of overburdening the court with quotations that are not absolutely necessary to establish your point. Doing so will lose focus and impact.

Avoid taking quotations out of context

The context of a case may well determine its utility as an authority in subsequent cases, and for this reason it is important not to take any part of a decision out of context.

Appreciate the weight a court is likely to give to each authority

Some authorities carry greater weight than others. In general terms, the greater the weight that can be attached to your authority, the more likely it is that the court will follow it. In Chapter 2, we discussed the doctrine of precedent and the hierarchy of the courts, and readers should remind themselves of these principles and of how they operate. The following additional points should be noted:

- A case that has been repeatedly followed is more likely to be followed than one that has received less judicial support.
- A case that was decided by a judge who was subsequently elevated to high judicial office may have greater following than one decided by a judge of equal standing who was not subsequently elevated.

Judicial comments

You need to be attentive to how your submissions are being received and to any comments made by the judge, and moderate your submissions or approach accordingly. Judicial comments can be just about anything, which makes it rather difficult to predict or to provide specific advice. You should review the guidance provided in the following table which contains the more common comments made by judges and the appropriate responses to them. This should enable you to appreciate the kind of comments you might encounter and how best to deal with them.

Judge	Mooter	Comments
'You can take it that I have read the papers and am familiar with the facts of the various cases noted in your skeleton arguments'	After citing a case, go straight to the point you want the court to consider and do not offer the facts.[a]	If you still offer the facts of the cases, it shows that you either haven't listened to what the judge has said or (more likely) lack flexibility probably because you are tied to your script.

Judge	Mooter	Comments
'I would find it helpful if you would address me on your second submission first'	Do it!	There is little excuse not to do as the judge asks and doing so will demonstrate your flexibility and good court manner. It will also demonstrate that you are not tied to a script.
'You are pushing on an open door with that submission and there is no need to address me further on it'	Respond with 'I am obliged, my Lord . . .' and move to your next point.	Again, there is little excuse not to do as the judge asks and doing so will demonstrate your flexibility and good court manner. It will also demonstrate that you are not tied to a script.
'I hear what you say but I just cannot accept that submission'	If you are confident that your submission is a good one but either you have not put it across sufficiently well or that the judge might have misunderstood it, you might respond with 'My Lord, I am obliged. In my respectful submission the point is a good one and I wonder whether I might have expressed it rather badly. If I may put the submission slightly differently . . .'.[b] If, on the other hand, you accept that the submission is a bad one or, for whatever reason, you cannot improve on it, you could respond with 'My Lord, [that is my submission on this point];[c] I will now move on to my next point'.	The context is all important here. You should ask yourself why you feel that the judge cannot accept your submission. You will need to form your own assessment as to the best approach to take which is likely to be influenced by the judge's body language and the context of the exchange. If in doubt, it might be sensible to err on the side of caution and move on.

a Subject to the specific advice given at pages 184–186.

b This is, of course, a rather brave response to make and should only be made if you remain convinced that either you have not put the point across sufficiently well or that the judge has misunderstood it. However, if you do respond this way and you get the impression that the judge remains strongly against you, it might be better to move on to your next point. In such a situation, you can do this by saying 'My Lord, I am grateful and will move on to my next point'.

c Depending on the circumstances, you may wish to omit the words in square brackets.

Mooting tip
Whenever a judge makes a good point during an intervention with either team, especially one that had not been raised by either team in argument,

consider if there is a way of making reference to it in your own submissions. However, you must avoid appearing oleaginous or obsequious in doing so. A good way of integrating a judge's point into your own submissions is 'As your Lordship has already noted . . .'. Judges (in common with most people) tend to be rather receptive to points they have themselves made.

Dealing with judicial interventions

Dealing with judicial interventions is seen by many mooters as being the most daunting part of the moot. This is because you will not know until the moot starts how the judge will deal with your submissions, how many questions he will ask or how difficult the questions might be. The only thing you can be reasonably certain about is that the judge will interrupt your submissions to ask questions. The judge might ask questions for one of two main reasons: first, because he needs to clarify the point you are making and, second, because he wishes to test your understanding of the issues and how you are able to respond. The judge is also likely to want to test how well you are able to depart from what you had prepared and how well you are able to recover the flow of your arguments once you have dealt with the questions.

Dealing with judicial interventions is one of the most important parts of any moot and is often the single most important factor that distinguishes the quality of the mooters and thus the determination of the winner.

Although moot judges differ in style, with some more interventionist than others, you should expect your oral submissions to be punctuated by a number of interventions of varying length and complexity.

Some mooters dread the prospect of having to deal with judicial interventions, although it is important to bear in mind that without them the activity would no longer be a moot but merely a monologue whereby you set out your case without challenge or interruption. Rather than dread the idea of having to deal with judicial interventions, you should relish the opportunity to engage with the judge and demonstrate your knowledge of the issues and ability to express them in a logical and coherent manner. Judicial interventions also test your ability to think on your feet and enable the judge to assess your skills as an advocate.

Mooting tip

Just because the judge interrupts your submissions, it does not mean that they are wrong; judicial interventions are simply part and parcel of mooting. During the practice stage of your preparations, it is important to enlist the help of your tutors and fellow students who should act as judges and test your submissions in the same way the judge is likely to do so. This will give you invaluable experience of answering questions and should help avoid any awkward silences on the day during interventions from the Bench.

The next section will explain:

- What constitutes a judicial intervention?
- Anticipating questions from the Bench
- Answering questions
- Questions you are unable to answer
- Sample questions with suggested responses.

What constitutes a judicial intervention?

A judicial intervention is a question, proposition or statement put to you by the judge during your submissions. You should expect a number of judicial interventions during the course of your submissions and possibly immediately after you have finished, before you sit down.

Anticipating questions from the Bench

Although there is no easy way of guessing what the judge will ask you, the questions are likely to fall into one of two broad categories:

1. questions relating to any weaknesses in your case
2. questions relating to the differences between your opponent's submissions and your own.

During your research, you will have given thought to how well your submissions will stand up to judicial scrutiny. This will have involved testing your submissions against a range of hypothetical objections. These are likely to be some of the questions that will also be on a judge's mind and could well result in questions during your moot.

Another way of anticipating judicial questions is to put yourself in the position of a judge and consider what questions you would ask.

By anticipating potential questions, you will be able to give thought to how you would answer them. Thinking about these questions is also an excellent way of preparing for your moot.

By remaining alert to the judge's body language, you may be able to anticipate that he is about to intervene with a question. Signs to look out for include direct eye contact, an intake of breath and hand movements. This is yet another reason why reading from a script is poor practice; having your head down in the papers is likely to result in you missing these cues. That said, some judges adopt a more direct and abrasive manner and give no indication that a question is looming. Either way, it is important to adhere to appropriate court etiquette which is that as soon as a judge speaks, you stop speaking, even if you are in mid-sentence. Competing with the judge to be heard has no place in a court setting.

Answering questions

Your ability to answer questions well will depend on a number of factors. These can be summarised as follows:

(a) Listen carefully to the questions

Before even considering your response, you must listen very carefully to the questions that you are being asked to deal with. You cannot possibly answer a question properly if you have failed to listen adequately to it, or if you try to anticipate what you are being asked by starting to answer the question before the judge has finished asking it. Not only is it poor court etiquette to interrupt the judge when he is talking, but doing so might also mean that you miss something that he says, which itself might be useful to you in answering the question.

(b) Clarify what you are being asked if you are not sure

Hopefully, you will understand what the judge has asked and you will not need to ask him to clarify or repeat it. If this is not the case, then you must ask for clarification. There is absolutely no point in trying to answer a question that you have not properly understood. There are several ways of asking for clarification, although it is important to stress that seeking *any* clarification should be an exceptional response. For example, you might say:

- 'I'm afraid that I didn't quite follow your Lordship's question', or
- 'I would be grateful if your Lordship would rephrase the question.'

(c) Think about your response before answering

Although you should answer the questions reasonably quickly, you should give yourself time to reflect and to consider how best to present your response in a convincing and coherent manner. This should only take a matter of seconds and is far better than panicking in the rush to speak immediately and risk giving a poor or incoherent response to the judge's questions.

(d) Answer the question

It ought to go without saying that when a judge asks you a question, you should answer it. Whatever you do, do not go into 'politician' mode and attempt to avoid answering the question or provide an answer to a question that you would have preferred to have been asked.

You should address the points raised as naturally as possible and, whatever you do, do not ramble! Deal with the questions as concisely as possible and then move on. Depending on the circumstances, it might be appropriate to ask the judge whether your response has addressed his concerns and whether you may now proceed with your submissions.

Mooting tip

Some mooters, especially those who are nervous, tend to waffle and give an overly lengthy response to a judge's question. To avoid doing this, you should always seek to answer a question as directly and succinctly as possible.

(e) Answer the question – now

You should answer any question put to you straight away and not tell the judge that you will deal with it in due course or when it is convenient for you. Far too many mooters answer a question from the Bench with 'I will deal with your Lordship's question later in my submissions'.

Simply telling the judge that you had intended to address the point later in your submissions is a weak and evasive response which might give the impression that you are too tied to your script to deal with it now. A weak mooter will fight hard to stay with their script, fearing that they might get lost if they depart from their structured plan.

Conversely, the judge will be impressed that you have been able to deal with the question straight away. This demonstrates not only your ability to think on your feet but also that you possess the flexibility of not being tied to a script and have a degree of mastery over the moot problem and the legal issues involved.

If you had intended to deal with the point raised by the judge later on in your submissions and cannot answer it now, then the best way of responding is: 'My Lord, I intend to address this point in some detail later in my submissions but, in short, the answer is . . .'. Of course, the best response would be, provided it makes sense to your overall submissions, to bring forward the submission you had intended to deal with later so as to answer the judge's question straight after he asks it. Once again, this demonstrates that you are not tied to your script and have an impressive command of the subject.

If, on the other hand, you still believe that there are good reasons for dealing with the question later in your submissions, then you should seek the judge's permission to do so and provide a very good reason for not dealing with it now. Having said this, it is hard to imagine what a good reason would be.

A better way of trying to postpone the answer until later on in your submissions might take the following approach: 'My Lord, this was a point I was intending to deal with later in my submissions but, if your Lordship prefers, I could deal with it briefly now.' You must then proceed in accordance with the judge's preference.

Mooting tip

If you do answer the judge's question earlier than you had intended, you must not repeat the same points at a later stage when you had originally planned to deal with them.

Questions you are unable to answer

No matter how much preparation you have done, you may still be faced with a question that you simply cannot answer or, worse still, cannot even understand. The first thing to do in such a situation is to keep calm and not panic. If you ever face this kind of situation, you must still provide a response as best you can. You should avoid attempting to 'blag' your way out of the situation or just talk for the sake of saying something as the judge is likely to smell 'waffle' from the far side of the courtroom. The embarrassment of owning up to not knowing the answer to the judge's question is likely to end far sooner than the prolonged agony associated with an enduring period of waffle.

Before giving up on a question that you are struggling to answer, you should consider the following strategies.

Consult with your teammate

This is just one example where good team work really comes to the forefront. When you are on your feet, your teammate should be paying close attention to the proceedings and ought to notice, or anticipate, that you are in, or might get into, difficulties. A simple glance towards your teammate should be enough to indicate whether they are likely to be able to assist.

However, a note of caution is needed here. You should not treat consulting with your teammate as anything other than wholly exceptional. On the other hand, when used appropriately, it can demonstrate good teamwork, provided it produces an answer to the question you have been asked to deal with.

Consult your notes or the authorities

Consulting your notes or the authorities will certainly give you valuable seconds in which to compose yourself and may also assist you in providing the answer to the judge's question. Once again, this should be seen as an exceptional response to a judge's question. That said, provided you are able to find the answer quickly, and the answer satisfies the judge's question, this approach could demonstrate how well you know your materials and/or your way around your bundle. If you think that consulting your papers might assist you, you should say to the judge: 'My Lord, may I please have a brief moment.'

Leave it to your teammate to answer the question

This option might be appropriate in cases where the judge asks you a question which is more suited to your teammate's submissions. You could respond with: 'My Lord, my learned friend will be dealing with this point in some detail in his submissions and it might be more appropriate for him to answer the question then.' Provided the judge is agreeable to this, it will give your teammate a short while in which to perfect his response. Better still, you should try to deal with the question yourself briefly, and explain to the judge that your teammate will be dealing with the point more substantially in his own submissions.

This approach cannot, of course, be used where you are the second speaker, simply because there is no one in your team speaking after you. In such a case, you will need to respond yourself using one of the approaches discussed in this section.

> **Mooting tip**
> It is important to re-emphasise that in any of these situations you should first seek the judge's permission. The appropriate way of doing this is to ask: 'My Lord, might I have a brief moment to consult with [my learned friend]/ [my notes]/[the authorities]?' Not only is this the appropriate thing to do, but it will also give you valuable seconds in which to gather your thoughts. Equally importantly, some judges will appreciate the difficulty you are in and either rephrase the question, ask a different one or, alternatively, invite you to move on with the remainder of your submissions.

If all else fails

If having done the above and you still cannot deal with the judge's question, then you should say so and move on as quickly as possible. You could do this in one of the following ways:

- 'My Lord, I regret that I am unable to assist with your Lordship's questions; might I return to my submissions?'
- 'My Lord, that is my submission and I am unable to take the point any further. If your Lordship pleases, I will now return to my submissions.'

Unless the judge feels that he can guide you towards a reasonable response, he is likely to allow you to move on as you have requested.

Do not ask the judge a question of your own

As tempting as it might appear to respond to a judicial question with one of your own, you must avoid doing so, no matter how impressive you feel your question is. Questions are very much a one-way street that is firmly closed to any coming from a mooter. Exceptions to the above include:

- asking the judge to clarify the question he has asked you
- asking the judge whether he requires a brief summary of the facts of a case
- asking the judge for permission to continue with your submissions
- asking the judge whether he has sight of the passage to which you wish to refer
- at the end of your submissions, asking the judge whether he has any further questions for you.

Sample questions with suggested responses

For current purposes, an analysis of judges' questions over the years tells us that they fall into one of three broad categories:

- **Type A: Clarification questions.** These questions are usually quite benign and simply seek clarification or further information about your submission. You should not look too deeply into straightforward questions or assume that every intervention has hostile intent. On the contrary, most don't.
- **Type B: Helpful questions.** These questions are usually the easiest to deal with. They are often asked in cases where a mooter gets into difficulties during their submissions and are intended to act as a kind of crutch to help them out. As with Type A questions, you should not look too deeply into these kinds of straightforward questions or assume that every intervention has hostile intent.
- **Type C: Disruptive questions.** These types of questions tend to focus on the weaknesses in your arguments as well as putting 'devil's advocate' questions to you about your opponent's arguments.

> **Mooting tip**
> You should not assume that just because a judge interrupts your submissions to ask a question it means that he believes there is something wrong with your argument. Judicial interventions are the norm in mooting and they are, in the main, intended to test your ability to think on your feet and respond appropriately in a persuasive manner.

We will now consider the three categories of questions outlined above.

Question type	Judge	Comment
A	*'I didn't quite hear your last point'*	This is an example of a perfectly benign question without any hidden trap. If you are asked to repeat something, just repeat it. Consider whether you need to speak more loudly to avoid having to repeat yourself again.
A	*'Am I bound by that authority?'*	This is a straightforward question that can be answered with little difficulty provided that you are familiar with the doctrine of precedent and how it applies to the authority in question.[a] Answer this kind of question as briefly as possible without elaboration unless needed.

Question type	Judge	Comment
A	*'What is the legal proposition that you say derives from this authority?'*	If you have followed the PASA method,[b] you will already have explained the legal proposition in stage one of your submission. This question tends to arise either if you have not explained the proposition or if you have done so but with insufficient clarity. In any event, you ought to be sufficiently familiar with your submissions to be able to answer this kind of question without any difficulty.
A	*'Am I right in understanding that your submission is . . . ?'*	A judge will typically ask this kind of question if he is struggling to follow your line of argument. In posing this kind of question, the judge will often reformulate your argument and seek your agreement to that reformulation. You should think carefully before answering this kind of question and not simply agree with the reformulated argument unless you are content with it. If the judge has not reformulated the argument correctly, then you must say so, politely. Simply agreeing with it because it has come from the judge is likely to create problems for you by taking you down a path that you never intended to travel.
A	*'You have cited a case that is now quite old. Has it been considered in a more recent case?'*	This is a rather basic question enquiring whether or not the case you have referred to has more recently been judicially considered. There is no hidden depth in this question; all the judge wants to know is whether or not the case and, in particular, the passage from the case upon which you seek to rely, remains good law. This question should not present a problem for you provided your legal research was sufficiently thorough.[c]
A or B	*'If I understand your submission properly, you are arguing that . . .'*	As noted above, this type of question often arises in cases where a mooter gets into difficulties during their submissions and is intended to act as a kind of 'crutch' to help them out. You should not look too deeply into straightforward questions of this kind or assume that every intervention has hostile intent.
C	*'Your opponent places a different interpretation on the authority. Why should I prefer your interpretation to theirs?'*	This type of question should not be too difficult to answer because you ought to have been aware, from your opponent's skeleton argument, of the way they were intending to interpret the authority and already considered why your interpretation was more appropriate. You simply need to explain why your interpretation of the case is correct and how your opponent has misinterpreted it.

Question type	Judge	Comment
C	*'Your opponent relies on a different authority in support of the point. Why should I prefer yours over theirs?'*	This is a very similar question to the one noted above and the same approach should be adopted. In addition, it is often the case that the authorities upon which each of you seek to rely appear to contradict the other. In such a case, it is perfectly normal for the judge to ask why your authority should be preferred over that of your opponent. Depending on the specific circumstances of the moot problem, there may be several possible responses to this, including seeking to persuade the judge that your opponent's authority should be distinguished from the facts of the moot problem. If this is your response, you should be able to explain where the cases differ and why this is sufficient for the judge to refuse to follow it.
C	*'Your opponent urges me to ... Isn't there some force in that argument?'*	Again, this is a very similar question to the ones noted above and the same approach should be adopted.
C	*'If I accept your submission, will that not lead to the following problem ... ?'*	This type of question can be quite tricky to answer because the judge may be attempting to extend your reasoning to a different set of circumstances, which are often less helpful to your argument. The judge is looking for two main things in your response: first, that you can think quickly on your feet; and, second, that you are sufficiently familiar with the material that you are able to provide a logical response that not only answers the question but also does not cause damage to your own submissions. The key to dealing well with this kind of question is to ensure that during the preparation stages of the moot you have thought through your arguments thoroughly, looking for any weaknesses and identifying appropriate solutions to any that you find.

a The doctrine of precedent is discussed in Chapter 2, page 32.
b Discussed in Chapter 6, page 151.
c See, also, the guidance provided at page 54 on the use of older cases.

8 Participating in the moot

Introduction

We are now at the stage where you are ready to participate in the moot. This chapter explains what you should expect when you arrive at the moot venue; a reminder of the running order of the moot; questions of etiquette such as dress code and appropriate conduct during the moot; a reminder about modes of judicial address; timekeeping issues during the moot; and a range of other matters relating to last-minute nerves and problems. The chapter concludes with advice on speed writing and shortcuts that should prove helpful to you during the moot.

Layout of a moot court

A properly designed moot court will be set out in a similar way to a real courtroom with the Bench at one end and the advocates' tables directly facing it. Some moots will take place in a real courtroom. Wherever the moot takes place, it will be helpful to arrive in sufficient time to be able to familiarise yourself with it. The picture below shows the layout of a moot room in England and Wales.

The Moot Room in the Redmonds Building at
Liverpool John Moores University

Scottish moot courtrooms are laid out differently to those in England and Wales to reflect the different layout of Scottish courtrooms.

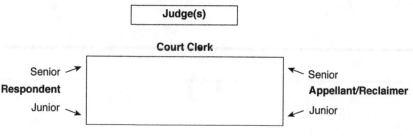

Typical layout of a Scottish moot courtroom

The running order of the moot

You should familiarise yourself with the running order of the moot. This was set out in Chapter 7 at pages 172–173.

Etiquette

By now it should come as no surprise that you must follow strict rules of mooting etiquette; these are almost identical to the rules of etiquette that practitioners must follow when appearing in court. For present purposes, there are several factors to consider.

Dress code

Smart, sober dress is essential when mooting. Black, navy blue or dark grey are the safest colours to wear. Women should wear a smart trouser suit or jacket and skirt of at least knee length. Men should wear a formal business suit, either with or without waistcoat. Shirts for both women and men should be formal and either white or a light neutral colour. Men should wear a sensible business-style tie. Striped shirts are fine, but avoid shirts with heavy patterns. Shoes should always be formal and smart. Dressing smartly will not only enhance the authenticity of the moot but will also present you in a professional manner and help improve your confidence. Where personal circumstances do not allow this, you should dress as smartly as you can and follow the above guidance as closely as possible.

Some moots require mooters to wear gowns, although this is not as common as it once was. When a gown is required, your (or a neighbouring) university or local practitioner might be able to assist with the loan of gowns.

Although it is unlikely that moot judges will mark you down specifically if your dress fails to conform to the appropriate standards (and dress code does not feature as a specific item on many mooting score sheets), an overall good impression might just tip the balance in a closely contested moot. As noted above, the strict rules of mooting etiquette are almost identical to the rules of etiquette that practitioners must obey when appearing in court. Not only will this demonstrate an advocate's respect for the court, but it will also create a positive impression on the judge by dressing as a legal professional would dress when appearing in court.

Make sure that you maintain the smartness of your dress throughout the moot, even after you have taken your seat having finished making your own submissions. Do not, therefore, loosen your tie or remove your jacket when you return to your seat. The same smart standard of dress should be maintained when returning to the moot room for the judge's decision.

The lack of an appropriate standard of dress can bring about unfortunate exchanges with the Bench, something which you would be well advised to avoid. In an often-quoted exchange which started when Counsel rose to make a challenge while the jury was being sworn in:

Croom-Johnson J:	I cannot see you, Mr Fearnley-Whittingstall.
Mr Fearnley-Whittingstall:	My Lord, I am before you, wigged and gowned.
Croom-Johnson J:	I still cannot see you, Mr Fearnley-Whittingstall.
Mr Fearnley-Whittingstall:	My Lord, is it my yellow waistcoat that you cannot see?
Croom-Johnson J:	Yes, it is.
Mr Fearnley-Whittingstall:	Well, my Lord, you can see me.
Croom-Johnson J:	Oh, very well, let's get on with the case.

In a more recent exchange in the Crown Court at Cardiff on 28 August 2014, His Honour Judge Morgan rightly objected to one of the advocates wearing ribbons and other memorabilia on his gown. The judge warned him:

If you ever appear before this court again dressed as you are at the moment, I shall exercise my right to decline to hear you. I did not raise any of these matters before this case started, although I wanted to, because I am mindful of the fact that a young man has died and I did not want to interfere with the dignity of the proceedings, but if you want to come into court looking like something out of Harry Potter, you can forget coming into this court ever again. Do I make myself clear?[1]

Appropriate conduct

It should go without saying that you must conduct yourself at all times with due respect for the moot court and the judge. In particular, you should note the following protocols, which again reflect the conduct expected of advocates in court:

- **Never interrupt the judge.** It should go without saying that you must never interrupt the judge. When the judge speaks, you don't – even if he interrupts

---

1 *R v Wojcicki*, Crown Court at Cardiff, 28 August 2014

you. Do not be tempted to start responding to the judge's intervention before he has finished asking the question. Not only can this be seen as rude, but you will run the risk of misunderstanding or misinterpreting his question.

- **Never interrupt your opponent.** Similarly, you must never interrupt your opponent when they are addressing the judge. If the judge wants you to speak out of turn, he will say so. This rule of etiquette includes refraining from engaging in acts of theatrics such as tutting, grunting or taking sharp intakes of breath when you disagree passionately with a point that your opponent are making.

- **Ensure mobile phones and other equipment are turned off.** It can be almost guaranteed to turn the judge incandescent with rage if your phone or other device rings or makes a noise during the moot. Double-check that all such equipment is turned off and not switched on again until you leave the moot room.

- **Do not leave your seat during the moot.** Unless you are addressing the judge, you should remain in your seat for the duration of the moot. If you need to leave the room in an absolute emergency, you should stand and explain briefly to the judge what the emergency is and seek his permission to leave the room.

- **Be careful with humour and wit.** You will only have a limited time to make your submissions, so do not waste time trying to entertain the court. Whatever you do, you must never direct your humour or wit at the judge. This ought to go without saying but the famous barrister and politician, F. E. Smith,[2] often entertained the court and doubtless generations that followed:

Judge:	I have read your case, Mr Smith, and I am no wiser now than I was when I started.
F. E. Smith:	Possibly not, My Lord, but far better informed.
Judge:	Are you trying to show contempt for this court, Mr Smith?
F. E. Smith:	No, My Lord. I am attempting to conceal it.
Judge:	Mr Smith, have you ever heard of a saying by Bacon – the great Bacon – that youth and discretion are ill-wedded companions?
F. E. Smith:	Yes, I have. And have you ever heard of a saying of Bacon – the great Bacon – that a much-talking judge is like an ill-tuned cymbal?
Judge:	You are extremely offensive, young man.
F. E. Smith:	As a matter of fact, we both are; but I am trying to be, and you can't help it.

2 1872–1930. Later to become Lord Birkenhead, Lord Chancellor.

| Judge: | What do you suppose I am on the Bench for, Mr. Smith? |
| F. E. Smith: | It is not for me . . . to attempt to fathom the inscrutable workings of Providence. |

Standing up and sitting down

When the judge enters or leaves the moot room, everyone (including the mooters), should stand. Where there is a court clerk, the clerk will announce the judge's entrance with an instruction 'Court rise'. Similarly, the clerk will give the 'Court rise' instruction when the judge is ready to leave the moot court – for example, to consider his decision – and again when he returns to the room. Before taking your seat, you should give a small bow of your head towards the judge.

If the judge is already seated at the Bench when you enter the moot room, you should walk to your place and stand. You should then give a small bow of your head and wait for the judge to invite you to take your seat.

You must stand whenever you are addressing the judge. You should only resume your seat when you have finished making your submissions and the judge indicates that no further assistance is required from you. This is likely to be when the judge says 'thank you' at the end of your submissions or otherwise indicates that you may sit down.

Although unlikely, the judge might pose a question to a mooter who is not at that time addressing him. In such a case, the mooter who is addressing the judge at that time should sit down and the mooter who is being addressed by the judge should stand. The original mooter only stands again once the exchange with the other mooter has concluded and he returns to his seat.

Finally, never interrupt your opponent (whether standing or seated!) when they are addressing the judge or, unless invited by the judge to do so, attempt to address him when it is not your turn to speak.

Mooting tip

If there is something pressing that you need to say – for example, in response to a point made by one of your opponent with which you strongly disagree – you should make a note of it and deal with it when your turn to speak arrives. Shouts of 'Objection!' have no place in our courts or in our moots.

Modes of address

It is very important that you use the correct form of address during the moot. This was discussed in Chapter 7 on pages 177–180.

Timekeeping issues during the moot

You need to know how long you have got to make your submissions and whether the clock stops for judicial interventions. Both of these points will be set out in the rules of the moot, and it is important that you familiarise yourself with them.

(a) Where the clock stops for judicial interventions

Where the clock stops for judicial interventions, you will have available to you the entire time allocated to your role. You should pace yourself to ensure that you are able to complete your submissions without running out of time.

(b) Where the clock does not stop for judicial interventions

Where the clock does not stop for judicial interventions, you will have to moderate your submissions to take account of the time that you will spend addressing the judge's interventions. Flexibility is the key. This might mean moving more quickly through some of your submissions or even leaving some out altogether. This is where a thorough knowledge of your case takes on a particular importance because it will assist you in deciding which submissions are less important to your case and can either be speeded up or omitted altogether.

Whatever you do, you should avoid running out of time as this runs the risk of being told to stop. Some judges are more tolerant to a mooter running over their allotted time, especially if they have taken up a lot of the mooter's time with their questions. Unfortunately, unless you are following other mooters, it is unlikely that you will know how the judge will manage the moot until your time has expired, which is then too late to alter your submissions to ensure your key points are dealt with.

> **Mooting tip**
> One helpful tip is to rank your submissions in terms of their overall importance to your case. This will make it easier for you to decide which parts of your submissions can be speeded up or omitted altogether in the event of you running short of time.

Although there will be a formal timekeeper to keep the time and notify the judge when the allotted time has expired, you should also make sure that you are aware of the time as you are speaking and moderate your submissions accordingly. You should consider placing your wristwatch or similar timing device on the desk in front of you or asking your partner to notify you when you are approaching particular stages in your submissions.

If you find yourself running out of time with important submissions still to be made, you should consider informing the judge of this fact; for example:

My Lord, I'm mindful that time is running against me and it might be helpful if I could use the time remaining to summarise my submissions.

Where the timekeeper has indicted that your time has expired, you could ask for the judge's indulgence to complete the point you are making:

My Lord, I note that my time has now expired. I would be obliged if I could quickly conclude the point I was making.

If the judge accedes to your request for a little additional time, make sure that you bring your point to an end as quickly as possible. Do not ramble on and run the risk of having the judge tell you to sit down.

Forgetting what to say or becoming 'tongue-tied'

By the time you get to your feet to argue your case, you will have spent a consider-able amount of time researching, preparing and practising your submissions. You should be extremely familiar with your material, and your skeleton argument will provide a good running order for your submissions. This can be supplemented with any additional notes you might need.

We discussed in Chapter 6 the reasons why you should not have in front of you a pre prepared script. An additional reason for not doing so is that the risk of becoming 'tongue-tied' is significantly reduced if you are not tied to a specific form of words, worrying about following them verbatim.

Mooting tip
For many students, the hardest part of the moot is actually getting started and the worry that once you get to your feet, you will not be able to utter a single word. However, experience tells us that once you do get to your feet and start making your submissions, you will find that you will quickly relax and settle into the role of Counsel. You might find it helpful, therefore, to write out your first two opening sentences – but no more – to ease yourself into your role. Having a glass of water on your desk will also help avoid dry-mouth syndrome.

Arrive in good time for the moot

Arriving early at the moot venue can be very helpful, especially where it involves a degree of travel. It can be very unsettling to experience any kind of travelling delays or problems associated with finding the venue. Leaving in good time will help ensure that none of these problems occur. Arriving early will help you settle in and familiarise yourself with the moot room and its layout. Arriving early should not be viewed as time wasted because the time can, and should, be put to good use. Rather than carrying out your final preparations 'at home', you can complete your preparations once you have arrived safely at the moot venue.

Feeling unwell during the moot

In the unlikely event that you feel unwell during the moot, then, if you are able to do so, you should inform the judge. Depending on the circumstances, you may wish to request the court's permission to make (or continue with) your submissions while seated, or to leave the moot room for a few moments.

If you take ill when you are seated while another mooter is addressing the court, you may feel it appropriate to interrupt the moot to explain the circumstances to the judge. Remember the principles of etiquette discussed at page 203 which require you (provided you are able to do so) to stand when asking the judge to be excused.

Mooting tip

Not being able to moot (or complete your moot) because of ill health is one of those rare problems that are very difficult to foresee. It is important, therefore, to make sure that your teammate (or team substitute if the rules permit a substitute) is sufficiently familiar with both grounds of the appeal and is able to take over in an emergency.

Speed writing and shortcuts

Whether in court or in the office, lawyers often need to make notes quickly. Learning shorthand can be both time-consuming and costly, and is therefore not a realistic option for many busy practitioners. Instead, many students and lawyers develop their own shortcuts and style of shorthand that help them to write more speedily. Typical shortcuts include 'C' for claimant, 'D' for defendant, 'CA' for the Court of Appeal, 'TJ' for trial judge and so on.

With practice, you should be able to learn how to shorten or abbreviate words yourself. Note that in all cases the context is important as this will help determine the true meaning of the words. For example, if the name of a witness is David, you might want to abbreviate it to 'Dv' so as to distinguish it from D (defendant). Consider the following:

- D ws askd 2 expln hw th acdnt hapnd – *The defendant was asked to explain how the accident happened.*
- TJ unimprsd wth ansr – *The trial judge was unimpressed with the answer.*

The following guide provides a quick and straightforward way of learning how to shorten or abbreviate words. The principle behind this guide is speed and simplicity. There are no rules or set formulae. Therefore, you do not need to adhere rigidly to the guide if doing so might make the words more difficult to read.

There are several tools in the guide which can be used alone or together.

Omit letters

Take out:

- **vowels in the middle of words:** chr (chair), wndw (window), bk (book), aslt (assault), mrdr (murder), dbl (double)
- **vowels that appear at the end of words (provided they are not sounded):** tbl (table), apl (apple)
- **one of two letters that are the same and appear together:** ltr (letter), chnl (channel), apl (apple)
- **letters that are unsounded:** smn (salmon), lm (lamb), lm (limb), clm (climb).

You will see from the final example that 'lm' could be either 'lamb' or 'limb'. As noted earlier, the context is important as this will help determine the true meaning of the words.

Abbreviate words

Consider the following abbreviations. What other words would be helpful to you to abbreviate?

a/c	account (as in 'to take account of') or accounts
co	company
dir	director
'ee	employee
'er	employer
gp	group
incl	include or including
neg	negligent or negligence
opp	opponent
sol	solicitor

Omit words

Many sentences remain perfectly comprehensible after certain words are omitted. In general, if the words are not needed to give meaning to a sentence, you should consider omitting them. For example, consider omitting the following words:

- the, a, an, and, or, but, was, is, that, which.

Leave in

- Vowels at the beginning of words: apl (apple), usr (user).
- Vowels that appear at the end of words (provided they are sounded): China, tree.
- Consonants: cnsnnts.

Change

- The letters 'gh' and 'ph' (provided they make an 'f' sound) to 'f': cof (cough), alfbt (alphabet), laf (laugh), grf (graph).
- The letters 'ck' with 'c' or 'k' (not both): chk (check), crk (crack), sk (sick).
- Words that end in 'dge' to 'g': hg (hedge), lg (ledge), plg (pledge).
- Words that end in 'aight', 'ate' or 'eight' to '8': str8 (straight), h8 (hate), pl8 (plate), g8 (gate), gr8 (grate), w8 (weight).

A personalised grid

The following grid can be used to add your own words which can then be referred to by the index letter. By including both upper- and lower-case index letters, you will be able to double the number of words available to you (although for simplicity you might prefer just to use a single case). We have included some examples of commonly used legal words. For example, using both upper- and lower-case index letters, 'A' is used as shorthand for 'appeal' whereas 'a' refers to 'arbitration'.

This is your grid and you should complete it using words that will be helpful to you.

A	appeal	a	arbitration
B	bailiff	b	breach
C	claimant	c	contract
D	defendant	d	damages
E		e	
F		f	
G		g	
H		h	
I		i	
J		j	
K		k	
L		l	
M		m	
N		n	
O		o	
P		p	
Q		q	
R		r	

S	s
T	t
U	u
V	v
W	w
X	x
Y	y
Z	z

In addition to the above, you should also consider using initials to replace phrases. Consider the following:

CA	Court of Appeal
CC	County Court
ChD	Chancery Division
DoC	duty of care
ECHR	European Convention on Human Rights
ECJ	European Court of Justice
ECtHR	European Court of Human Rights
HC	High Court
HL	House of Lords
IH	Inner House (Court of Session – Scotland)
JR	judicial review
KBD	King's Bench Division
OH	Outer House (Court of Session – Scotland)
QBD	Queen's Bench Division
SC	Supreme Court

9 Organising a moot or mooting competition

Introduction

This section of the book is aimed at anyone who is concerned with the organisation of mooting. The aim of this and the following chapter is to provide a comprehensive guide to setting up and running a mooting competition or other mooting activity, including mooting that is assessed as part of a student's course of study.

Responsibilities

Organising a moot or mooting competition comes with a number of key responsibilities. If you get it wrong, you run the risk of causing damage to the goodwill that you had built up with those who have supported you in organising the event, such as your own and other institutions, judges, sponsors and mooters. On the other hand, a well-organised mooting event will help cement relationships and goodwill for the benefit of all parties.

An organiser's responsibilities include:

- Setting the date and finding a venue for the moot. In the case of a competition that runs over a number of different dates, you will also need to make sure that arrangements for dates and venues are available throughout the period of the competition.
- Setting or agreeing the moot problem or problems.
- Setting out the rules for the moot.
- Setting out who is eligible to participate.
- Organising or facilitating the provision of judges.
- Agreeing responsibilities for those who act as hosts.
- Arranging refreshments where appropriate (but always provide a jug of water and a drinking glass for the judge and court clerk).
- Providing for an adjudication process in the event of a dispute.
- All financial arrangements relating to the moot or competition.
- Scheduling and timetabling matters.

The format of the mooting competition

There are several important preliminary decisions that you will need to make in relation to the running of your mooting competition. These relate to the structure and operation of the event.

There are two main types of mooting format: knockout and league. A knockout format is by far the most common.

Knockout format

With a knockout competition, mooters are entered into a draw and compete against each other through a series of rounds until there is an eventual winner. The figure on the next page shows a typical knockout table, for 64 teams, and can be adapted depending on the number of mooters or teams involved.

If fewer than 64 teams enter the competition, in order to make the numbers work, some of them will need to be given a bye to the second round. This presents both advantages and disadvantages for the mooters concerned. The advantage is that they will progress to the next round without having to moot; this can be weighed against the disadvantage that they may then be drawn against competitors who have had the experience of mooting in the previous round. Where more than 64 teams enter, a preliminary round will need to be held to reduce the number to 64.

With a competition that is open to mooters nationally or internationally, organisers will often arrange the earlier rounds of the draw regionally so that the teams do not have to travel too far, at least until they progress further into the rounds.

When organising the draw, the organiser will need to determine which team will moot at 'home', with their opponent travelling to them as the 'away team', as well as which team will represent the appellant, with the other team representing the respondent. The organiser will also need to set a date by which each round needs to be completed.

Alternatively, each round could be arranged centrally, with each team travelling to a neutral venue where they will moot at the same time.

League format

If the competition is organised as a league event, the teams are placed into groups with each team mooting against every other team in their group. A typical group will consist of four teams. The team with the greatest number of wins proceeds to the next stage of the competition which is usually a knockout stage followed by the final.

League mooting formats have advantages and disadvantages. The main advantage is that each team gets to moot more than once, which, in the knockout format, is not guaranteed. The main disadvantages with a league format is that it requires far greater resources in terms of the number of rooms and judges required, as well as more input from the organisers. Determining the winner can

English-Speaking Union – Essex Court Chambers National Mooting Competition

also be problematic. First, it will not be possible to utilise the 'bye' method in the event that the number of teams is not divisible by the number of groups. Second, at the end of the initial (or group) stage of the competition there may be more than one team with the same number of wins, which will then require a mechanism to determine which of these teams progresses through to the knockout stage.

Ad hoc or smaller informal moots

Ad hoc or smaller informal moots are particularly useful if the organiser doesn't want to be tied to one of the more formal structures described above or where there are too few mooters who wish to participate in the event. This may be particularly useful for student law societies or similar groups who wish to offer mooting experience to students without having to follow the stricter procedures that are associated with more formal mooting competitions.

With an ad hoc or smaller informal moot, the organiser simply has to arrange the mooters into teams or groups, arrange the moot problems and judges, and help facilitate the moot when the students are available.

Eligibility to enter the competition

The organiser is also responsible for determining who is eligible to enter the competition. The principal consideration is to ensure a level playing field between mooters. To achieve this, it makes sense to ensure that all entrants are reasonably matched in terms of their level of study. In practical terms, this will mean that a competition aimed at undergraduate students will not generally allow postgraduate students to enter. If a sufficient number of postgraduate students are interested in mooting, the organiser should consider putting on a separate competition for them.

More difficult questions arise in relation to students following the Graduate Diploma in Law (GDL) degree. This is because these students are already graduates, albeit not in law. Many competitions allow GDL students to enter an otherwise undergraduate event, and organisers need to make clear their position with regard to these students. Below is shown an extract from the English-Speaking Union–Essex Court Chambers National Mooting Competition in relation to eligibility to enter their mooting competition.

Entry to the Competition

A participating institution may enter a team consisting of two eligible students at that institution. The members of the team may be varied between rounds; however, the members of a team that wins a semi-final round must also represent the institution in the grand final. Students are regarded as eligible if they are registered students at the participating institution and are not graduates in law. GDL students are eligible to take part in the competition. Students are not eligible if they hold or are studying for professional legal qualifications (i.e. Legal Practice Course, Bar Professional Training Course or ILEX courses). No individual may enter the competition if he or she has participated in a semi-final of this competition in any previous year.

Alternatively, where the organiser wishes to allow entries from both postgraduate and undergraduate students, they may wish to consider a system of points ranking to even out any advantages that the more experienced students may have.

Authority limits

Another consideration for the organiser is whether or not to impose a limit on the number of authorities each team may use and, if so, what that limit is. Most moots impose a limit of around eight authorities per team. Some competitions state that an authority may consist of cases, statutes, journal articles and textbooks, although others state that, for the purpose of numbers, only cases will count as an authority. If an authority is cited as part of the moot problem itself, it is usually classed as a court authority which may then be used by either team without it being counted as one of their own authorities.

It is sensible to impose a limit on the number of authorities each team may cite as this prevents the mooters from selecting too many which they will not have the time to use.

Skeleton arguments

The organiser will also need to consider whether or not the mooters need to prepare skeleton arguments and, if so, whether to impose a word or page limit. Where skeleton arguments are required, the organiser also needs to decide on the process and deadlines for their exchange with the opposing team and for providing copies for the judge.

Bundles

Organisers also need to consider whether to impose a rule that requires mooters to prepare bundles or whether this should be left to the teams' own judgement. Since good advocacy is assisted by the use of bundles, organisers might take the view that leaving it to the teams' own judgement is no bad thing; a good team is likely to want to make good use of bundles whether required by the rules to do so or not. This might, however, present a problem for novice mooters who may need prompting about the advantage of using bundles.

Speaking order

Although the order of speaking is reasonably standard, it would nevertheless be sensible to remind mooters of this in the rules or competition literature. For a detailed discussion on the order of speaking, see pages 171 and 172.

Timing

The organiser should also set out how long each mooter will have to deliver their submissions and whether or not the clock is stopped for judicial interventions. A detailed discussion on this topic is provided on pages 204 and 205.

Appeals

Many mooting competitions stipulate that there will be no appeal on any grounds from the decision of a judge or upon the conduct of the moot itself. If, however, you wish to provide a route for appeal, this should be clearly set out in the rules.

Competition rules

It is incumbent on moot organisers to provide a set of rules under which the moot or mooting competition will operate. Although there are no standard rules that you must follow when organising a moot, most moots tend to follow similar procedures and the various competitions have devised their own rules which apply to those who enter their competitions.

The following rules are those devised for the English-Speaking Union–Essex Court Chambers National Mooting Competition which readers may choose to consider when devising the rules for their own event.

Entry to the competition

The competition is known as the 'ESU–Essex Court Chambers National Mooting Competition'. The National Adjudicator is responsible for setting the moot problems and any matters of a legal nature relating to the competition.

Entry to the competition is open to all universities or higher education colleges involved in the teaching of law in the United Kingdom. To qualify for entry, an institution must:

- register online at www.nationalmooting.org
- pay the entry fee of £50.00.

A participating institution may enter a team consisting of two eligible students at that institution. The members of the team may be varied between rounds; however, the members of a team that wins a semi-final round must also represent the institution in the grand final. Students are regarded as eligible if they are registered students at the participating institution and are not graduates in law. GDL students are eligible to take part in the competition.

Students are not eligible if they hold or are studying for professional legal qualifications (i.e. Legal Practice Course, Bar Professional Training Course or ILEX courses). No individual may enter the competition if he or she has participated in a semi-final of this competition in any previous year.

There shall be no appeal on any grounds from the decision of a judge or upon the conduct of the moot itself in any round.

Any complaints about, or problems with, the conduct of the teams during a round must be made in writing to the National Adjudicator, who may then investigate and resolve the problem as he thinks is in the best interests of the competition. The National Adjudicator and the Competition Administrator have the discretion to disqualify at any stage any institution that fails to comply with these rules or with the spirit of the competition. An institution may be disqualified either on the basis of its own acts or omissions, or on the basis of the conduct of the team representing it in a given round. The complaint must be made within 24 hours of the end of the moot it concerns.

Any questions regarding the interpretation of these rules shall be submitted to the National Adjudicator who may, at his discretion, in consultation with the Competition Administrator, resolve the problem.

In the event of a dispute involving the institution from which the National Adjudicator is drawn, the National Adjudicator shall refer the dispute to one or more of the members of the Competition Advisory Panel.

Communications

For the purposes of any communication in connection with this competition, it is sufficient if the communication is sent, as appropriate, to the email of either of the contacts listed in the contact sheet supplied by the Competition Administrator, save where a specific rule below requires communication in a particular way. If an institution wishes to change either of its contacts, it must inform the Competition Administrator and the opposing team.

Competition format and timetable

The competition is run on a simple knockout basis for 64 teams. The six rounds of the competition will conform as closely as possible to the following pattern:

FIRST ROUND – (64 teams) to be held by [date]
SECOND ROUND – (32 teams) to be held by [date]
THIRD ROUND – (16 teams) to be held by [date]
QUARTER-FINALS – (8 teams) to be held by [date]
SEMI-FINALS – (4 teams) to be held by [date]
GRAND FINAL – (2 teams) to be held by [date]

Please pay careful attention to these deadlines. If it is impossible for a team to comply with these dates, the team will withdraw from the competition and offer its opponent a bye, unless a change of date has the consent of both their opponent and the Competition Administrator. Extensions are not guaranteed, and will only be granted in extenuating circumstances.

If an extension has been granted, and the moot still has not proceeded, the Competition Administrator shall decide who progresses by tossing a coin, unless the reason that the moot has not proceeded is the fault of one team in which case the other team shall proceed to the next round.

Where more than 64 teams enter, a preliminary round will be held to reduce the number to 64. The teams required to participate in the preliminary round will be chosen by the Competition Administrator in an order determined by the receipt of entry fees.

Rules for all rounds except the semi-finals and grand final

The following rules apply to all rounds except the semi-finals and grand final. Participating institutions will be informed of their opponent and moot problems at least two weeks before the deadline set for the moot. Host teams are selected at random and are required to follow the procedure set out in these rules.

In the first round of the competition, the Host team also takes the position of the moot problem's Appellant (or equivalent), but this is only the case in the first round.

In each of the subsequent rounds (except the semi-finals and grand final) the decision on which team is to be the Appellant and which team is to be the Respondent will be made by the Competition Administrator, independent of whether or not an institution is hosting a round. This decision will be released to each section of the draw for the next round when either:

(a) both teams in a specific part of the draw can carry out the next round of the competition as they know who their opponent will be, or

(b) the deadline date for the completion of the previous round has passed, whichever is earlier.

Semi-finals and grand final

The semi-finals and grand final will be held in London on the same day. The same problem will be used for both the semi-finals and grand final. This is seen as having two advantages. First, it alleviates pressure on the timetable, enabling the first round to be later in the academic year. Second, it will be an advantage for all four teams in the semi-finals to have to prepare both sides of the argument, in case they reach the grand final.

There will be a special procedure for skeleton arguments and authorities for both the semi-finals and grand final, which will be provided to the semi-finalists immediately after the results of the quarter-final rounds are known.

The semi-finals will be held at Dartmouth House, and the grand final will take place in the Royal Courts of Justice.

Supporters are encouraged to attend the semi-finals in the morning and to stay on for the grand final in the afternoon even if their institution does not reach the grand final.

The semi-finals will take place concurrently. Immediately after their conclusion there will be a draw to determine which team acts for which side in the grand final. The Competition Administrator will be responsible for the distribution of skeleton arguments and copies of authorities to the judges for the semi-finals and grand final as appropriate.

Moot format

All moot problems are set as a case on appeal to the Court of Appeal or the Supreme Court, represented by a single judge.

Each round consists of two teams. In the first round, the Home team represents the Appellant and the Away team represents the Respondent. In subsequent rounds, sides will be allocated at random, as detailed in the above Competition Format and Timetable section.

Two judges will sit at the semi-final and three judges will sit at the grand final.

Each team consists of two speakers: a leader and a junior. The leader takes the first ground of appeal and the junior takes the second. The four speakers will be heard in the order and for the times in Figure 9.2 in the first column. On an occasion where the moot takes the form of an appeal and cross-appeal, the order and timing of speeches shall be as in the second column of the figure below.

	Leader for the Appellant 20 minutes
Leader for the Appellant 20 minutes	Leader for the Respondent 20 minutes
Junior for the Appellant 15 minutes	Junior for the Cross-Appellant 15 minutes
Leader for the Respondent 20 minutes	Junior for the Cross-Respondent 15 minutes
Junior for the Respondent 20 minutes	Reply by the Appellant 5 minutes
Appellant's Right to Reply 5 minutes (not obligatory)	Reply by the Cross-Appellant 5 minutes

Problems

The moot problems will be on 'core' legal subjects that do not require additional specialist knowledge. Examples of 'core' subjects are criminal law, contract, tort (or delict), company and commercial law, constitutional law, employment law, consumer protection law, EU law and any area of law based on a UK statute. Problems should be on legal issues that are common to all the legal jurisdictions of the United Kingdom.

The moot problems will be solely concerned with points of law. They will be cases heard on appeal by the Court of Appeal or the Supreme Court and will have no less and no more than two grounds for appeal clearly stated.

No objection to any moot problem will be sustained unless communicated to the National Adjudicator within seven days of the receipt of the moot problem. If the National Adjudicator is satisfied with the objection, he may direct that another moot problem be used.

Authorities

A team may rely on no more than eight authorities of its own choosing, which it must cite in a list of authorities. All authorities cited may be used by either the Appellant or the Respondent for any purpose. If an authority is cited as part of the moot problem, it is classed as a court authority which may be used by either team and which need not be included in either side's list.

A single case which has been decided in more than one court (e.g. a case that has started in the High Court and then gone to the Court of Appeal and then to the House of Lords/Supreme Court) counts as one authority, although all references must be cited if a team wishes to use them.

For the purposes of this competition, only cases count as authorities. However, if a team intends to cite statutes, texts or other legal literature then, notwithstanding that these do not count towards the maximum of eight authorities, the team must disclose them by provision of copies to the opposing team at the time of the exchange of skeleton arguments.

Both lists of authorities must be exchanged by email, to the email address provided on the contact sheet, at least 3 working days before the moot. Their arrival and contents must be confirmed by the sender by email to the contact email address. No variation of authorities will be allowed unless the opposing team agrees.

Each team must bring to the moot copies of its own authorities for both the opposing team and the judge. The Host team must additionally supply copies of the 'court authorities' referred to in the problem for the judge.

See below for details as to the provision of the teams' authorities and skeletons to the judge in advance.

Cases should be cited as authorities in the following descending order of priority:

- The Law Reports
- The Weekly Law Reports or All England Law Reports
- Others

A team that cites an authority which is not in the Law Reports, the Weekly Law Reports or the All England Law Reports must provide copies of that authority to their opponent, at the time of the exchange of lists of authorities.

Skeleton arguments

A team must also submit a skeleton argument setting out the main propositions and submissions in support of their case.

The skeleton arguments must be exchanged by email to the contact email address provided on the contact sheet at least 3 working days before the moot. The arrival of the skeleton must be confirmed by the sender by email to the contact email address. The skeleton argument should not be longer than one side of A4, and should be word processed.

The main grounds of argument should be set out concisely together with the authorities relied on to support the argument.

The Host team, when arranging for the judge, should ask the judge whether he wishes to be provided with copies of the skeleton and of any of the authorities in advance. If so, the Host team must ensure that the judge receives the material asked for.

Teams in the semi-finals and the grand final

Immediately after all of the quarter-finals are completed the teams that reach the semi-finals will be given instructions as to the procedure for the semi-finals and grand final.

Host responsibilities

The organisers greatly appreciate the hospitality of the institutions that host the rounds of the competition.

All participating institutions undertake to host a round if allocated the position of Host team. A Host institution has a number of responsibilities:

- to locate a judge who meets the criteria described below in the section on Selection of Judges. The Guest team must give their consent to the judge, whose identity and background should be made known to them with as much notice as possible;
- to provide the judge with a copy of the moot problem and this handbook, drawing their attention to these rules and the scoring sheets;
- to provide the judge with the skeleton arguments and court authorities prior to the moot;
- to communicate details of the round venue, date and time to the Guest team, and to confirm that they have been received;
- to prepare a moot courtroom and provide water for the judge's and mooters' use;
- to provide a clerk to the moot court, who is required to keep time. The clerk shall inform the judge when the time periods have elapsed, preferably by means of a note. Mooters should also be alerted, through

the display of a card, when they have 5 minutes left to speak and also 1 minute left. The clerk should use a stopwatch to keep time;
- to inform the Competition Administrator of the result within 24 hours of the completion of the round.

Please note that the clock is not stopped for interruptions by judges.

All institutions should work towards identifying a suitable judge as soon as possible, as each institution may be asked to host the rounds of the competition.

Selection of judges

Judges shall be qualified legal practitioners (barristers, solicitors or advocates – not pupil barristers or trainee solicitors) or lecturers in law, and must be experienced in the judging of moots. Unless agreed in advance by both competing institutions and the National Adjudicator, the judge in a given round other than the semi-final and grand final (for which a panel of judges must be arranged before the finalists are known) may not be an employee, former employee, student or former student of either competing institution. An employee of a neighbouring institution is an appropriate judge.

Judges should be selected based on their relevant experience of the fields of law upon which the moot is set. For example, a practitioner or academic who has acted solely in the area of civil law would not be considered an appropriate judge in a criminal moot problem.

Guidelines for judges

A judge has the following duties:

- to give judgment on the various points of law argued by the mooters;
- to give a reasoned judgment as to the merits and faults of each mooter; and
- to decide upon and announce the winning team.

The winning team of the round is at the sole discretion of the judge. The decision of the judge on any point cannot be appealed.

It is suggested that, in order to ensure an element of consistency throughout the competition, the judge should use four criteria to decide upon each team's performance: Content, Strategy, Ability to Respond and Style. It is hoped that these criteria can best evaluate each team's relative strengths. An optional scoring sheet has been provided for judges to assess each mooter and allocate them individual marks. In the end, however, it is the overall impression of which team made the most convincing presentation of their case that will determine the outcome. The better team will not necessarily be the team for whom judgment is given on the points of law. The following areas can be considered as relevant guidelines for assessment of the mooters:

Content:

- the insight into and analysis of the moot problem and grounds of appeal
- the relevance of the authorities cited and the fluidity with which they are adduced
- the ability to summarise facts, cases or law where appropriate.

Strategy:

- the presentation and structure of the legal arguments, including skeleton arguments, where used (rigidly scripted speeches, in particular, should be penalised)
- the ability of the mooters to work as a team
- the effective use of the mooter's limited time.

Ability to respond:

- the rebuttal of an opponent's arguments
- the ability to answer questions from the Bench.

Style:

- the mooter's skill as an advocate
- the proper use of court etiquette.

The judge may retire to consider the decision. Since this is a team competition, it is expected that the best all-round team will be chosen. When announcing the decision, it is greatly appreciated if, in addition to the questions of law, the judge makes some comment on the merits of the performance of each of the mooters. This advice is always listened to very carefully and the mooters will value such balanced assessments.

Judges are encouraged to interrupt mooters at any time where the judge requires clarification of the legal argument being presented; interruptions also test the mooter's ability to respond as an advocate. However, the clock is not stopped during interruptions by judges so they are asked to treat all four mooters equitably. Questions should not be unduly difficult at this level. None of the stated grounds of appeal should be thought to be unarguable by the mooters or the judge, and judges should not refuse to hear an argument for that reason. However, if a team fails to produce cited authorities, the judge has the discretion to render the citation inadmissible. Finally, judges should not ask so many questions that mooters are unable to complete the points raised in their skeleton arguments. Although it is proper for judges to assess the quality and appropriateness of arguments, mooters should not be prevented from putting forward arguments in their own way.

Judge's scoresheet

Appellant

	Speaker	Content	Strategy	Ability to respond	Style	Total	Comments
Leader							
Junior							
Reply speech							
TOTAL							

Respondent

	Speaker	Content	Strategy	Ability to respond	Style	Total	Comments
Leader							
Junior							
Reply speech							
TOTAL							

Selecting the moot problem(s)

The choice of moot problem will typically be determined by the nature of the moot. Some moots are subject-specific, such as the Property Law Mooting Competition,[1] whereas other competitions tend to include a wider choice of moot problems covering a range of core subjects taught during the course of legal study.

In Chapter 10, we have included a number of moot problems covering a range of legal subjects. With many moots, the law will fall on one side or the other of

---

1 Described at page 262.

the arguments, and when drafting a moot problem it is important to make sure that the moot is capable of argument. Sometimes moot problems are 'reused' from one year to another. When this is done, it is important to make sure that nothing has occurred (i.e. new cases or legislation) since the original moot was drafted that now makes the problem difficult to argue or, worse still, unarguable.

Choosing the judge(s)

The organisers will need to provide the judges for the moot or alternatively provide a mechanism for the judges to be selected. In either case, judges need to be chosen carefully so as to avoid any possibility of bias or apparent bias. In a competition setting, this means avoiding inviting as judges anyone who has or has had any material connection with either institution.

In addition to judging the moot and determining the winner, the judge plays an important part in the event by providing valuable feedback to the mooters.

Judges can be drawn from three main sources: students, academic staff and those invited externally. Before discussing each of these categories, it is important to emphasise that whichever category of judge is used for the moot they must be thoroughly briefed both in terms of the moot problem and in how they will be expected to discharge their role as judges.

Students

Provided you choose the students carefully, they can be a valuable source of judges, especially in the earlier rounds of a competition. Many students who have had experience of mooting will be only too pleased to assist as judges. Because student judges tend not to be able to carry the same degree of authority as more experienced judges, they might require a degree of supervision.

Academic staff

Academic staff from one's own institution often act as judges in internal moots and mooting competitions, although for the reasons outlined above they may not generally be considered to be suitable to act as judges in external mooting events.

External judges

External judges are used in the majority of mooting competitions. They can be academics from other institutions, legal practitioners or members of the judiciary, either current or recently retired. The experience that external judges bring to a moot can be considerable. In most major competitions, the final round is judged by a Bench consisting of three judges, one or more of whom are members of the judiciary.

Judges must be experienced in judging moots and preferably in the area of law covered by the moot problem. That said, most competent lawyers should be able to appreciate the issues in a moot that is not directly within their own specialism.

Both legal practitioners and members of the judiciary bring with them their experience of professional practice. Members of the judiciary can deliver the added gravitas of first-hand judicial experience as well as giving in their feedback to the mooters the most authoritative guidance on what does and does not persuade them when sitting as a judge.

Judging the moot

Judges should familiarise themselves with the rules of the moot, noting that not all moots or mooting competitions operate with identical sets of rules. Organisers should brief the judges thoroughly before the moot and point out the key issues that they would like them to consider when judging the moot.

Judges often have their own style when judging moots and the following guidance is provided to help ensure the smooth running of the moot and the fair treatment of all mooters:

Judicial conduct

In the same way that mooters try to act as an advocate would act in court, judges should also conduct themselves as a judge would behave in court. This provides a degree of authenticity and realism to the proceedings.

Judicial interventions

Judicial interventions are fundamentally important in mooting. Indeed, in a significant number of moots, judicial interventions (or, to be more precise, how the mooter deals with them) represent the single most important factor in determining the winner of the moot as it requires mooters to think on their feet and depart from their notes. Although it is impossible to provide anything like definitive guidance as to the number of interventions judges should make or what kind of questions should be asked, judges should bear in mind the points considered in this section.

Judges must allow mooters to develop their arguments without continually interrupting them. On the other hand, without interventions from the Bench, the mooter will be doing little more than delivering a well-rehearsed presentation: this is not what mooting is about. It is a question of balance. One would generally expect to see a larger number of interventions with more difficult questions being asked during the final round of a major competition than during an early-round moot aimed at first-year undergraduates.

Generally, judges should confine their interventions to the submissions being advanced by the mooters rather than seek to widen the discussion to a wider exploration of the law.

Treat all mooters fairly and equally

The principal role of a moot judge is to determine which team has won the moot. Dealing fairly with all mooters is an essential part of this task. In treating all mooters fairly and equally, judges should ask them all roughly the same number of questions with similar complexity.

Timekeeping

Although judges are likely to be assisted by a court clerk and/or timekeeper, it is always a matter for the judge to determine how strictly to apply the time constraints laid down in the rules. Some judges will choose to apply the time rules strictly and stop a mooter immediately their allocated time has expired; others may allow them some latitude to finish making the point they were dealing with. Judges often prefer the latter approach if they have intervened a lot during the moot and thereby eaten into a mooter's time. The important consideration is, of course, to treat all mooters fairly.

Have regard to the mooter's level of study

Wherever possible, judges should have regard to the mooter's level of study, especially with regard to judicial interventions which is often seen as the most difficult and daunting part of the moot. Consequently, judges should not expect the same level of skill and competence from first-year students as they would from students in their final year of study.

Dealing with students who are struggling during the moot

Judges should give mooters every opportunity to deal with interventions from the Bench. However, when it is clear that a mooter is struggling to respond to a particular intervention, judges should, where appropriate, encourage them to move on rather than insist they deal with the intervention to a satisfactory standard. Similarly, where a mooter makes a fundamentally bad point, it might be helpful to guide them by saying something like 'I am unlikely to be persuaded [by that submission] and suggest you move on to your next point'. Judges should not, however, insist that the mooter moves on and should leave it to the mooter's own discretion how they argue their case.

Giving your judgment on the law

Judges should deliver a reasoned judgment on the law but it should not be too lengthy. The amount of detail in the judgment is a matter of personal choice, although this is often determined by the time available and the audience who have come to watch the moot. Some judges prefer to deliver their judgment in summary form by way of bullet points whereas others prefer to deliver it with more detail.

The mooters, as well as members of the audience, are entitled to know how the law has been decided, even if that is not the most important part of the day. When delivering their judgment, judges should consider making particular reference to any difficult points that arose during the moot. Where there is more than one judge on the Bench, they might each wish to deliver their own short judgment, perhaps taking a different ground or point of appeal.

Whichever way judges decide to discharge this part of their role, they should remember that it is the next part of their decision that the teams are most interested in!

Judges will often retire to consider their judgment and decide who has won the moot, although any such retirement should be as short as possible.

Declaring the winner of the moot

This is, of course, the main purpose of the moot. Organisers should emphasise to judges that the team that wins the law should have no bearing on the outcome of the moot. In other words, the party that wins the law may lose the moot and vice versa. This is simply because with many moots the law will be on one side or the other[2] and it is a matter of luck as to which team is chosen to represent the party with the stronger legal position. For this reason, it is important for judges to determine the winner of the moot by the quality of each side's mooting and advocacy skills. In short, the successful team is the one that presents their case, whatever its merits, the most ably and persuasively.

Organisers should provide a marking scheme for the judges and decide whether this needs to be followed or is only provided as a guide. An example of a marking scheme is shown on page 223.

In addition to declaring the winner of the moot, judges should also provide feedback on the particular strengths and weaknesses of the individual mooters. Whether this is done before or after the winner is announced is a matter of personal choice, although many judges prefer to maintain a degree of suspense until the very end. A reasonable amount of time should be devoted to providing feedback as this can prove invaluable to mooters in their effort to improve their performance. Judges should try to avoid concentrating only on the positive (or negative) aspects of a mooter's performance or giving bland and uninformed feedback, such as telling the mooters that the moot was very close, but team X wins by a whisker. When giving their feedback, judges should not only concentrate on the mooters' oral presentations but should also provide comment on other aspects of the moot, such as the skeleton arguments and bundles and the mooters' use of these during the moot.

Experience tells us that mooters benefit more when judges provide specific examples of both good and poor mooting practice. It might be helpful to start with

---

2 Although this can be avoided by drafting the moot in such a way that each side has a ground of appeal that is stronger than their opponent's.

some examples of good practice, such as: 'I was particularly impressed by the way you referred me back to your skeleton argument as this enabled me to appreciate where you were up to with your submissions and where they were going.' Where the judge identifies areas of poor mooting practice, it is always beneficial to explain to the mooters how they might avoid making such mistakes in the future and provide them with some examples of what they could have done differently.

The court clerk

The court clerk has a number of functions to perform, all of which are designed to ensure the smooth running of the moot. Depending on the layout of the moot room, the clerk either sits at a table immediately in front of the Bench or on the Bench next to the judge. It is normally helpful to discuss with the judge the precise functions he wants the clerk to perform, but in general these will include the following:

Instructing the Court to rise

The clerk will announce the judge's entrance with an instruction 'Court rise'. Similarly, the clerk will give the 'Court rise' instruction when the judge is ready to leave the moot room – for example, to consider his decision – and again when he returns to the room.

Calling on the case

Once the judge has taken his seat and has indicted that he is ready for the moot to start, the clerk will call on the case. To do this, the clerk will stand and announce:

In the Supreme Court,[3] in the matter of Smith and Jones.

Assisting the judge with the authorities

Whether the judge requires assistance with the authorities is a matter of the judge's preference and, to some extent, where the clerk is seated and whether bundles have been prepared. Some judges are content to handle bundles themselves whereas others prefer the authorities to be handed to them the first time they are cited by the mooters.

Keeping the time

Unless there is a separate timekeeper, the clerk should keep the time. To do this, the clerk will need a stopwatch or timepiece with a second hand. It is often

---

3 Or whichever court the moot is held.

helpful for the clerk to give time warnings to the mooters, by informing them when they have, say, five minutes and one minute left, and then when the time allowed has expired. These warnings are often prescribed by the rules of the moot. At each of these time stages, the clerk should hold up a sign informing the court of the time remaining for the mooter then speaking. The clerk should ensure that the mooter, and the judge, can see the notice. Where a mooter has run out of time, the clerk holds up the 'time up' sign in such a way that the mooter and judge can see it, but it is for the judge alone to decide whether the mooter must stop speaking or can have a little more time to finish the point they are making. Under no circumstances should the clerk tell the mooters to stop speaking.

The rules of the moot will set out whether or not the clock stops for judicial interventions. Organisers should ensure that whoever is responsible for keeping the time is aware of how the rule is to be applied. Where the rules stipulate that the clock stops for judicial interventions, the timekeeper's task is somewhat more exacting in that they will need to stop the clock each time a judge asks a question and then restart it as soon as the mooter has finished answering. This is likely to occur quite frequently during the moot and, especially where there is more than one judge, it is likely to keep the timekeeper busily occupied. In such cases, organisers should consider using a separate timekeeper, leaving the clerk to carry out their other clerking duties.

In all cases, the person keeping the time needs to know how many minutes each mooter has been allocated by the rules.

Moot problems

There are two main ways of obtaining a moot problem for your moot or mooting competition. The first is to write one yourself (or ask a colleague to write one for you) and the second is to use or adapt a problem from a previously held moot. Whichever way you decide to obtain the moot problem, it is important that it reflects the stage that the prospective mooters have reached. It is also important to ensure that the moot problem is reasonably well balanced and capable of being argued by both sides.

Writing your own moot problem

Writing your own moot problem has the obvious advantage that you will be able to tailor the problem to the specific circumstances of the students or programme of study. It also enables you to reflect into the problem specific issues of interest.

You do not have to write the moot problem from scratch as many problem-based seminars or past exam questions could easily be amended for this purpose. If you decide to amend a seminar or past exam question, you will need to set up the appeal process by writing into the problem a brief judgment of the trial judge (if the moot is to take place in the Court of Appeal) and of the Court of Appeal (if the moot is to take place in the Supreme Court). It is necessary to add these judgments into the moot problem because seminar questions or exams generally do not include this detail. Once you have done this, you will then need to draft appropriate grounds of appeal. Again, these are not usually present in seminar or exam questions.

Adapting an existing moot problem

There is no shortage of moot problems that you can use as a basis for your moot. In the case of a long-established mooting event, you are likely to have a bank of old moot problems that are easy to adapt to bring them into line with any changes in the law since the problem was first written. You might find that since the problem was first written, there has been a significant change in the law that now provides a definitive answer to one or both grounds of the appeal. In such a case, you might find that altering part of the problem (typically the factual background) will make the moot once again arguable by the mooters. Alternatively, you could introduce a cross-appeal into the moot problem. This is often helpful where the first ground of appeal strongly favours one of the parties. The inclusion of a cross-appeal could balance out the moot by writing it in such a way that it favours the other party.

Finding a sponsor

A number of mooting competitions are supported by sponsors. Sponsorship provides a cost-effective and efficient means of promoting and broadening a firm's competitive edge by improving their image and prestige as well as broadening their appeal to prospective lawyers from the student fraternity. Ideal sponsors include:

- solicitors' firms
- barristers' chambers
- employers, especially those whose business involves an element of legal work
- anyone who has a connection with your institution.

In addition to supporting the sponsor by enhancing their public profile relatively cheaply and helping them to foster closer relationships with your law school, sponsorship also has numerous benefits for mooting organisers, including:

- financial benefits, such as the sponsoring of prizes or prize money
- fostering relationships between sponsor and institution
- fostering employability and work-placement opportunities
- potential for assistance with public relations and other kinds of publicity
- administrative support.

Because sponsorship is often considered to be the preserve of large businesses which have significant marketing budgets, it is likely to prove helpful to let your prospective sponsor know what you are looking for from them, both in terms of financial commitment and anything else that might impact on their resources.

Organisational matters

The smooth running of the moot rests with the organiser. The following is a non-exhaustive list of tasks that organisers will need to consider.

Securing and setting up the moot room

Most institutions require rooms to be booked in advance. Once the room has been booked, the organiser will need to make sure that it has been set up correctly. The photograph on page 200 shows a typical layout of a moot room, designed to replicate the layout of a real courtroom.

Where a number of moots will take place in different rooms at the same time, it will be helpful for notices to be placed on the door to each room identifying the names of the mooters and any other relevant information.

Technical assistance (audio-visual)

Many moot rooms have the facility to record the proceedings, and some of this equipment can be quite complex to set up and use. Organisers should ensure that there is someone available on the day of the moot who is able to use the equipment and that any assistance that may be needed from the IT department has been organised in advance.

Lecterns

If lecterns are available, they should be provided. Ideally, one lectern should be provided for each team; if there is only one available, then arrangements should be made either to place it centrally so that the mooters approach it when addressing the Bench or for the mooters to pass it amongst themselves when the next mooter is due to speak. Where lecterns are not available, it might be possible to improvise by providing something that the mooters can use to rest their papers.

Water

Organisers should provide the judges and the mooters with jugs of water and drinking glasses. Nothing looks less professional than people swigging from plastic bottles during a formal activity such as mooting.

The audience

Some moots attract large audiences whereas others struggle to attract anyone other than those directly involved in the moot. This presents something of a challenge for organisers. Where possible, organisers should advertise the event well in advance of the moot and request that anyone who is interested in attending should let them know. In any event, it makes sense for organisers to arrange sufficient chairs for a reasonably anticipated number of spectators so as not to discourage from staying anyone who does turn up.

In addition to the seating arrangements, providing copies of the moot problem and each team's skeleton argument should help ensure that the audience remains engaged during the proceedings.

After-moot refreshments

Consideration should be given to whether refreshments and light snacks will be provided to the participants and the audience after the moot. In addition to the problem of knowing how many people are likely to attend, there is also the issue of funding. The advantage of providing after-moot refreshments is that it provides an excellent opportunity for networking and discussing the moot. This can be especially valuable where practitioners or members of the judiciary are in attendance (as judges or otherwise).

Scheduling and timetabling matters

Scheduling

Having decided upon the structure for the mooting event, organisers will then need to schedule the various moots or rounds. This will be far more straightforward where the event is open only to students from your own institution because you will have access to all of the information needed to ensure that there are no clashes with assessments and general students' workloads, room bookings, end-of-term dates and the like. Where the event is open to other institutions, then these considerations become far more complex, not least because of the different academic calendars each may follow.

Timetabling

Setting the timetable for the moot or mooting competition is an important task, as is the requirement for it to be complied with. Although the precise stages of the timetable will necessarily differ from event to event, the following table should serve as a workable example of what is required, and by when.

Stage and detail	Timescale (expressed as working days prior to the moot)	Responsibility of
Announcement of moot/draw	20–30	Organiser
Details of the moot/round/draw are circulated to all participants, typically by email. This should include, where relevant, names and contact details of participants, moot venue, which team represents which side, dates/times of the moot or the date by which it must be held and, in the case of an inter-university competition, which team is 'home' and which team is 'away'.		
Distributing the moot problem to the mooters	14–30	Organiser
This is often distributed at the same time as the announcement described above but, if not, at least 14 days prior to the moot.		
Exchanging skeleton arguments/authorities with opponent	3–5	Mooters/organiser
Skeleton arguments/authorities are usually exchanged simultaneously with one's opponent, ordinarily by email. Alternatively, organisers may wish to become involved in this stage by acting as a 'post box' and then forwarding copies on to the relevant parties.		
Providing judges with relevant material	2–4	Organiser
Once all of the materials for the moot have been settled, and exchanged with opponent, copies of the same should be forwarded to judges.		
Meeting judges/clerks and providing final briefing	0	Organiser
It is often helpful for the organisers to meet briefly with the judges/clerks on the day of, but prior to, the moot starting. This will help ensure that the judges have received all relevant material and are familiar with the rules of the moot and the clerks (or timekeepers) are aware of the rules pertaining to the timing of each mooter's submissions. Organisers should also take this opportunity to ask whether the judges/clerks, etc. have any queries that need dealing with before the moot starts.		
Issues after the moot has concluded	0	Organiser
After the mooters have completed their submissions, it is usual for judges to retire to consider their decision. Organisers should provide separate rooms for this purpose. A member of the organising committee should make themselves available to judges in case any issues arise or guidance is required. Under no circumstances should any attempt be made to influence the decision of the judges as to their determination of the moot.		

Stage and detail	Timescale (expressed as working days prior to the moot)	Responsibility of
Issues post-moot	N/A	Organiser
Once the moot has concluded, organisers should consider publicising the results and, in the case of a competition that has been organised in rounds, advertise the next round of the event. Mooting winners, especially those who win one of the major events, are usually only too pleased to assist with publicity, including publicity for the following year's event, and can also serve as valuable ambassadors to their institutions.		

Mooting as part of a student's course of study

An increasing number of institutions now offer mooting as an assessed module. At Liverpool John Moores University, for example, mooting is offered as a level 6 option for final-year undergraduate law students where it ranks equally with other options in terms of the number of credits awarded. Not only is mooting popular with students and staff, but external examiners also commend its inclusion for its practical application and diversity of assessment.

Because mooting differs quite considerably from most of the other modules offered, it is important that students appreciate precisely what it involves. All students who intend to enrol on the mooting module should be encouraged to attend an initial briefing session where they will be told what is involved and the amount of commitment they will need to put into it.

10 Sample moot problems

This chapter sets out a number of moot problems covering a range of different law subjects. They vary in layout and complexity and are provided to illustrate the different styles and approaches used in mooting competitions and to give you an idea of how to draft moot problems for your own mooting event. In particular, you will see that some of the moots are set out more formally than others and some don't expressly state which party is the appellant and which is the respondent. Where the parties are not expressly set out, it will be necessary to work out from the moot problem which party is which. Advice on this is provided at page 8.

We are particularly grateful to the following for allowing us to publish mooting problems that they drafted for competition use:

Helen Morton of Essex Court Chambers, who drafted the contract/commercial law moot on page 254. This moot featured in the finals of the ESU–Essex Court Chambers National Mooting Competition, held in the Royal Courts of Justice on 22 June 2016. This moot consists of an appeal and cross-appeal, and readers are referred to page 7 for the different order for speakers when a cross-appeal is introduced.

Meredith Major, barrister, who devised the family law moot on page 251. This moot was used in the finals of the Magna Carta Moot held in the Inner Temple on 24 October 2016. We decided to include this moot because of its unusual features as regards the parties involved, there being two appellants and four respondents. The child, X, is a party to the proceedings (and the appeal) and in lieu of oral submissions has submitted a skeleton argument via her guardian, the fourth respondent. This requires the appellants, in particular, to be mindful of the points made in that skeleton and to focus on the human rights arguments applicable to the appellants rather than those of the child. The third respondent (the Secretary of State for Health) is an intervener, who did not participate when the case was considered at first instance. He is the only active respondent, seeking to have the appeal dismissed on both grounds noted in the problem. Submissions should focus on general points, using the facts of this case as examples of wider issues; permission for the state to intervene is only given where there are points of overarching importance to be addressed. The first and second respondents play no role at all in the case, aside from giving their consent to the making of the

Parental Order; their lack of participation is significant when it comes to supposition as to their views.

In addition, we would also like to express our thanks to the English-Speaking Union for their permission to reproduce some of the mooting problems that have been submitted during the course of the ESU–Essex Court Chambers National Mooting Competition and to the hard work of tutors who drafted them (and, of course, the students who had to argue the cases): in particular, Marc Howe (Oxford Brookes University), Norma Hird (University of Manchester), Adam Slavny (University of Warwick), Dr Tracey Elliott (University of Leicester), Peter Ward (Open University) and Jeffrey Hill (Manchester Metropolitan University).

If you wish to draft your own moot problem based around one contained in this chapter, it is important that you check whether there have been any changes in the law since the problem was first written that will require you to take a different approach to how the problem should be drafted. Guidance on this is provided at page 230.

Criminal law

IN THE SUPREME COURT

R v Bamber and Jones

Rob Bamber and Mike Jones were both convicted under section 18 of the Offences Against the Person Act 1861 after a trial at Ambridge Crown Court. Both had attempted, unsuccessfully, to raise the defence of duress by threats.

On 15 April 2015, Bamber and Jones were out having a drink in a local pub with Bamber's father, Tommy Bamber. Rob Bamber knew that Tommy had a very long list of previous convictions, many for offences of violence. Rob had always been a little frightened of his father, but also admired him. Because of Tommy's record for violence, Rob had only maintained minimal relations with him over the previous ten years. Mike Jones had never met Tommy Bamber before he was introduced to him at the pub that night.

During the course of the drinks, the conversation was going well. Mike told Tommy that he had a five-year-old daughter who lived alone with him and that they only lived a few hundred yards away from Tommy. Later on in the evening, however, Tommy explained to Rob and Mike that he had recently become involved with a violent criminal gang and that he wanted their help to 'kneecap' a member of a rival gang called Kenny Smith. Both Rob and Mike refused to help, causing Tommy to become aggressive towards them. Tommy told Rob that he would cut his throat if he did not help, and said to Mike that he would snatch his daughter and keep her in a secret place where he would never find her. As a result, both Rob and Mike reluctantly agreed to help in the attack on Kenny Smith, which resulted in him suffering two broken legs and a broken jaw.

At their trial for causing grievous bodily harm with intent under section 18 of the Offences Against the Person Act 1861, both Rob and Mike pleaded duress by threats.

The trial judge, HHJ Boggis, made the following comments when summing up to the jury:

1. Following *Hasan* [2005] 2 AC 467 and *Ali* [2008] EWCA Crim 716, the defence of duress by threats was not available where the defendant had voluntarily associated with those engaged in criminal activity and ought to have known that he might be compelled to act by threats of violence. The fact that Tommy Bamber was Rob Bamber's father was irrelevant;
2. Following *Dao* [2012] EWCA Crim 1717, a threat of false imprisonment was not enough for a defence of duress by threats. The threat must be a threat of either death or serious bodily harm. The defence of duress by threats was therefore not available for Mike Jones.

Rob Bamber and Mike Jones were subsequently convicted under section 18. The Court of Appeal (Criminal Division) dismissed their appeals and commended the trial judge's summing up to the jury. The Court of Appeal certified the following as points of law of general public importance upon which Rob Bamber and Mike Jones now appeal to the Supreme Court:

1. Whether the defence of duress by threats should be unavailable where a defendant is threatened by a close relative, even where the defendant only maintained minimal relations with that relative;
2. Whether the defence of duress by threats should be extended to cover situations where the defendant acts to avoid a threat of false imprisonment.

IN THE SUPREME COURT

R v Thrasher

Mr and Mrs Thrasher have been happily married for 40 years during which time they have developed a fascination for sado-masochism practices which they record on video for their own sexual entertainment. These practices include slapping each other using pieces of plastic piping, pouring very hot water on each other's genitals and engaging in partial strangulation. To celebrate their wedding anniversary, they booked themselves into a nudist hotel and, following her husband's request, Mrs Thrasher used a red-hot knitting needle to carve her name across his buttocks. They were both delighted with the result. Later that night, Mr Thrasher noticed that his buttocks were continually bleeding and that he had sustained bruising to his neck from the strangulation games they played. No medical treatment was needed.

A couple of months later, they were watching the video they had recorded when the vicar popped around for tea. The door had been left ajar and the vicar was able to walk straight in. When he saw what the Thrashers were watching, he left in disgust and reported the matter to the police who raided the Thrashers' home and seized the video recording.

Mrs Thrasher was subsequently charged with offences contrary to sections 47 and 20 of the Offences Against the Person Act 1861. Mr Thrasher told the police that nothing occurred without his consent and he therefore refused to testify against his wife at trial. He provided a written statement confirming that they had engaged in these practices for almost four decades and both of them had always fully consented to the other's actions, including during the evening when he sustained the injuries that are the subject of the prosecution. At trial, the prosecution relied solely on the video evidence.

The trial judge, Frisky J, felt bound to follow *R v Brown* [1994] 1 AC 212 and directed the jury that consent was not a defence to actual bodily harm. Mrs Thrasher was convicted on both counts and her appeal to the Court of Appeal was allowed. Happydays LJ concluded that her convictions were unsafe because: 'Consensual activity between husband and wife, in the privacy of the matrimonial home, is not, in our judgment, a proper matter for criminal investigation, let alone prosecution.'

The Crown now appeals to the Supreme Court on the following grounds:

1. In accordance with *R v Brown*, Mr Thrasher cannot, as a matter of law, consent to the infliction of such bodily harm as was caused by his wife.
2. In a democratic society, it is necessary to criminalise sado-masochistic practices for the protection of health and/or morals as permitted by Article 8 of the European Convention on Human Rights.

Contract law

IN THE SUPREME COURT

Giovanni Fashion House Ltd v Western Fabrics Ltd

Giovanni Fashion House (GFH), a new brand in the fashion industry, is launching their arrival in the fashion industry at the London Fashion Week by exhibiting and putting on a catwalk display showcasing its latest formal-wear designs.

To establish its brand, GFH decided to use a high percentage of silk as the base material for all of its creations. For the London Fashion Week display, GFH decided to use a special and precise blend of silk and linen for its designs. The blend is called 'Panache'. Panache is made from 65 per cent silk and 35 per cent linen. GFH selected Panache, as it would ensure a superior degree of fabric flow on its models with little or no creasing when the designs are being modelled on the catwalk.

GFH contracted with Western Fabrics, a specialist and experienced fabric supplier and garment manufacturer in the fashion industry, to make the clothes for the London Fashion Week display. A full specification was agreed for the work, which was to cost £350,000. Western Fabrics agreed to manufacture GFH's creations entirely in Panache for the display.

One week before GFH's display date, Western Fabrics informed GFH that it had finished manufacturing the designs. Western was paid the full amount of the contractual price. Upon delivery of the designs from Western Fabrics' factory in Newcastle, GFH noticed that the inner lining of all the garments for the display was not made with Panache but with 'Exquisite'. Exquisite is a blend of 60 per cent silk and 40 per cent linen and is cheaper than Panache and creases more. The outside layer of the garments was made with Panache.

To remedy the defect in the specification, GFH would have to spend £200,000 to reproduce all the garments using Panache only.

It transpired that the reason Western Fabrics used Exquisite was that although they had manufactured Panache, they had then sold it to another fashion house, Formosa Es, who paid a very high price, enabling Western Fabrics to make a profit of £20,000.

GFH brought an action for damages against Western Fabrics for the cost of having the garments replaced. GFH also brought an action for account of profits for the £20,000 profit Western Fabrics made by deliberately reselling the Panache material to Formosa Es.

In the High Court, Salander J held:

1. That the action for damages failed, as the cost of replacing the garments was disproportionate to the benefit to be obtained. GFH was instead awarded damages of £5,000 for loss of amenity.
2. No account of profits should be awarded as the circumstances of this case did not fall within the principles laid down by the House of Lords in *AG v Blake* [2001] 1 AC 268.

GFH's appeal to the Court of Appeal was dismissed. GFH now appeals to the Supreme Court against both of the above decisions.

IN THE COURT OF APPEAL

Shazia v Billy

Shazia is looking to buy a second-hand car. She sees a car for sale on a notice placed in her local newsagent's window. The price is £2,000. She phones the number on the card and makes an appointment to see the car.

Billy lives next door to Shazia and has done so for four years. They know each other and pass the time of day whenever they meet, but they are not close friends. Shazia knows that Billy is a retired motor mechanic. She asks him if he would mind coming with her to look over the car; he agrees. Billy lifts the bonnet and looks at the engine. They take it for a short test drive. Billy tells Shazia that the car is in good condition and worth the price. Shazia buys the car for £2,000 cash. When they get back home, Shazia offers Billy £20 for his trouble. He is reluctant to take the money but agrees to do so when she insists.

The next day, Shazia decides to take the car out for a run in the country. On the way back she intends to call into a shop and buy a ticket for that night's lottery draw. She has played identical numbers in the lottery every week for the past five years, never missing a week.

While she is on a country road, the engine cuts out and the car comes to a stop. She cannot restart it. She calls a garage but has to wait two hours for the mechanic to arrive. When he arrives, he takes one look under the bonnet and tells Shazia that 'the engine is shot. It is not worth repairing. It is only good for scrap.' By the time Shazia finally gets home, she is too late to buy a ticket for that night's lottery.

That night several of her numbers come up in the lottery draw. If she had bought a ticket, she would have won £15,000.

Shazia tries to contact the seller of the car but is unable to trace him.

Shazia sues Billy in negligence alleging that he gave advice about the state of the car which was negligent and which she relied upon. She seeks to recover from him the £2,000 she paid for the car and also the £15,000 which she claims she would have won on the lottery in the absence of his negligence.

Clarkson J finds in favour of Shazia on both heads of loss. In relation to the cost of the car, he considers the case to be materially indistinguishable from *Chaudhry v Prabhakar* [1989] 1 WLR 29 by which he considers himself bound. As to the lottery win, he finds there is a direct causal link between the defendant's breach of duty and the loss.

Billy appeals to the Court of Appeal on two grounds:

1. *Chaudhry v Prabhakar* [1989] 1 WLR 29 was wrongly decided and should not be followed and/or is distinguishable from the facts of the present case.
2. Clarkson J erred in regarding the recovery of the lottery winnings to be merely a question of causation. The lottery winnings are not recoverable because the claim fails for remoteness and/or the loss is not within the scope of any duty the defendant may owe to the claimant.

IN THE COURT OF APPEAL (CIVIL DIVISION)

Rory Wideboy v Parking Services Ltd

Rory owns a number of luxury cars including a custom-built Rolls Royce worth £2 million. On 30 September 2015, he parked his Rolls Royce in a multi-storey car park owned by Parking Services Ltd (PSL). He was content to park his car there as he had done so many times over the past few years without incident.

At the entrance to the car park there is a barrier and automatic ticket machine. There is also a sign which reads: 'Parking is subject to our terms and conditions.'

Rory entered the car park and took a ticket from the machine. On the rear of the ticket was printed: 'For our terms and conditions of parking, please see the notice board which is situated on the fifth floor.' Rory did not read what was printed on the ticket and simply put it in his wallet. In very small letters at the bottom of the fifth-floor notice board, it reads:

> PSL excludes all liability for damage to car owners' property, howsoever caused, as well as liability for any other loss including economic loss. Anyone leaving their vehicle in the car park for more than 5 days will be charged up to £50 per day, in addition to the usual parking charges.

Rory did not go to the fifth floor and therefore did not read the notice. The above text from the fifth-floor notice board also appears prominently on PSL's website.

Rory left his Rolls Royce in the car park for 30 days while he holidayed in the Caribbean. On the thirtieth day, the roof of the car park collapsed onto his car, completely destroying it. PSL were aware of defects to the roof and the risk of it collapsing, but took no action to remedy it.

Rory commenced proceedings in negligence against PSL for the cost of replacing his car (£2 million). PSL brought a counterclaim in the sum of £1,250 (calculated at £50 per day for 25 days).

Beavis J dismissed Rory's claim and upheld PSL's counterclaim. He held that:

1. The relevant statements contained in the notices were incorporated into the contract between Rory and PSL.
2. On its proper construction:

   (a) the contract excluded PSL's liability for negligence;

   (b) the contract entitled PSL to charge £50 per day for late collection of vehicles;

   (c) the terms were neither unreasonable for the purposes of the Unfair Contract Terms Act 1977 nor unfair for the purposes of the Unfair Terms in Consumer Contracts Regulations 1999.

Rory appeals to the Court of Appeal arguing that:

1. As a matter of law, the relevant statements were not incorporated into the contract between him and PSL.
2. Even if the relevant statements were incorporated into the contact, they were ineffective either to exclude PSL's liability or to entitle them to charge £50 per day for late collection.

Tort law

IN THE COURT OF APPEAL (CIVIL DIVISION)

Davies v The Martial Arts Academy

The Martial Arts Academy (MAA) is an academy that promotes martial arts at all levels. It employs a number of high-ranking martial arts instructors who have, over the years, trained students to an extremely high level, with many going on to represent their country in international competition.

Following a recent major competition in which students from the MAA won a number of medals, the instructors went out to celebrate. Unfortunately, the celebrations went on for longer than they had planned and as a result they missed their flight home that evening. This meant that the MAA was without any instructors for the following day's classes, which, as it happened, were being filmed for promotional purposes. To avoid having to cancel classes, the MAA decided to engage the services of an external martial arts instructor, Mr Lee. Mr Lee had been used by the MAA a number of times over the past 12 months when the MAA needed cover for holiday-related absences. The MAA stressed to Mr Lee that in accordance with MAA procedures no students were to be allowed into the training hall (the Dojo) unless he was himself present and could therefore supervise them. It was also a requirement that Mr Lee only use MAA's equipment and attached MAA's badge/emblem on his uniform. Mr Lee was also required to teach the classes himself and not delegate the work to anyone else.

The following morning, Mr Lee commenced the training and then gave the students a break. During the break, he left the Dojo unattended and a number of students stayed on the mats practising what he had taught them that morning. Unfortunately, one of the students, Sam Davies, suffered a broken arm when he was thrown to the ground by another student. It transpires that this other student used an advanced throwing technique on Sam for which he was not prepared. The throwing technique used was not one that had been taught. Mr Lee says that had he been there he would not have allowed this to have happened.

Sam Davies commenced proceedings against the MAA. At trial, Sensei J held that:

1. Mr Lee was negligent in leaving the students in the Dojo unsupervised.
2. Mr Lee was an employee of the MAA.
3. The MAA was vicariously liable for Mr Lee's actions.
4. In disregarding the MAA's instructions, Mr Lee was acting in the course of his employment.

The MAA appeals to the Court of Appeal on the following grounds:

1. Mr Lee was not an employee of the MAA but was an independent contractor.
2. By disregarding the MAA's instructions, Mr Lee put himself outside of the course of his employment and the MAA cannot therefore be liable for his actions.

IN THE COURT OF APPEAL (CIVIL DIVISION)

Gladys Arkwright v Grand Gas Turbines Ltd

Granville Hamilton was 17 years of age and was employed by Grand Gas Turbines Ltd as a maintenance operative. His foster mother, Gladys Arkwright, had encouraged him to apply for the job as she had previously worked for the company, before giving up her employment to become a full-time foster mother to Granville when he was placed with her at the age of 14.

On 25 September 2015, Granville was at work when an explosion took place. The factory foreman had fallen asleep on duty and had failed to carry out crucial safety checks. Dangerous levels of gas had built up and a spark from switching on a light caused the explosion. Granville was thrown several feet in the air and landed on a hard floor. He suffered extensive burns and a spinal injury. The incident occurred at 2.00pm. The factory manager, Rufus, had to telephone the families of several injured employees. By the time he rang Gladys, who was listed as next-of-kin, it was 3.30pm.

Gladys arrived at 4.00pm and discovered several ambulances, fire engines and police cars outside the factory. Rufus recognised her and took her to where Granville was waiting for the air ambulance to arrive. He was strapped to a spinal board, covered by a foil blanket and had obvious burns to his face. He did not appear to be conscious. He was attached to an emergency drip. A paramedic informed Gladys that Granville had been sedated and they were waiting for the air ambulance.

The air ambulance landed shortly afterwards close to where they were. As it came down, the wind from the rota blades dislodged a metal sheet from the roof that had been damaged in the explosion and it landed close to where Gladys was standing. At this point, Gladys became hysterical and had to be taken away from the area by Rufus. Granville remained in hospital for six weeks and after skin grafts and some surgery he was discharged. Gladys suffered long-term insomnia and experienced frequent flashbacks of the scene she encountered at the factory. She was prescribed a lengthy course of medication to control her symptoms. She was subsequently diagnosed with Post Traumatic Stress Disorder and depression.

A claim for nervous shock was brought by Gladys against Grand Gas Turbines Ltd. Liability had been accepted for injuries to all of the employees who were caught in the blast.

At trial, it was agreed that Gladys had suffered nervous shock and that Post Traumatic Stress Disorder and depression were recognised psychiatric conditions.

Wideview J held that Grand Gas Turbines Ltd was liable to Gladys on the grounds that:

1. Gladys's apprehension of injury through witnessing the roof panel flying towards her was sufficient to place her in the zone of danger and be classed as a primary victim, for which it was not necessary to show reasonable foreseeability of illness within the definition in *Page v Smith* [1996] 1 AC 155.

2. That even if taken as a secondary victim, Gladys had come across the immediate aftermath of the incident at the factory and was proximate in time and place. Furthermore, Gladys had been acting *in loco parentis* as Granville's foster mother and thus there was a presumption of a close tie of love and affection.

Grand Gas Turbines Ltd appeals on the following grounds:

1. The force exerted by the rota blades to dislodge the roof panel was a *novus actus interveniens,* thus breaking the chain of causation between the defendant's actions and the claimant's loss, and this prevented her from claiming to be a primary victim: *Alcock & Others v Chief Constable of South Yorkshire Police* [1992] 1 AC 310 should apply.
2. Due to the two-hour time delay between the time of the explosion and Gladys seeing Granville in the factory, who was sedated on a stretcher, it cannot be said that she had witnessed the immediate aftermath of the incident and that, at any rate, the concept of acting *in loco parentis* did not extend beyond legal rights and responsibilities such that there was no automatic presumption of a close tie of love and affection with the injured person in such circumstances.

IN THE SUPREME COURT

Brooke v Middlemarch Medical Group

In October 2010 Dorothea Brooke developed a bacterial infection. The bacteria seeded into her proximal femur resulting in osteomyelitis (infection of the bone) on 10 or 11 October. Within a couple of days, she was lethargic and feverish, and on 13 October she went to see her local GP, Dr Sprague, at Middlemarch Medical Group. Dr Sprague failed to arrange for Dorothea to be referred to hospital, and a few days later on 15 October, when her feet had started to swell and turn blue, she made another appointment at Middlemarch Medical Group. The doctor who saw her referred her immediately to Lydgate Hospital.

At the hospital, Dorothea was not seen by a consultant for three days and was initially given the wrong antibiotics by the junior doctors. As a result, she suffered permanent damage to her hip. She brought an action against Middlemarch Medical Group for negligence.

Allowing Dorothea's claim, the trial judge, Chettam J, held the following:

1. Applying *Wright v Cambridge Medical Group* [2013] QB 312, Dorothea enjoyed the presumption in law that she would have been treated competently had she been referred in good time.
2. On the presumption that she would have been treated competently at the hospital had she been referred by the defendants on 13 October, the delayed referral had caused her injury.

3. Even if it were to be presumed that she would have been treated negligently at the hospital had she been referred by the defendants on 13 October, the delayed referral still reduced her chances of full recovery from 40 per cent to 10 per cent.

Middlemarch Medical Group appealed to the Court of Appeal, which allowed the appeal, holding that Dorothea did not enjoy the presumption that she would have been treated properly had she been referred in time, and therefore the delay did not cause the injury. Additionally, she could not claim for the reduction in her chances of recovery.

Dorothea now appeals to the Supreme Court on the following grounds:

1. She is entitled to the presumption that she would have been treated competently had she been referred in good time.
2. Alternatively, she is entitled to claim damages for losing a chance of full recovery.

IN THE SUPREME COURT

Starsky v Chief Constable of NJ Police

The NJ Police received a tip-off that two men, who had convictions for burglary and firearms offences, were planning a night-time raid on particular premises. Police officers were stationed in the vicinity of the premises and two police marksmen, Hutch and Starsky, were positioned inside the building. Two intruders were seen to enter the building, and one of them was shot and fatally injured by Hutch. The victim turned out to be a 15-year-old boy, Huggy, who was carrying out a burglary with his 17-year-old brother, Bert. Neither of them had previous convictions and neither was armed. Starsky, who had already apprehended Bert without any resistance, was horrified when he saw the younger boy gunned down by Hutch. Hutch had wrongly assumed that Huggy was carrying a gun: in fact, it was a large torch.

Starsky suffered a severe psychological illness as a result of the incident and has had to retire from the police service. He claims that the whole police operation was 'botched'. The police officers outside the premises should have realised that the two boys were not the men the police were hoping to apprehend, and the fatal shooting of an unarmed 15-year-old boy was completely unjustified. Starsky is now suing the Chief Constable of the NJ Police, seeking to hold him vicariously liable for the negligence of the police officers and, in particular, Hutch.

On a preliminary ruling as to whether Hutch (or other police officers) owed a duty of care to Starsky not to cause him injury through shock, Dodgy J held that no such duty arose. He gave two reasons for his decision:

1. It was not reasonably foreseeable that a mere bystander would suffer nervous shock through witnessing the death of a fellow human being in the absence

of a close relationship to the victim. It made no difference that the victim was still only a child or that the death arose from a deliberate act.

2. Starsky was employed as a police marksman. He knew that circumstances might arise in which he or his colleague would have to use their guns. He was also aware that in these difficult situations there was always a possibility of a miscalculation being made. These were risks which Starsky could be taken to have voluntarily assumed. It was not, therefore, just and reasonable to hold that Starsky was owed a duty of care.

3. The Court of Appeal upheld Dodgy J's judgment. Starsky now appeals to the Supreme Court against each of the above rulings.

IN THE SUPREME COURT

Sybil v Fawlty Fireworks Ltd

Basil and Sybil were a married couple, but were having difficulties with their relationship. After months of disagreement, Basil moved out of the family home in September 2006 and moved into rented accommodation while working as a foreman at Fawlty Fireworks Ltd.

During the early morning of 8 November 2011, Basil was working a night-shift in a bunker at Fawlty Fireworks' workshop in Torquay. Unfortunately, at 3.30am, due to an electrical short-circuit, a number of firework containers exploded, resulting in the ignition of the bunker. The site manager, Manuel, raised the alarm and contacted the emergency services. Basil was trapped in the bunker and had to be rescued by the fire brigade.

Manuel used the personnel records to find the details of Basil's emergency contact, who was still recorded as being Sybil. He rang Sybil at 4.15am, saying, 'There's been a bit of an accident; can you come to the workshop?' Sybil's first reaction to the news was to presume the accident was not very serious. Knowing that Basil had worked within the fireworks industry for some considerable time, she had become used to him suffering minor burns on a fairly regular basis.

Sybil arrived at the factory at 6.00am. She was horrified to be faced with numerous fire engines and ambulances. She was directed towards a mess room, where emergency treatment had been administered to Basil. Most of his body was covered by a blanket, but his blackened face, singed hair and moustache, and burnt hand were visible. At the sight of her husband in this state, Sybil broke down, and started weeping and shaking uncontrollably. It was explained to Sybil by the attending doctor that he had suffered a degree of smoke and soot inhalation and his injuries included burns which affected his right hand, his legs and his face. Basil's burns had been treated to a degree, and he had been given a high dose of morphine to try and control the pain.

At 8.00am, Basil was transferred to Poole Hospital where he was stabilised. Sybil remained with Basil, keeping an almost constant vigil, for over a week, before he returned to the family home. She subsequently displayed symptoms of PTSD, suffering frequent flashbacks of the scene.

Sybil brought a claim as a secondary victim for psychiatric harm against Fawlty Fireworks Ltd, who accepted liability for Basil's injuries.

At first instance, Cleese J found that:

1. It was accepted that Sybil had suffered nervous shock in the form of a recognised psychiatric disorder.
2. When first seen by Sybil, Basil was in a controlled state and was not being treated.
3. Basil and Sybil had subsequently divorced.

Cleese J found that Sybil could recover as a secondary victim on the grounds that:

1. As a spouse, it was clear that she had had a close tie of love and affection with her then husband.
2. Arriving at the workshop, Sybil had witnessed the immediate aftermath of the explosion, and was therefore proximate to the accident in time and space.

The Court of Appeal dismissed Fawlty Fireworks Limited's appeal. They now have permission to appeal to the Supreme Court on the following grounds:

1. Whether Sybil previously had a close tie of love and affection with Basil was irrelevant; at the time of the accident, Basil did not live at the marital home and so the spousal presumption of relationship could be rebutted.
2. As there was a two-and-a-half-hour time delay between the time of the accident and Sybil seeing Basil, who had been treated and was in a controlled state, it cannot be said that Sybil had witnessed the immediate aftermath of the accident.

Human rights law

IN THE COURT OF APPEAL (CIVIL DIVISION)

Igor Gove v Daily Torygraph

Following the outcome of the EU referendum, and resignation of the Prime Minister as leader of the Conservation Party, the party decided to elect a new leader. A leading candidate was former Home Secretary, Igor Gove, who had led the successful campaign for the UK to leave the EU. His election as party leader was opposed by the *Daily Torygraph*, which had supported the failed campaign for the UK to remain in the EU. The *Daily Torygraph* was backing the current, pro-European, Home Secretary, John Osborne, in the leadership campaign.

In the course of the party leadership campaign, Duncan Smith, a junior official and assistant to John Osborne in the Home Office, went to the police and to the editor of the *Daily Torygraph*. Duncan Smith alleged that when Igor was Home Secretary, he had accepted bribes from a Russian businessman, Vladimir Tolstoy, to ensure that Russian oligarchs living in London, who were the subject of extradition requests, were not extradited to Russia. The *Daily Torygraph* published an article setting out these unverified allegations, and revealing that when he was Home Secretary, Igor had had a series of private meetings with Tolstoy. The article was accompanied by covertly taken pictures of Igor at Tolstoy's London home, including several photographs which appeared to depict Igor having sex with Russian prostitutes.

Igor lost the leadership election, but a subsequent police investigation and parliamentary inquiry both concluded that there was no evidence that he had accepted bribes from Vladimir Tolstoy. Igor brought proceedings in the High Court for (1) defamation and (2) infringement of his right to privacy, relying on *Campbell v Mirror Group Newspapers Ltd* [2004] 2 AC 457.

At trial, Benson J held that:

1. The *Daily Torygraph* was not liable in defamation because the issues in the article were matters of public interest and the newspaper had satisfied the 'responsible journalism' test in publishing the information.
2. Igor had no reasonable expectation of privacy with regard to his meetings with Tolstoy, and any right to privacy that he might have had was outweighed by the public interest in publication of the story and the accompanying photographs: *Lord Browne v Associated Newspapers Ltd* [2008] QB 103.

Igor now appeals to the Court of Appeal on both points.

IN THE COURT OF APPEAL (CIVIL DIVISION)

Branson and Parry v Hot! Magazine

Amy Parry is a pop singer, who recently got married in India to the actor and broadcaster Russ Branson. Amy and Russ had hoped to keep their marriage a secret from their respective families, who disapproved of their relationship. However, Amy's friend Kate Joss, the fashion model and a former girlfriend of Russ, sold her story about their relationship to *Hot! Magazine*, which published photographs of their wedding, together with a photograph of the two of them apparently smoking cannabis from a cannabis pipe.

The wedding photographs in *Hot! Magazine* were accompanied by an interview in which Kate Joss made clear that she had ended her relationship with Russ because his drug addiction (which he had always denied) had left him sexually impotent. The *Hot! Magazine* feature also included confidential details about Russ's private treatment for drug addiction, accompanied by photographs taken in a hotel bedroom, in which he was photographed apparently injecting heroin into a young fan's arm.

Amy Parry and Russ Branson brought proceedings in the High Court for infringement of their right to privacy, relying on *Douglas v Hello! (No.1)* [2001] QB 967 and *Campbell v Mirror Group Newspapers Ltd* [2004] 2 AC 457.

At trial, Ramsey J held that:

1. Amy Parry and Russ Branson were celebrities who regularly courted publicity, and they had no reasonable expectation of privacy with regard to the fact of their wedding, the details of their relationship or any photographs taken at their wedding.
2. Any right to privacy which Russ Branson might have had with regard to his drug addiction and treatment was outweighed by the public interest in the publication of the story and of the photographs taken of him with a young fan in a hotel bedroom.

Amy Parry and Russ Branson now appeal to the Court of Appeal on the grounds that:

1. They both had a reasonable expectation of privacy with regard to the fact of their wedding, the details of their relationship and all photographs taken at their wedding.
2. The right to privacy which Russ Branson had with regard to his drug addiction and treatment was not outweighed by any public interest in the publication of the story and/or of the photographs taken of him in the hotel bedroom.

IN THE SUPREME COURT

R (on the application of X) v Walford Crown Court, Y

The accused, Y, is awaiting trial at the Walford Crown Court, London, on an indictment containing one count of sexual assault, contrary to section 3 of the Sexual Offences Act 2003, on X, a Muslim woman (date of birth 1 May 2000), during the early evening of 26 January 2016. The assault allegedly happened while X was travelling home from her work in Central London, on a very full underground train. X alleged that, as she was standing in the crowded train carriage, a male stranger (later identified as Y) had sidled up to stand behind her, and had rubbed his body against hers in a sexual manner and fondled her bottom with his hands. As he did this, X alleged that she was able to feel that the man was sexually aroused. X was very distressed, and immediately objected to this, telling the man to leave her alone, but the man left the train at the next station.

Following scrutiny of CCTV evidence obtained from video cameras on the underground train, X identified the man alleged to be her assailant. Police, having ascertained his whereabouts, name and address, and obtained an arrest warrant, arrested Y for the offence of sexual assault. At the police station, an identification procedure was conducted, and X formally identified Y as the man who had sexually assaulted her. Y admitted being the person shown in the train at the relevant time, but denied sexually assaulting X, and the CCTV evidence does not show the alleged assault because the view is obscured by other passengers. There is no forensic evidence or other eyewitness testimony in relation to what occurred on the underground train.

At the time of the alleged sexual assault, X was wearing the hijab. In April 2016, X began to wear the niqab and, when the prosecution of Y was listed for trial in October 2016, she indicated that she wished to testify wearing her niqab. The trial judge, HHJ Flame, at a preliminary hearing in October 2016, held a voir dire to resolve the issue of whether X should wear the niqab when giving evidence at the jury trial. X was called to give oral evidence during the voir dire, and wore her niqab when taking the oath and testifying. She gave evidence that she had become more religious in April 2016, and that since then her religious belief had required her to wear a niqab in public where men (other than certain close family members) might see her. She admitted that she had removed her niqab for the photo on her passport to be taken, which was taken in June 2016 by a female photographer, and that, if required, she would remove it for security checks – for example, at a border crossing.

In the light of this evidence, HHJ Flame concluded that this was a case in which the relative credibility of X and Y was key, and the assessment of credibility was dependent not merely upon what the witness said, but how the witness said it. Allowing X to testify with her face covered would interfere with the ability of the trier of fact to assess her credibility as a witness. In the circumstances, permitting X to wear a niqab while she was giving evidence would create a serious risk to the fairness of Y's trial and would breach his right to a fair trial under Article 6 ECHR. X's religious belief could be adequately protected by the use of special measures pursuant to Part II, Chapter I of the Youth Justice and Criminal Evidence Act 1999 (such as by giving evidence via a video link or behind a screen). Accordingly, he directed X to remove her niqab during cross-examination, although he also made an order that she should give her evidence via a live video link.

X instituted judicial review proceedings, claiming that the refusal of HHJ Flame to allow her to give evidence wearing the niqab amounted to a breach of her rights under Article 9 ECHR. Y was joined as an interested party to the proceedings. X was granted permission to proceed with her claim, but the Administrative Court dismissed the claim, holding that although HHJ Flame's decision refusing to allow X to wear the niqab while she was being cross-examined as a witness during Y's trial engaged her right to manifest her religion under the ECHR, that right had not been infringed, and even if it had been, the decision was objectively justified under Article 9(2) because it was a necessary and proportionate measure to protect Y's Article 6 right to a fair trial.

X appealed to the Court of Appeal, who upheld the decision of the Administrative Court. She now appeals to the Supreme Court, on the grounds that:

1. The refusal to permit X to wear the niqab at all times while giving evidence during Y's trial amounted to an interference with her Article 9 rights, which was not a permissible limitation under Article 9(2); and

2. Permitting X to wear the niqab at all times while giving evidence:

   (a) did not amount to an interference with Y's Article 6 right to a fair trial; alternatively,

   (b) did not amount to a disproportionate interference with Y's Article 6 rights.

For the purposes of this moot, counsel for the appellant will represent X and counsel for the respondent will represent Y.

Family law

IN THE COURT OF APPEAL (CIVIL DIVISION)
ON APPEAL FROM
THE HIGH COURT OF JUSTICE
FAMILY DIVISION

Mr A and Ms B
1st and 2nd Appellants

v

Mrs S and Mr S
1st and 2nd Respondents
and
The Secretary of State for Health
3rd Respondent
and
X (a child through her guardian)
4th Respondent

Facts (as found by Mrs Justice Von Trapp)

The appellants, Mr A and Ms B, applied for a Parental Order under the Human Fertilisation and Embryology Act 2008 (HFEA) in relation to the child, X, who was born as the result of a surrogacy agreement, carried by Mrs S who is married to Mr S.

In January 2015, discussions began between Mr A's and Ms B's respective families as regards the prospect of arranging a marriage between them. Ms B's family own a successful clothing production business, with factories in Pakistan, and Mr A was keen to develop his own clothing distribution business in the UK using these links.

Mr A holds dual British and Pakistani citizenship, has a British passport and has lived in the jurisdiction of England and Wales for 20 years, since he was 15. Mr A already has a wife in the UK, whom he married in England (legally, according to the law of England and Wales, and religiously) 15 years ago and has lived with ever since, along with their four children. He agreed to take Ms B, who is a Pakistani citizen, as his second wife and a religious ceremony was performed between the two in England, shortly after she travelled to this country in 2015 on a six-month work visa, which has since expired. Her application to regularise her immigration status is currently awaiting determination.

Ms B lives near Mr A but at a separate address, at which Mr A has never lived. Their marriage has been consummated, they do spend some time together each week, and Mr A does provide financially for Ms B. It was known prior to the marriage that Ms B is unable to carry her own children, following earlier health problems, and the appellants explored the opportunity of using a surrogate prior to Ms B travelling to the UK.

They entered into a surrogacy arrangement with Mrs S and her husband, who live in Pakistan, via an agency; Mrs S was implanted with an embryo created using Mr A's sperm and a donor egg at a clinic in Pakistan. Mr A and Ms B returned to Pakistan shortly before the birth of X in February 2016 where all the relevant paper work was signed, including consent forms by both Mrs and Mr S. The appellants were entrusted with the day-to-day care of X as soon as she was discharged from hospital and brought her to this country on a Pakistani passport.

Upon their return, Mr A and Ms B applied jointly for a Parental Order, under section 54 of the HFEA. Mrs S and Mr S supported the application and played no further part in the first instance hearing, Von Trapp J being satisfied that they were aware of the proceedings and had been given notice of the hearing.

First instance decision

At first instance, Von Trapp J was satisfied that the requirements of section 54(1), (3), (5), (6), (7) and (8) were met.

However, she held that seeing as the marriage between Mr A and Ms B was bigamous, and therefore void according to section 11 of the Matrimonial Causes Act 1973, they did not fulfil section 54(2)(a). Further, they were not in a committed relationship, did not live together and overall did not fulfil section 54(2)(c); as a matter of public policy, bigamous relationships should not qualify.

Grounds of appeal

Mr A and Ms B were given leave to appeal on the following grounds:

1. Von Trapp J failed to apply the appropriate law in considering the question of fact of whether the appellants were in an 'enduring family relationship', as a matter of domestic statutory interpretation a public policy exception for bigamous relationships cannot be read into the HFEA, *A and Anor v P and Ors* [2011] EWHC 1738 (Fam) considered.
2. Von Trapp J had disproportionately interfered with Mr A and Ms B's Article 8 rights by refusing their application for a Parental Order and in so far as

section 54(2)(c) is incompatible with the European Convention on Human Rights, it should be read down in order to ensure compliance, *Z (a child) No. 2* [2016] EWHC 1191 (Fam) considered.

Mrs S and Mr S, the first and second respondents, make no submissions in this appeal. X, through her guardian, the fourth respondent, is entirely aligned with the position of the appellants; the guardian's attendance, along with that of his representatives, has been excused at the appeal hearing, although a brief skeleton argument adopting the submissions on behalf of the appellants has been filed.

The Secretary of State for Health was given permission to intervene and is the only active respondent, seeking to have the appeal dismissed on both grounds of appeal.

Examples of an appeal and cross-appeal

The following two moots consist of an appeal and cross-appeal. Readers are referred to pages 172 and 173 for a discussion on cross-appeals which includes a table setting out the different order for speakers with this kind of moot.

IN THE SUPREME COURT

Makemoney Ltd v Risky Advisers Plc

Mr Shiftykov was a former trader and prominent business figure at an investment house in his native country of Dazokstan. He moved to London in the early 2000s; sometime afterwards, the investment house collapsed after discovering a large black hole in its accounts. He then became a director of and later CEO of MakeMoney Ltd ('MakeMoney'), an investment company which was often advised by Risky Advisers Plc ('RAP') on financial investment opportunities. In January 2014, RAP advised MakeMoney of a high-risk, high-return property investment. The investment needed at least £200 million worth of investment to be viable, and the fees payable to Risky Advisers Plc for the referral were 10 per cent of the profit made by each investor.

In March 2014, Mr Powder, a junior Vice President at RAP, was enjoying a night out at an exclusive London nightclub with his friend, Mr Wylde. Mr Wylde had worked with Mr Shiftykov back in Dazokstan, and after several rounds of tequila, told Mr Powder, 'Mate, I can't believe you're getting into bed with Shiftykov. The man's a crook. He ripped off the last company he worked for, and he'll rip off this one.' However, before Mr Powder could enquire further, Mr Wylde ordered another round of drinks. The next day, (an obviously hungover) Mr Powder told the Board of RAP of this conversation. The Board had heard rumours that Mr Shiftykov was behind the collapse of his last company, but they took no action. Two weeks later, Mr Shiftykov told RAP he wanted to put £20 million 'of his own money' into the investment. This took the total sum to the

£200 million required. RAP asked no questions and advised him how to make the investment. The investment proved a success, and in August 2014 Mr Shiftykov sold his stake for £50 million. In total, RAP made a total profit of £32 million from fees earned from all of the investors.

In November 2014, it was discovered that Mr Shiftykov had in fact been using MakeMoney's funds for his own benefit, including the £20 million he used for participating in the investment. However, Mr Shiftykov had disappeared. MakeMoney sued RAP in dishonest assistance. At trial, Mr Justice Precedent held that RAP had a general suspicion that Mr Shiftykov was engaged in fraudulent activity against MakeMoney, but not a specific suspicion that Mr Shiftykov's participation in the investment was the product of any fraud against MakeMoney. Therefore, following *Abou Rahmah v Abacha* [2007] 1 Lloyd's Rep 115, MakeMoney's claim failed to make out dishonesty. However, had he found that RAP was liable in dishonest assistance, he would have held, following *Novoship (UK) Ltd v Mikhaylyuk* [2015] 2 WLR 526, that the £200 million requirement would not have been reached without Mr Shiftykov's participation (such that the investment would not have progressed and RAP would have earned no fees) and that there was therefore a sufficient causal link to entitle MakeMoney to an account of RAP's profits of £32 million. Permission has been granted for a 'leapfrog' appeal and cross-appeal directly to the Supreme Court on two points:

1.   **The Appeal:** MakeMoney contends that a general suspicion of fraudulent activity is sufficient to constitute dishonesty for the purposes of dishonest assistance even in the absence of a specific suspicion that the relevant acts were part of a fraud.
2.   **The Cross-Appeal:** RAP contends that an account of profits is not available as a remedy for dishonest assistance.

IN THE SUPREME COURT

Pear Ltd v Sloth Inc

1.   Pear Ltd is a company which manufactures and sells mobile phones across Europe, including smartphones. In January 2014, it was announced that a new 4GS mobile network would be launched on 1 February 2015. This new network would have a faster internet connection but use much more of the battery life of smartphones than the normal 4G network. In February 2014, Pear Ltd announced that it would be developing a new smartphone for release on 1 February 2015, to coincide with the 4GS network launch. Their main competitor, Pineapple Ltd, announced a few days later that they would also be developing their own new smartphone for launch on 1 May 2015.
2.   In April 2014, Pear Ltd approached Sloth Inc, a mobile technology engineering firm they routinely dealt with, to develop a new battery with increased battery life for the new smartphone. There was an existing agreement between the

parties, dated 1 January 2014, for Sloth Inc to research and develop a new software system for Pear Ltd, including the design of a tablet device to connect with smartphones (the 'System Agreement'). The first designs for this new system and tablet were not due to be sent to Pear Ltd until November 2016. On 1 May 2014, the parties entered into a second agreement for the design of a new battery (the 'Battery Agreement') which contained an express term at Clause 8 that the final battery design must be completed and delivered to Pear Ltd by 1 September 2014. This was to ensure that the new smartphone could be developed by the 1 February 2015 launch date. It also contained the following clause:

> Clause 15: Liquidated Damages, In the event that the final design for the Battery is delayed by a period of over 1 month, Sloth Inc is liable for liquidated damages calculated on the basis of 30% of Pear Ltd's forecast annual profits on the sales of the new Smartphone for 2015. For delays of over 2 months, the liquidated damages calculation will increase to 50% of Pear Ltd's forecast annual profits for the sales of the new Smartphone for 2015.

3. Despite the importance of timing, Sloth Inc did not deliver a final battery design until 2 December 2014, and Pear Ltd had to delay the launch until 1 May 2015. As a result and in accordance with the terms of the Battery Agreement, Pear Ltd terminated that Agreement and commenced proceedings against Sloth Inc for the breach on 1 January 2015. On 2 January 2015 Sloth Inc ceased work on the development of the new software system and tablet. Pear Ltd refused to accept this repudiation and amended their claim to include continued performance of the System Agreement.

4. In proceedings at first instance, Pear Ltd claimed that they were entitled first to liquidated damages in accordance with Clause 15 of the Battery Agreement, and second to performance of the development of the new system design pursuant to the System Agreement. Sloth Inc contended that Clause 15 was a penalty clause and therefore not enforceable. In addition, they argued that Pear Ltd was not entitled to specific performance of the designs for the new software since damages would be an adequate remedy. Mr Justice Jones decided on two preliminary issues of law and held, in accordance with *Cavendish Square Holding BV v Talal El Makdessi* [2015] UKSC 67, that Clause 15 was not a penalty clause since it did not impose a detriment on Sloth Inc out of all proportion to the legitimate interest of Pear Ltd in ensuring the designs were completed on time. It was therefore enforceable. However, he held that Pear Ltd were not entitled to specific performance of the new software design since, although there were difficulties in valuing the software and tablet designs, an estimated award of damages was preferable to forcing the parties to continue with a hostile and damaged commercial relationship. The Court of Appeal upheld Jones J's judgment for substantially the same reasons as he gave.

5.   Permission has been granted by the Supreme Court for an appeal by Sloth Inc and cross-appeal by Pear Inc on the following points:

   5.1 **The Appeal:** Whether Clause 15 is a penalty clause and should not be enforced; and

   5.2 **The Cross-Appeal:** Whether Pear Ltd should be entitled to specific performance of the new software and tablet designs.

11 Interactive videos

Analysis of a live moot

To complement the guidance provided throughout this book, we have provided full coverage of a moot together with feedback on the performance of each of the mooters. To access this resource, visit www.routledge.com/cw/baskind.

The videos will provide comprehensive guidance by analysing each mooter's presentation, identifying their strengths and weaknesses, their use of cases and other materials, their interaction with the judges, the respondent's ability to respond to the appellant's arguments, the appellant's right of reply and generally each mooter's style and overall performance. The videos will also provide helpful feedback for each of the mooters and advice on how to improve.

The structure of the online resource is as follows:

Video 1: the moot

This is the full moot in *Davies v The Martial Arts Academy* which can be found on page 242. It starts with the mooters entering the room, followed by the judges, and the court clerk 'calling on' the case. The entire moot is shown, uninterrupted, followed by a brief judgment on the law and individual comments on the performance of each of the mooters. Finally, the winning team is announced.

Before moving on to consider a series of excerpts identifying and commenting on good and poor mooting practice, the author provides his own overall observations on the moot.

Video 2: high points of the moot with commentary

This video shows excerpts from the moot identifying a number of areas where a mooter's performance was particularly impressive, together with advice to enable you to follow these good examples.

Clip 1:

Note how the lead appellant introduces the case to the court which is made up of one female and two male judges. This is discussed at page 176 in the book and further on the online commentary.

Clip 2:

The mooter in this clip cites, introduces and deals particularly well with an authority later to be relied upon. This is discussed at page 183 in the book and further on the online commentary.

Clip 3:

This is an excellent example of how to answer a question on a point that has not yet been addressed by the mooter. This is discussed at page 195 in the book and further on the online commentary.

Clip 4:

The mooter in this clip demonstrates considerable skill in moving on to the next point following an intervention from the Bench indicating that they do not require any further assistance on the point being discussed and inviting the mooter to move on to the next point. The mooter could not have achieved this fluidity had he been tied to a script. This is discussed at pages 188 and 189 in the book and further on the online commentary.

Clip 5:

This clip shows a particularly skilful interaction with all three members of the Bench. Note, in particular, how the mooter engages with all members of the Bench while directing the responses to the particular judge who asked the question. This is discussed further on the online commentary.

Video 3: low points of the moot with commentary

This video shows excerpts from the moot identifying a number of areas where a mooter's performance could have been better, together with advice to help you avoid the issues identified.

Clip 6:

The mooter in this clip fails to wait until the judges have found the passage cited, and continues with the submissions while they are still trying to locate the text. Had the mooter maintained sufficient eye contact with the Bench, it would have been obvious that the judges were not ready and were not concentrating on the submission. You will also see that the passage quoted was unnecessarily lengthy, which had the effect of diluting the effectiveness of the point being addressed. This is discussed at pages 187 and 188 in the book and further on the online commentary.

Clip 7:

The mooter in this clip introduces a case to the court giving its full citation before explaining either its relevance and context or where it can be located in the bundle. This prompts a rather obvious question from the Bench as to its purpose. Furthermore, as the case had already been cited earlier in the appeal, it was unnecessary to repeat its full citation. This is discussed at page 183 in the book and further on the online commentary.

Clip 8:

The judge raises a question with the mooter which interrupts the prepared submissions. Rather than dealing with the question straight away, the mooter informs the judge that it will be dealt with in due course. The best way of dealing with judicial interventions and especially those which take the mooter away from their planned order of submissions is discussed at page 193 in the book and further on the online commentary.

Clip 9:

The judge raises a straightforward question which required an equally straightforward 'yes' or 'no' (or similarly brief) answer. Instead, the mooter goes around the houses in answering the question and, in doing so, gets tied up with further discussion that eats into the time and was wholly avoidable. Answering straightforward questions such as this is discussed at page 196 in the book and further on the online commentary.

Clip 10:

The mooter takes the Bench to an authority but the citation in the skeleton argument is different from that cited orally and used in the bundle. The importance of using the correct version of a law report and ensuring that the citations used in your skeleton argument and bundle are identical are discussed in pages 136 and 137 in the book and further on the online commentary.

12 Useful resources

This chapter contains a list of useful resources for anyone involved in the process of mooting. It covers competitions, sponsorship and other resources that will be of interest to mooters as well as to those organising mooting competitions.

Competitions

There are numerous mooting competitions each offering a slightly different approach and focus. We have listed below some of the best-known and longest-established competitions together with some of the more specialist and newer events. We will start with UK-based competitions.

UK-based mooting competitions

English-Speaking Union–Essex Court Chambers National Mooting Competition

http://nationalmooting.org
The ESU–Essex Court Chambers National Mooting Competition is one of the most prestigious and longest-established national mooting competitions in the UK, with the first final being held in 1972. It operates on a knockout basis with rounds conducted over the winter and spring, culminating in the semi-finals held at the ESU headquarters at Dartmouth House, Mayfair, London, and the Grand Final in the Royal Courts of Justice, London, in June each year.

The winning team is presented with the Silver Mace, with the two winners being given £1,000 each and a further £1,000 for their institution. Runners-up are presented with the Scarman Shield and awarded a cash prize of £750 each, with a further £500 going to their institution. All four finalists are offered mini-pupillages at Essex Court Chambers.

Oxford University Press & BPP National Mooting Competition

https://global.oup.com/ukhe/mooting/?cc=gb&lang=en
Another prestigious and popular mooting competition, the OUP & BPP National Mooting Competition offers undergraduate law and GDL students the

opportunity to practise and perfect their advocacy skills. Like the ESU–ECC competition, it operates on a knockout basis.

Lincoln's Inn Inter-Provider Mooting Competition

www.lincolnsinn.org.uk/index.php/education/bptc-student-information/competitions

Preliminary selection rounds are held for Lincoln's Inn students at all the BPTC providers, using a 'speed-mooting' system, with the two highest-scoring students going through to represent their provider in the later rounds when the teams will be pitted against each other to decide which provider will be the holder of the Shield. Selection for those at London providers will be held at the Inn and for those at providers outside London selection will be organised locally by the relevant Lincoln's Inn Student Representatives.

UK Supreme Court moot finals

www.supremecourt.uk/moots.html

The Supreme Court moot finals are specifically for accredited higher education law programmes and student-run societies. Every year the UK Supreme Court offers 12 graduate law schools and university law societies the opportunity to hold the final of their mooting competition at the Supreme Court in front of a Supreme Court Justice.

UK Law Students' Association

www.uklsa.co.uk/mooting

The UKLSA Annual National Advocacy/Mooting Competition provides training and other opportunities for all those training to become lawyers. Only one representative team for each university, generally the winning one, can enter the competition which is organised across a series of six rounds.

Sir Alexander Stone Mooting Competition

www.gla.ac.uk

The Sir Alexander Stone Mooting Competition is open to all law schools in Scotland which provide an LLB programme. It runs on a knockout basis from October to March, with the finals held in Glasgow, presided over by a senior member of the Scottish judiciary.

The Times 2TG Moot

www.2tg.co.uk/timesmoot

The Times 2TG mooting competition differs from existing national mooting competitions in that there is no pre-set limit to the number of applications generally or from any particular establishment. As well as generous cash prizes, all four finalists will be invited for mini-pupillages at 2 Temple Gardens Chambers.

UK Environmental Law Association Moot Competition

www.ukela.org/law-student-moot-competition
The UKELA holds two annual mooting competitions which are hosted by King's College London and sponsored by No. 5 Chambers. The Senior Competition is open to students undertaking the vocational part of their training and the Junior Competition is open to undergraduate, postgraduate and GDL students.

University of Leicester Medical Law Mooting Competition

www2.le.ac.uk/departments/law/news-events/medical-law-moot
This is a specialist medical law mooting competition. One moot problem will be set for the competition for which teams will prepare both sides of the problem. Heats will take place during the day, with a final in the late afternoon/early evening. Only undergraduate students and those registered on either an LLM/MA law course or a GDL course may enter the competition. The competition is not open to students studying on a practice course.

Property Law Mooting Competition

www.landmarkchambers.co.uk/property_moot
The Landmark Chambers annual Property Law Mooting Competition is a specialist property law mooting competition that provides students who have a particular interest in property law with an opportunity to develop their understanding of the subject and to gain some insight into the realities of practice through meeting members of Chambers' property law team.

The competition comprises of a number of knockout rounds followed by a grand final. The two individual competitors who obtain the highest scores in the final will each be awarded £500 and the opportunity to undertake a mini-pupillage in Chambers.

The Inner Temple Mooting Society

www.innertemple.org.uk/education/students/societies?showall=&start=2
https://twitter.com/innermooting
The Inner Temple Mooting Society runs a number of mooting events, the largest being the Lawson Moot and the Inter-Varsity Moot, both of which are held within the Inn. The Lawson Moot is an internal moot for student members of the Inn. Attracting 64 participants, the moot runs over five knockout rounds. The Inter-Varsity moot is contested between 32 university teams across five rounds on a knockout basis. Each team consists of two student competitors who must not be studying a vocational postgraduate legal course (BPTC or LPC).

The Rosamund Smith Mooting Competition

www.middletemple.org.uk/members/student-information-and-services/mooting
The Middle Temple hosts an annual mooting competition for its student members which is open to both BPTC and CPE/GDL students. The competition is run on a knockout basis with the winning team from each round progressing to the next round of the competition. The initial rounds are not open to spectators but the semi-finals and final take place in Hall after dinner, usually in front of a large audience.

International mooting competitions

As with UK-based competitions, there is no shortage of international events. Some of the best-known international competitions are listed below.

Philip C. Jessup International Law Moot Court Competition

www.ilsa.org/jessuphome
Organised by the International Law Students' Association, and now in its fifty-eighth year, the Philip C. Jessup International Law Moot Court Competition is the world's largest moot court competition, with participants from over 550 law schools in more than 87 countries. The Competition is a simulation of a fictional dispute between countries before the International Court of Justice, the judicial organ of the United Nations. One team is allowed to participate from every eligible school. Teams prepare oral and written pleadings, arguing both the applicant and respondent positions of the case.

Oxford Intellectual Property Moot

www.oiprc.ox.ac.uk
www.law.ox.ac.uk/centres-institutes/oxford-intellectual-property-research-centre
Participation in the oral rounds of this competition is by invitation only, on the basis of two written submissions (of 3,000 words each) prepared by teams wishing to compete.

The oral proceedings comprise four preliminary rounds, quarter-finals, semi-finals and a grand final. Teams may comprise two or three students, with any two team members speaking in any given moot. The grand final is held before senior members of the judiciary.

The Essex Court Chambers–Singapore Academy of Law International Mooting Competition

https://essexcourt.com/news-events/mooting/international-mooting
The ECC–SAL International Mooting Competition, co-organised by the members of Essex Court Chambers and the Singapore Academy of Law, presents an ideal

opportunity for young lawyers to showcase and hone their skills as advocates. Now in its sixth year, the contest is open to young advocates and has received entries from Australia, India, Hong Kong, Malaysia, Pakistan, Singapore and South Korea.

The winning team is offered an all-expenses-paid two-week internship at Essex Court Chambers in London. Awards will also be given for the Best Orator and Best Memorandum submitted in the competition.

The European Law Students' Association Moot Court Competition

http://elsa.org

http://emc2.elsa.org

The European Law Students' Association Moot Court Competition on World Trade Organisation Law is a simulated hearing of the WTO dispute settlement system. Participants from around the world send in written submissions, for the complainant and respondent, in a fictitious case. After sending their submissions, all the teams are given the opportunity to present oral arguments in front of panels which consist of WTO and trade law experts. Winning teams from five Regional Rounds (two European Rounds; an Asia-Pacific Round; an All-American Round; and an African Round) compete against each other in the Final Oral Round, held in Geneva, Switzerland at the WTO headquarters.

Manfred Lachs Space Law Moot Court Competition

www.iislweb.org/lachsmoot

Since its inception by the International Institute of Space Law (IISL) in 1992, the Manfred Lachs Space Law Moot Court Competition now covers four world regions: North America, Europe, Asia-Pacific and Africa. The winners of each region attend the world finals in October, held in conjunction with the International Astronautical Congress and the IISL Colloquium on the Law of Outer Space.

The world finals take place within the framework of the IISL's annual colloquium and judged by three sitting members of the International Court of Justice.

The International Air and Space Law Academy Space Law Moot Court Competition

http://spacemoot.org

The IASLA Space Law Moot Court Competition is aimed at students wishing to learn more about international and space law, and to gain some experience in international advocacy.

The competition is divided into regional rounds in which teams from universities compete. Each team participates in four preliminary rounds in a round-robin format, scoring points for their oral arguments and written submissions, with the top eight scoring teams advancing to the regional quarter-finals. The winners of these quarter-finals advance to the semi-finals and the winners of the semi-finals advance to the regional final. The regional champions advance to the international finals.

The Jean-Pictet Competition

www.concourspictet.org
The Jean-Pictet Competition is not a traditional mooting competition but is a week-long training event on international humanitarian law (IHL) intended for students (undergraduate or above in Law, Political Science, military academies, etc.). It consists in 'taking law out of the books', by simulations and role plays, allowing the jury of the competition to evaluate teams' theoretical knowledge and practical understanding of IHL. To register, teams must consist of three students, from the same institution, none of whom has taken part in the competition before and all of whom should generally be under 30 years old.

The Thomas A. Finlay Moot Court Intervarsity Competition

www.ucd.ie
Named after the former Irish Chief Justice, the Thomas A. Finlay Moot Court Intervarsity Competition is hosted by University College, Dublin. It operates over a number of preliminary rounds followed by a knockout format.

Telders International Law Moot Court Competition

www.universiteitleiden.nl/en/events/2016/05/telders-international-law-moot-court-competition
Originating in 1977, the Telders International Law Moot Court Competition is described as the most prestigious and important moot court competition in Europe. Annually, teams from more than 40 universities compete in the national rounds, with the winning teams going on to represent their countries in the international rounds held at the Grotius Centre and the Peace Palace in The Hague.

The Willem C. Vis International Commercial Arbitration Moot

https://vismoot.pace.edu
Law students from all countries are eligible to participate in this competition. The moot involves a dispute arising out of a contract of sale between two countries that are party to the United Nations Convention on Contracts for the International Sale of Goods. The contract provides that any dispute that might arise is to be settled by arbitration in Danubia, a country that has enacted the UNCITRAL Model Law on International Commercial Arbitration and is a party to the Convention on the Recognition and Enforcement of Foreign Arbitral Awards. The arbitral rules to be applied rotate yearly among the arbitration rules of co-sponsors of the Moot.

The competition is divided into two stages: the written stage and the oral stage, and recognises the business community's preference for resolving international commercial disputes by arbitration. The format involves the writing of memoranda for both claimant and respondent and the hearing of oral argument based upon the memoranda.

Sponsorship

We discussed, in Chapter 9, the advantages of sponsorship. The Incorporated Council of Law Reporting for England and Wales used to run their annual ICLR Mooting Competition but have recently decided to support legal training in a more general way that is open to all.

ICLR Annual Mooting Sponsorship

www.iclr.co.uk/news-events/sponsorship
The ICLR offers sponsorship to universities, colleges and law societies who run their own in-house mooting competitions. They do this in one of two ways. The first is to provide the winners of the moot with a free year's subscription to their most comprehensive series, The Weekly Law Reports, on ICLR Online. The second is to provide the university, college or law society with a small financial contribution to help in the running of their own in-house mooting competition.

Online resources

There are many resources on the internet that will be of interest to mooters. These include videos of moots and advocacy as well as a number of websites maintained by various universities and student law societies. These are of varying quality and too numerous to mention.

Every mooter should take the opportunity of visiting either the Court of Appeal or the Supreme Court to observe appellate advocacy in the same courts as the vast majority of moots are notionally set. The UK Supreme Court (www.supremecourt.uk) provides live footage of its cases as well as an archive of decided cases that can be viewed at a later stage. This resource should be considered a must for anyone looking to moot, especially for the first time.

Index